Psychology in Sport

Contemporary Psychology Series

Psychology in Sport

John MD Kremer
and
Deirdre M Scully

Taylor & Francis
Publishers since 1798

UK Taylor & Francis Ltd., 4 John Street, London WC1N 2ET

USA Taylor & Francis Inc., 1900 Frost Road, Suite 101, Bristol, PA 19007

First published 1994

A catalogue record for this book is available from the British Library

ISBN 0 7484 0181 4
ISBN 0 7484 0182 2 (pbk)

Library of Congress Cataloging-in-Publication Data are available on request

Cover design by Amanda Barragry

Typeset in 9.5/11 pt Garamond by RGM, Southport PR8 1PU

Printed in Great Britain by Burgess Science Press, Basingstoke on paper which has a specified pH value on final paper manufacture of not less than 7.5 and is therefore 'acid free'.

Contents

This book is dedicated to

Jane, John and our families

List of Tables and Figures

Series Editor's Preface

For reasons which are explored in *Psychology in Sport* the development of sports psychology has been somewhat distant from developments in 'mainstream' academic psychology. This has occurred despite a recognition by those involved in sport that psychological factors are of immense importance in determining sports performance, and a recognition by psychologists that sport (both through direct and vicarious participation) is an important aspect of human behaviour and experience. Much of the work that has been done in sports psychology until recently has been by keen sports men and women who have borrowed ideas and techniques from psychology (eg., personality tests) in order to investigate or explain performance. In chapter one of this book by John Kremer and Deidre Scully, the ground-breaking research of Norman Triplett is described which stemmed from his observations, as a cyclist, that even though cyclists pushed themselves as hard as they possibly could when racing against the clock, they went even faster when racing against each other. This is a very early (1898) example of a recognition, by a sportsman, of the importance of psychological factors in maximising performance. More recently, physiologists have shown that when athletes run on a treadmill until total exhaustion — so that they just cannot run another step, direct electrical stimulation of the leg muscles will still produce a vigourous contraction — hence exhaustion is a psychological state not a physical condition.

There have been any number of books written on sports psychology many of which are referred to in this volume. A large number of such books are practically orientated texts for coaches, trainers, athletes and sports educators which can be dismissed by 'pure' psychologists as superficial cook books. Such books may achieve wide circulation and admiration in sports circles but rarely, if ever, find their way on to reading lists for psychology courses. On the other hand, standard psychology textbooks aimed at undergraduate psychology students contain few, if any, references to sport even though they cover topics where sporting examples and applications would be directly relevant.

Kremer and Scully have, as is common throughout the Contemporary Psychology Series, written their book as psychologists and for psychologists but in a way that will be accessible for those who are commencing their encounter with psychology and for those who are mainly orientated towards sports science. As the title and the structure of the book makes clear this is an attempt, which I believe to be unique, to take fundamental research in nine key areas of psychology and to explore what each of these bodies of theory, data and methodology can offer in terms of insights into sporting endeavour. Thus, the book is organised as an introductory psychology text with chapter subheadings that mirror those to be found in a large number of introductory texts, but with consideration of possible applications to sport being at the forefront of each chapter.

When you have finished reading this book you will know a lot more about sports psychology and, equally important, you will have encountered a great deal of basic psychology that is also relevant to other aspects of human behaviour.

Ray Cochrane,
Birmingham, January 1994

Chapter 1

Introduction

For a great many readers of this book, it is likely that sport psychology must be something of an enigma, part of the discipline of psychology yet also apart from it. With this in mind, we would like to begin with two very basic questions. First off, what is sport psychology and second, what is it for? Taking these questions one at a time, we would like to think that by the time you finish Chapter 9 you will have some grasp of the content and concerns of sport psychology — what it is. Put most simply, sport psychology can be any example of psychological knowledge, principles or methods as applied to the world of sport. As for who it is for then we immediately hit more troubled waters. According to two eminent sport psychologists there is little doubt as to who sport psychology is for, and who it is not for: 'Sport psychology is not for psychologists . . . Psychology is for sport and its participants' (Bunker and Maguire, 1985: 3).

To say that personally we find it hard to support this proposition would be an understatement, yet in writing this book we have tried to look upon such sentiments not as a barrier to progress but as a source of inspiration and motivation. Indeed one explicit aim of this book is to challenge this type of bunker (*sic*) mentality within sport psychology and show that the subdiscipline does not have to plough a lonely furrow. Instead, and with a little imagination, sport psychology can be for psychologists, just as it can be for sports scientists, managers, teachers, administrators, coaches and last but by no means least, the athletes themselves.

To those already steeped in the culture of sport psychology, given the number of texts which are already on the market it is unlikely that the publication of another introductory sport psychology text will precipitate a stampede to the local bookstore. Fortunately for us, sport scientists are not identified as the primary target for this book. Instead this introductory text has been compiled for those who have an interest in sport but who come to regard their parent discipline as psychology itself. To this population, the world of sport psychology has often remained uncharted territory. It is rarely mentioned in general undergraduate psychology textbooks and until recently was almost never identified as a topic for separate study within a typical psychology curriculum. When contemplating this gaping hole in our knowledge, any psychologist with even a passing interest in sport may have pondered the same question which we have posed ourselves (Kremer and Scully, 1991). Put simply, why is it that general psychology degrees, textbooks and courses include so few references to sport? One temptation which psychologists must avoid right away is somehow to blame themselves. They may think that during their training they have inadvertently ignored or missed relevant material but it is nevertheless ready and waiting to be picked up. In one sense this is actually true for there is a huge literature available on sport psychology. At the same time, working as a psychologist (but not a sport psychologist) it is more than likely that students will not have had the opportunity to encounter this material, for sport psychology simply has not formed a natural part of the common stock of psychological knowledge. For example, which of the following journals would the average psychology student refer to in the course of her or his studies?

> *British Journal of Sports Medicine*
> *International Journal of Sport Psychology*
> *Journal of Applied Sport Psychology*
> *Journal of Human Movement Studies*
> *Journal of Leisure Research*
> *Journal of Sport and Exercise Psychology*
> *Journal of Sport Behavior*
> *Journal of Sports Sciences*
> *Quest*
> *Research Quarterly for Exercise and Sport*
> *The Sport Psychologist*

Without a shadow of a doubt, sport psychology has and does stand apart from the discipline of psychology as a whole. Its history is different, its concerns are often different, its centres of learning and teaching are different, and its professional training is different. Yet despite this, at the end of the day it remains permanently bonded to psychology through its common interest in the bedrock of psychology, human behaviour and experience. Through all the discourse, debate and discussion of academe, we should strive never to lose sight of this fundamental tenet.

It would probably not be stretching a point too far to describe the separate development of sport psychology as a prime example of academic apartheid. It is debatable as to why and how the situation has developed but clearly guilt does not reside solely with one party or the other. One possibility which cannot be ignored is that within psychology the study of sport and exercise is taken to be somewhat trivial when set alongside the weighty, longstanding preoccupations of academic and professional psychologists. Put very bluntly, separate development reflects upon a form of academic snobbery but in turn as we all know this snobbery bears no relation to the day to day concerns of our primary focus, men and women in their social and sport oriented worlds. No one could possibly deny the significant role which sport and recreation plays in every culture and society across the globe. In the western and eastern worlds alike, sport and leisure continue to support huge industries and take up massive amounts of individual time, effort, money, energy and emotion. Within the media, competitive sport is afforded enormous attention and despite this the public's appetite for yet more sport never appears to be sated. For example, it has been estimated that around two thirds of all newspaper readers in Great Britain first turn to the sports pages when they pick up their daily paper. Beyond this, when one considers the number of people who actually engage in sport or even take regular exercise then the significance of sport to all our lives cannot be denied.

To blame the current state of academic affairs on mainstream psychology would be to tell only half the story. Sport psychologists, normally coming from a background in physical education and sport sciences, have certainly never been slow to draw selectively on psychological theories and methods in order to advance their understanding. At the same time there may have been an element of what is best described as protectionism from within the ranks of sport psychologists. For some, the zone of demarcation which separates sport psychology from the discipline as a whole could be regarded as a welcome safety buffer, with breaches to the protective shield not always greeted warmly. This defensive mentality sees its natural end-product in the encouragement of theories and methods which are unique to sport psychology (Feltz, 1987), an approach which we believe can do nothing other than drive the wedge between sport psychology and sport ever deeper. It could be that this defensiveness reflects upon a general anxiety that sport psychology may not stand close scrutiny from the wider psychological community. Sport psychologists can rest assured that this anxiety is not well founded. Indeed, the scientific rigour which characterizes so much empirical research within sport psychology is extremely commendable and could often serve as a good example for many other branches of professional and applied psychology which choose to adhere closely to the scientific method.

A more common problem with sport psychology research lies not in its scientific rigour but in its somewhat myopic, or short-sighted, appreciation of present day accumulated psychological knowledge. Scanning across sport psychology, you are confronted by a landscape of knowledge which rises and falls often suddenly and dramatically. At certain times, massive peaks of understanding rise up before our eyes yet at other times huge tracts of psychology remain untouched to the horizon. In this respect at least, it is to be hoped that some sport scientists may find this text useful for opening new vistas and charting the full range of psychological territory more thoroughly.

To trace the history of sport psychology is not an easy task and is beyond the scope of this book. Most historical accounts record significant landmarks in sport psychology throughout this century but truthfully these cannot be regarded as milestones which chart a smooth and natural development of the subject. Instead, they serve to demonstrate the opportunities which sport has always afforded to psychological study but far too often they now appear as wasted opportunities, episodic enterprises with a beginning and, regrettably, an end. This is not to deny the valuable work carried out by early explorers in sport psychology but in terms of the history of the subject they are probably best regarded as adventurers rather than genuine 'fathers' of sport psychology (the sexism is deliberate given that they were all men!), given that the line of descent was extremely fragmented until at least the 1960s. It was at this time that scientific traditions, institutions and publications which prosper to this day first came into being and it was this era which truly marked the structural genesis of modern day sport psychology.

Before that time, psychology departments and occasionally physical education departments may have included on their staff certain individuals with an interest in the psychology of sport but unfortunately it was rarely possible for these individuals to develop permanent facilities or centres of academic excellence. The one exception to this general rule was the area of motor skills which has continued to bridge the gap between sport and psychology over the years (see Chapter 5).

From the turn of this century, there were examples of sport-related research, probably the most famous early example being Norman Triplett's archival and experimental work on 'dynamogenic factors' involving cycling and reeling fishing line (1898; see Chapter 6). Leaving aside these early forays, almost without exception sport psychologists regard the mid-1920s as the most significant formative landmark in sport psychology and this is due almost entirely to the work of one man, Dr Coleman Roberts Griffith. Griffith taught psychology at the University of Illinois, introducing a course entitled 'Psychology and Athletics' in 1923, and later, in 1925, establishing and subsequently directing the Athletic Research Laboratory. It would be reassuring to describe Griffith's work as marking the launching pad for contemporary sport psychology. Sadly the truth is more depressing for in 1932, due to lack of funds, Griffith felt obliged to resign his post and the Athletic Research Laboratory closed.

In the USA, the decades which followed (between the 1930s and the 1960s) represented something of a hiatus, filled only partially by motor learning research. Similarly, in eastern Europe this was a period of stagnation, although by the 1960 Melbourne Olympics it is probably true that sport psychologists were accompanying eastern European teams (Salmela, 1984) and certainly by 1972, it was the case that Olympic competitors from East Germany and the Soviet Union were using sport psychologists as a matter of routine (Roberts and Kiiecik, 1989).

In the western world, the mid-1960s marked the true watershed in the history of sport psychology (Wiggins, 1984). It was at this time that there was a rapid growth of the subject within physical education departments in the United States, and the dominant themes which still concern practising sport psychologists came to the fore. These included individual differences and personality in sport, mental rehearsal and practice, stress, motivation, team spirit, audience effects and motor development. Throughout these early stages of growth, the parent discipline of psychology maintained a discreet distance. This distance between psychology and the fledgeling subject of sport psychology is perhaps revealed most starkly by the fact that it was not until 1986 that the American Psychological Association (APA) finally took official cognizance of sport psychology as a subdiscipline within psychology.

Generally speaking, developments in other western countries have followed the early lead taken by the USA. For example, in the United Kingdom, the road to recognition and respectability has been considerably longer. The players involved have also been far fewer in number but in essence the story line remains remarkably similar. This story began in 1984 with the formation of the British Association of Sports Sciences (BASS; since 1993 known as the British Association of Sport and Exercise Sciences or BASES), and moved forward apace in 1988 when BASS implemented a register of sport psychologists, a final draft of which became available in 1992. To gain accreditation, BASES members must normally have either a primary degree in sport science together with a postgraduate degree (by course or research) in sport psychology, or a primary degree in psychology plus a postgraduate degree (by course or research) in sport science. In addition applicants must have gained at least three years of supervised experience in the field.

The professional body which oversees psychology in general in the UK, the British Psychological Society (BPS), has mirrored the caution of the APA in taking its time to recognize sport psychology. Indeed, it was only in 1992 that the BPS finally agreed in principle to the establishment of a sport and exercise psychology interest group, a decision followed by the formation of a separate BPS Sport and Exercise Section in 1993.

Almost since sport psychology first came into existence, a fundamental divide was apparent in the work carried out by sport psychologists. In its crudest form, a distinction exists between academic or pure sport psychology and applied sport psychology. The former is the concern of those sport psychologists who busy themselves with basic research and teaching while the latter forms the hunting ground for those who use their skills, wit and knowledge to aid directly the world of sport. Often there has been friction between those who are reluctant to practise or offer professional advice without a sound theoretical grounding and those who are attracted by the practical results, and rewards, which they are able to realize through immediate action or intervention. This is not a new problem for sport psychology, indeed Coleman Griffith combined his research with consultancy work, for example with the Chicago Cubs baseball team and the University of Illinois football team (Furlong, 1976). However, the more recent seeds of conflict between theory and practice can be traced back to the mid-1960s, highlighted by the publication of *Problem Athletes and How to Handle Them* by Bruce Ogilvie and Thomas Tutko (1966). Despite the considerable criticism and hostility which the book provoked from within academic sport psychology, it quickly gained popularity within the world of sport. Indeed, their Athletic Motivation Inventory (AMI) became established as the most commonly used inventory for measuring personality dimensions which were believed to be associated with sporting success (see Chapter 2 for further details), and Bruce Ogilvie duly took on the somewhat controversial mantle of the father of applied sport psychology.

Over recent years, the heat of this pure/applied debate has cooled somewhat, perhaps as it has become obvious that the lines of demarcation between the different brands of sport psychology are difficult to draw and the whole labelling process increasingly has been seen as rather sterile and unproductive. Given the time lag between developments in sport psychology on either side of the Atlantic it is to be hoped that the history of conflict in the US is not replayed in the UK. Certainly the number of British self-help and popular sport psychology publications has mushroomed during the 1980s while at the same time the BASES accreditation process for registration as a sport psychologist can appear irrelevant to many applied sport psychologists working directly in the field (Anshel, 1992). These practitioners regard accreditation with a degree of scepticism and particularly as they often have not the time, resources or the inclination to further their academic careers or maintain a healthy publication count because they are so busy doing what they do best, working with athletes. Are we already witnessing the first murmurings of discontent from practitioners, or has the potential for conflict been successfully avoided? Time alone will tell but it is to be hoped that the quest for professional rigour does not serve to marginalize further those who may already feel that they are working alone.

From these diverse roots and structural machinations, what is the current state of play? In the first instance it is important to recognize that the term sport psychology now encompasses a wide range of institutions and individuals with different backgrounds, goals and approaches to the subject. In the UK as elsewhere, the demand for sport psychology has never been greater. Coverage of the Barcelona Olympics in 1992 and the emphasis which commentators and competitors alike placed on the 'mental' side of sport bears ample testimony to this demand. However, this popular interest in itself can be beguiling and dangerous, and caution must be exercised in promoting and developing the subject with due regard to its limitations and weaknesses, alongside its strengths. To many laypeople and sports coaches, professional sport psychologists are already viewed with a degree of suspicion. At times they have failed to deliver the goods which they over-optimistically promised, or have packaged the goods in a way that clients have found unappealing. At other times sport psychologists have been regarded as manipulators or puppet masters who attempt to pull athletes' strings with one goal in mind, performance enhancement, at whatever price and with little regard to the sensitivities or wishes of the individual or team concerned (Patmore, 1986).

The reality of professional sport psychology is somewhat different. Increasingly sport psychologists would work hand in glove with athletes, coaches, administrators, dieticians, physiotherapists, physiologists, biomechanists and other technical specialists as part of a team devising packages and programmes which the athlete feels will be of benefit to him or her. There is little cloak and dagger or behind-the-scenes manoeuvring, and it is to be hoped that the continuance of this 'up front' approach will help to sweep away any lingering worries and apprehensions.

Undoubtedly, lurking on the fringes of the subject there may be those whose professional conduct leaves a great deal to be desired but as professional and amateur sport continues to become ever more systematic, and athletes become increasingly sophisticated and knowledgable in their approach to their chosen sport then the scope for sharp or poor practice becomes that much more limited. Professional bodies may feel that it is their sole responsibility to oversee standards in their disciplines but make no mistake, the customers themselves, working and playing out there in the sporting community, are equally capable of maintaining quality control and should be actively encouraged to continue to do so.

Presenting Sport Psychology

As an introductory sport psychology book it would have been very tempting, and much easier, for us to adopt the format which most sport psychology texts follow. These books are primarily geared to the needs of students of physical education or sport science, or those with a direct interest in practising sport psychology. As a consequence they often assume little background knowledge across psychology. We do not intend to denigrate these texts but it is important to signpost the way in which they put across sport psychology, and thereby make understandable the selection and categorization processes which authors and editors employ. Inevitably certain fields are given prominence while others are largely ignored, and the selection process may appear strange to those with little knowledge in the area itself. To start to provide some guidance to the available literature, a list of the more popular sport psychology texts which have appeared since 1988 is presented at the end of this chapter.

Clearly there is no shortage of choice from a list which contains both general introductory texts and more specialist books, some written exclusively for the academic market, others for the expert practitioner. Unfortunately the psychological insight which is offered in some, but certainly not all, may be somewhat disappointing to anyone who is other than a complete newcomer to psychology. The depth of analysis is therefore one dimension along which these books differ. A further but equally significant dimension is the relative importance which is attached to either pure research or applied work. This distinction can be clearly seen in the contrast between teaching texts prepared for general sport psychology students and those written with the more lucrative applied sport psychology market in mind. To highlight this distinction, a list of contemporary applied sport psychology texts which have appeared since 1988 appears at the end of this chapter, a list developed from the earlier work of Sachs (1991).

As can be seen immediately, there is little overlap between the two book lists, a stark reminder of the two faces of sport psychology. In the subsequent chapters, while aiming to cover a broad range of material, our main focus has been on the pure or academic sport psychology research, with examples of applied techniques discussed if and when appropriate. In terms of the sport psychology texts geared towards an academic audience, a survey amongst BASS members was designed to discover which texts were most popular amongst those who organize or teach sport psychology courses in the UK (Biddle, 1992). The most cited general introductory texts (in order of citation) were those by Silva and Weinberg (1984), Schmidt (1988), Cox (1990), Carron (1980, 1984, 1988), Gill (1986), and Williams (1986). Unless you are familiar with these books, obviously this list tells you little of the content of existing sport psychology courses. Therefore to give you a greater feel for the primary areas of interest, we have listed the chapter headings from one of the most popular and up-to-date single author texts below (Cox, 1990):

Introduction
Personality and the Athlete
Attention in Sport
Arousal in Sport
Anxiety in Sport
Intervention Strategies
Achievement Motivation
Causal Attribution Theory
Aggression in Sport
Audience Effects
Team Cohesion
Leadership in Sport

To condense the key areas of primary interest yet further, it would be fair to say that sport psychology (which is that version not defined exclusively as motor skills and motor learning, see Schmidt, 1988) would still tend to focus on six primary issues. These are motivation, personality, aggression, arousal/stress/anxiety, psychological skills training/ intervention practices, and finally, team processes. Depending upon your point of view, it is either reassuring as a sign of continuity or it is alarming as an indication of inertia that this is a list which would not have been unfamiliar to Coleman Griffith almost 70 years ago!

To help foster links between psychology and sport psychology we felt that it would be helpful to reframe this literature using categories which were familiar to psychologists from many diverse backgrounds. This may help psychologists feel comfortable with this material while at the same time it may also give sport scientists the opportunity to incorporate more recent research from within and beyond sport psychology into an expanded framework or mental set. In addition this framework may show professional psychologists where opportunities for further work may lie and at the same time inevitably shows the constraints imposed by existing knowledge frameworks. To move forward effectively, sometimes it is necessary to break with tradition and partially deconstruct certain 'topics' which may have formed the core of traditional sport psychology but which now inhibit rather than facilitate research intiatives. One prime example is motivation in sport which we have deliberately not treated as an isolated topic but have broken down into smaller and more manageable themes, themes which are then set in the context of relevant literatures from across psychology. Thus motivational themes emerge and are discussed in relation to individual differences and achievement motivation (Chapter 2), cognitive styles (Chapter 3), precompetition arousal (Chapter 4), work motivation and job satisfaction (Chapter 7), participation motivation and drop out (Chapter 8), and the psychophysiology of emotion and arousal (Chapter 9). The same is true for issues such as stress, anxiety and arousal in sport, topics which appear in many guises in many chapters. We make no excuse for this approach; instead we see it as a positive step which may help towards breaking free from traditional labels and outmoded research constraints and which eventually may encourage the development of models which can genuinely accommodate multiple perspectives.

Taken as a whole, the book represents an interchange between sport, sport psychology and the discipline of psychology, presenting current research in sport psychology and seeing how this fits within the wider frame of mainstream psychology. Lines of demarcation between subdisciplines within psychology are never clear cut and there are bound to be occasions where material does not fit tidily under one label, or it could be argued is more appropriate elsewhere. Where there are overlaps then it is important not to ignore these territorial disputes and we certainly do not regard the boundaries between the branches of psychology as set in stone. Instead, the book's structure represents a heuristic framework which is permeable and amenable to change but which also provides some convenient and readily identifiable categories with which to segment the array of material which now constitutes sport psychology.

If nothing else, *Psychology in Sport* should help you appreciate the diversity and the dynamism of sport psychology. The scene continues to change rapidly, and there are many significant research initiatives which point the way towards a very healthy future for the subject as a whole. Boundaries between disciplines and between interest areas no longer seem quite so daunting and the distance between psychology and sport psychology shrinks perceptibly by the day. These are all positive signs but at the same time there are a number of old chestnuts which continue to roast away in the fire. Professional issues still occupy a great deal of time and energy, centring most recently around the question of certification or chartering. At least sport psychologists can take comfort from the fact that they are not alone here, with many branches of psychology wrestling with similar sorts of professional problems. In a broader sense, the relationship between theory and practice, and between pure and applied research is a long way from being resolved. However, this conflict or tension may not always be counterproductive, and in some ways it may be a useful source of both energy and checks and balances. One very good example is the work on stress, arousal and anxiety, highlighted in Chapter 4, where empirical research and practical interventions seem to be converging yet from entirely different directions.

For those encountering the sport psychology literature for the very first time, the diversity of interests of sport psychologists must be bewildering. It is no longer possible to call yourself a general sport psychologist and be capable of keeping abreast of all developments across all these areas. The era of the research specialist is dawning, yet it is to be hoped that with an expanding student demand and with a growing market in sport itself that the corporate identity of sport psychology is not lost. At the present time, the field is showing definite signs of bifurcation, with sport psychology continuing to concentrate most heavily on competitive sport while a newer and extremely vigorous offshoot, exercise psychology, now focuses on the psychology of physical exercise and activity. We have tried to keep our focus on competitive sport but at the same time we have included signposts towards the exercise psychology literature, and have delved into that material in greater depth when we felt it was important. The split between exercise and sport psychology was inevitable and represents yet one more saga in an ongoing story of development for the subject area. It is likely that this division will become more and more obvious over the coming years and particularly given the speed with which exercise psychology has developed during the late 1980s, and the good relationships which have already been established with other health related branches of psychology. This distinction between sport and exercise psychology is entirely understandable yet the original links are also so important to both areas that it is to be hoped that a state of peaceful coexistence and cooperation prevails for the foreseeable future.

At the end of the day, whether or not we have been successful in first of all pulling apart and then weaving together the strands which go to make up contemporary sport psychology will eventually be left to you to decide. We remain convinced that the enterprise has been worthwhile, if for nothing else as a way of encouraging yet closer cooperation between psychology and sport psychology and through this to help develop a deeper understanding of sport research within the wider psychological community. Separate development rarely leads to long term happiness; more often it is a step on a long road to acrimony. A healthier alternative is to encourage open and frank communication, to recognize strengths and weaknesses, similarities and differences, and through this process to help to marry good theory with good practice. Whether you call yourself a psychologist, a sport scientist, a coach, an athlete or merely someone with a general interest in sport, it is in this spirit of 'sport psychology for all' that *Psychology in Sport* is presented.

References

ANSHEL, M. H. (1992) 'The case against the certification of sport psychologists: In search of the phantom expert', *The Sport Psychologist*, 6, pp. 265–86.

BIDDLE, S. (1992) 'Psychology on sport science/sport studies degrees', *British Association of Sports Sciences Newsletter*, 2, 1, pp. 12–13.

BUNKER, L. K. and MAGUIRE, N. (1985) 'Give sport psychology to sport', in BUNKER, L. K. *et al.* (Eds) *Sport Psychology: Psychological Considerations in Maximizing Sport Performance*, Ithaca, NY: Movement Publications, pp. 3–14.

CARRON A. V. (1980) *Social Psychology of Sport*, Ithaca, NY: Movement Publications.

CARRON, A. V. (1984) *Motivation: Implications for Coaching and Teaching*, London, Ontario: Sports Dynamics.

CARRON, A. V. (1988) *Group Dynamics in Sport*, London, Ontario: Spodym.

COX, R. H. (1990) *Sport Psychology: Concepts and Applications*, Dubuque, IA: Wm Brown.

FELTZ D. L. (1987) 'Advancing knowledge in sport psychology: Strategies for expanding our conceptual frameworks', *Quest*, 39, pp. 243–54.

FURLONG, W. B. (1976) 'Psychology of the playing fields', *Psychology Today*, July.

GILL, D. L. (1986) *Psychological Dynamics of Sport*, Champaign, IL: Human Kinetics.

KREMER, J. and SCULLY, D. (1991) 'Psychology and sport: Past, present . . . and future?' *The Psychologist: Bulletin of the British Psychological Society*, 4, pp. 147–51.

OGILVIE, B. C. and TUTKO, T. (1966) *Problem Athletes and How to Handle Them*, London: Pelham Books.

PATMORE, A. (1986) *Sportsmen under Stress*, London: Stanley Paul.

ROBERTS, G. C. and KIIECIK, J. C. (1989) 'Sport Psychology in the German Democratic Republic: An interview with Dr Gerd Kanzag', *The Sport Psychologist*, 3, pp. 72–77.

SACHS, M. L. (1991) 'Reading list in applied sport psychology: Psychological skills training', *The Sport Psychologist*, 5, 1, pp. 88–91.

SALMELA, J. H. (1984) 'Comparative sport psychology', in SILVA, J. M. and WEINBERG, R. S. (Eds) *Psychological Foundations of Sport*, Champaign, IL: Human Kinetics, pp. 23–34.

SCHMIDT, R. (1988) *Motor Control and Learning*, Champaign, IL: Human Kinetics.

SILVA, J. M. and WEINBERG, R. S. (Eds) (1984) *Psychological Foundations of Sport*, Champaign, IL: Human Kinetics.

TRIPLETT, N. (1898) 'The dynamogenic factors in pacemaking and competition', *American Journal of Psychology*, 9, pp. 505–23.

WIGGINS, D. K. (1984) 'The history of sport psychology in North America', in SILVA, J. M. and WEINBERG, R. S. (Eds) *Psychological Foundations of Sport*, Champaign, IL: Human Kinetics.

WILLIAMS, J. (1986) *Applied Sport Psychology: Personal Growth to Peak Performance*, Palo Alto, CA: Mayfield.

Further Reading

Basic Sport Psychology Texts (1989–1993)

BAKKER, F. C., WHITING, H. T. A. and VAN DER BRUG, H. (1990) *Sport Psychology: Concepts and Applications*, Chichester: John Wiley and Sons.

BIDDLE, S. and MUTRIE, N. (1991) *Psychology of Physical Activity and Exercise*, London: Springer-Verlag.

CARRON, A. V. (1988) *Group Dynamics in Sport*, London, Ontario: Spodym.

COX, R. H. (1990) *Sport Psychology: Concepts and Applications*, 2nd edn, Dubuque, IA: Wm C. Brown.

DAVIES, D. (1989) *Psychological Factors in Competitive Sport*, London: Falmer Press.

DIAMANT, L. (Ed.) (1991) *The Psychology of Sports, Exercise and Fitness: Social and Personal Issues*, New York: Hemisphere.

DIAMANT, L. (Ed.) (1991) *Mind-Body Maturity: Psychological Approaches to Sports, Exercise and Fitness*, New York: Hemisphere.

DISHMAN, R. K. (Ed.) (1988) *Exercise Adherence: Its Impact on Mental Health*, Champaign, IL: Human Kinetics.

HEIL, J. (1993) *Psychology of Sport Injury*, Champaign, IL: Human Kinetics.

HORN, T. S. (Ed.) (1992) *Advances in Sport Psychology*, Champaign, IL: Human Kinetics.

LE UNES, A. and NATION, T. (1989) *Sport Psychology*, Chicago, IL: Nelson-Hall.

MARTENS, R., VEALEY, R. S. and BURTON, D. (1990) *Competitive Anxiety in Sport*, Champaign, IL: Human Kinetics.

OSTROW, A. C. (1990) *Directory of Psychological Tests in the Sport and Exercise Sciences*, Morgantown, WV: Fitness Information Technology.

REJESKI, W. J. and KENNEY, E. A. (1988) *Fitness Motivation: Preventing Participation Dropout*, Champaign, IL: Human Kinetics.

ROBERTS, G. C. (Ed.) (1992) *Motivation in Sport and Exercise*, Champaign, IL: Human Kinetics.

SCHILLING, G. (Ed.) (1992) *Sport Science Review: Volume 1(2), Sport Psychology*, Champaign, IL: Human Kinetics.

SALMELA, J. H. (1992) *The World's Sport Psychology Sourcebook*, 2nd edn, Champaign, IL: Human Kinetics.

SINGER, R. N., MURPHEY, M. and TENNANT, L. K. (Eds) (1993) *Handbook of Research on Sport Psychology*, New York: Macmillan.

THOMPSON, R. A. and TRATTNER-SHERMAN, R. (1993) *Helping Athletes with Eating Disorders*, Champaign, IL: Human Kinetics.

WEINBERG, R. S. and RICHARDSON, P. A. (1990) *Psychology of Officiating*, Champaign, IL: Human Kinetics.

WILLIS, J. D. and CAMPBELL, L. F. (1992) *Exercise Psychology*, Champaign, IL: Human Kinetics.

Applied Sport Psychology Texts (1989–1993)

ALBINSON, J. G. and BULL, S. J. (1988) *The Mental Game Plan*, London, Ontario: Spodym.

BULL, S. J. (Ed.) (1991) *Sport Psychology: A Self-help Guide*, Wiltshire: The Crowood Press.

BUMP, L. (1989) *Sport Psychology Study Guide (and Workbook)*, Champaign, IL: Human Kinetics.

CURTIS, J. D. (1989) *The Mindset for Winning*, La Crosse, WI: Coulee Press.

HARDY, L. and FAZEY, J. (1990) *Mental Training*, Leeds: The National Coaching Foundation.

HEMERY, D. (1991) *Sporting Excellence: What Makes a Champion?* London: Harper Collins.

KUBISTANT, T. (1988) M*ind Pump: The Psychology of Bodybuilding*, Champaign, IL: Leisure Press.

LIVINGSTON, M. K. (1989) *Mental Discipline: The Pursuit of Peak Performance*, Champaign, IL: Leisure Press.

NIDEFFER, R. M. (1992) *Psyched to Win*, Champaign, IL: Leisure Press.

ORLICK, T. (1990) *In Pursuit of Excellence: How to Win in Sport and Life Through Mental Training*, Champaign, IL: Leisure Press.

TERRY, P. (1989) *The Winning Mind*, Nottingham: Thorsons.

WEINBERG, R. S. (1988) *The Mental Advantage: Developing your Psychological Skills in Tennis*, Champaign, IL: Human Kinetics.

Chapter 2

What Makes an Athlete?

(Personality and Individual Differences)

Introduction

In many people's minds, first and foremost sport psychology is about charting the relationship between personality and sport. Whether in the context of motivation, aggression, stress and anxiety, cognitive processes, development or social influence, each could be said to discuss how individuals differ in their response to sporting situations. To pursue this argument to its natural conclusion, almost the entire book could be described as an examination of the relationship between personality and sport. Intuitively, such an approach may be appealing; in reality, to use personality as the prime focus would almost certainly create more confusion than clarity and the reason why this is the case is not difficult to discover.

Put quite simply, so long as psychology wrestles with, or at least accommodates, so many conflicting personality theories then sport psychology cannot hope to develop a comprehensive appreciation of the effects of personality on sport. If you turn to classic overviews of the study of personality within the discipline of psychology, such as provided by Mischel (1971) and Maddi (1976), or any introductory text of today, the problem becomes readily apparent. What these writers demonstrate emphatically is that psychologists are still a very long way from reaching consensus as to what it is that makes us who we are — what makes us human and what makes us social. What is more, a great many of these theories are diametrically opposed. To Sigmund Freud, we are selfish animals, thrown together into our social world through biological necessity, yet to Carl Rogers we are inherently noble and good but diverted from the royal road to self-actualization through the intervention of significant others in our lives. To Erving Goffman, personality is nothing more than a series of roles or personae which we present to the world, yet to Raymond Cattell there is a stable core to our personality. To George Kelly, above all else we are each unique, with idiosyncratic priorities and special world views, yet to Hans Eysenck we all comprise a finite number of personality traits. To George Herbert Mead, we are what we are through the meaning we impute to our interactions, yet to B. F. Skinner we are mindlessly conditioned by our environment.

We could go on but hopefully the point is clear. Nowhere do the unique qualities of psychology as a special brand of science reveal themselves more vividly than in the multiple perspectives which are encountered in the personality literature. Psychology students over the years have learnt to live with, and select from, these competing views and their fundamental contradictions. There is little evidence of a coming together of minds, nor, it could be argued, should there be. Psychology as a discipline may not be motivated to resolve these fundamental disagreements, but where does this leave applied areas, including sport psychology? The answer is in a real pickle for sport psychologists, as applied scientists, are expected to provide answers to customers' questions, questions such as: Is there a psychological profile of the successful athlete? What set of characteristics set the champion apart from the also-ran? Does sport make the person, or is it only a certain type of individual who can ever succeed in sport?

These are all questions which practising sport psychologists routinely encounter, and when they turn to psychology for answers they are hit by a welter of theories but little by way of definitive conclusions. What has been their response? Using diplomatic parlance, their strategy has traditionally been to be 'economical with the truth'. Lip service is normally paid to competing theories of personality but then the cut and thrust of theoretical debate is left swiftly behind as one approach is afforded prominence above all others, namely the trait or dispositional approach, more latterly looked at from an interactional perspective. This approach has dominated the sport psychology literature for decades, despite longstanding scepticism of the approach from within psychology as a whole (Mischel, 1979) and indeed it is only in recent years that the inherent weaknesses in the trait approach have been seriously placed under the spotlight in sport psychology itself (for example Vealey, 1989; Vanden Auweele, *et al.* 1993).

The momentum to continue this type of research undoubtedly derives from a consumer demand for player profiling. Our old friend Coleman Griffith was one of the earliest to tread the well worn path of categorizing athletes through the determination of significant psychological traits. As a consultant for the Chicago Cubs he was asked to produce the psychological prototype of a champion baseball player. From interviews and observations he was prepared to offer a general description of the sporting champion, couched in terms including ruggedness, loyalty, buoyancy, optimism, alertness and courage (Griffith, 1928). Unfortunately, at the same time he was singularly unsuccessful in coming up with a personality blueprint which would actually predict success. However, his failure did little to quench the ardour of numerous sports scientists who yearned to discover the elusive psychological formula for predicting sporting achievement. The marketplace for these research endeavours has always been there, and presumably will always exist so long as the world of sport maintains a belief that a personality formula or recipe awaits discovery, and that despite the failures of the past, the quest remains legitimate, and the goal realizable. To what extent psychology has itself contributed to this process is debatable. Certainly the popular image presented of the subject as a deterministic science with ready-made answers for complex questions has done little to harm the cause.

In many respects this branch of the subject is the most controversial within sport psychology. Psychological profiling data have the potential to be used in many different ways; some are benign while others have the potential to be positively dangerous. At one extreme is the practising sport psychologist who has the genuine interest of his or her client at heart. This individual may legitimately turn to standard psychometric measures to facilitate understanding and subsequently to help develop suitable intervention programmes. In this context personality profiling is used for the immediate benefit of the individual athlete. At the other extreme, there is evidence, often anecdotal, that attempts have been made over the years to use psychological tests as screening or selection devices within sport. It is here that a range of ethical and professional issues come to the fore. For example, according to Neil Amdur (writing for the *International Herald Tribune* on 26 January 1978; cited in Patmore, 1986: 233), the Dallas Cowboys kept 25,000 separate dossiers on every professional American football prospect, files which included ratings on their aggressiveness, competitiveness, mental alertness and even their biorhythm charts. To imagine that the professional career of a highly paid athlete may have hung on his biorhythm chart should send shivers down the spine of any self-respecting psychologist! In former Eastern bloc countries, and most notoriously East Germany, it has long been rumoured that psychological tests were routinely used to screen and select potential athletes from a very early age, although hard evidence to substantiate these claims is difficult to obtain. Closer to home, a growing number of professional soccer clubs now hire consultants to carry out psychological profiling of players, although these aptitude and personality tests are not overtly used for the purposes of selection but in the more general context of player management where they may well play a useful role. However, once these data have been generated, how those data are controlled and protected must be a matter of some concern.

Although it is possible to find many and varied examples of profiling research in sport, it would be mischievous and misleading to argue that the majority of applied work has always explicitly or indeed implicitly been carried out as part of a selection process, to sort the wheat from the sporting chaff as some have suggested (Patmore, 1986). The majority of personality research in sport psychology is at worst benign, at best positively helpful to the athlete. Most professional sport psychologists use tests sensibly, and at the same time have at least some awareness of their limitations. It is an undeniable fact that the literature offers little encouragement to those who believe they can turn to sport psychology for reliable tests and measures which will discriminate between the good and the not-so-good. In the words of Richard Cox (1990: 22),

> A coach or teacher should never make a decision to cut or bench an athlete based solely on personality testing. With the best research available and sophisticated testing procedures, only 70 to 80 percent of élite athletes can be correctly categorized using psychological testing procedures. This is not good enough. It would be unethical to act contrary to this recommendation.

To some, this may appear as an accurate, if damning, indictment of decades of fruitless research. To them, a figure of 70 per cent may seem optimistically high, or even a meaningless statistic. To others the statement may be seen as a pragmatic appraisal of the current state of play, and to others it may act as yet another spur to do further but yet more rigorous research in the same vein! Whichever is the case, the significant role played by psychological testing in sport psychology cannot be ignored and this chapter will endeavour to offer a flavour of this material. We begin by considering work on psychological traits in sport, before looking at the more recent work which considers these enduring characteristics alongside psychological states and how these impact on performance in particular sports. Beyond this, the issue of causality will be discussed before finally considering alternative approaches to personality in sport, at the same time suggesting directions in which the subject may head in forthcoming years.

To end this introduction, we return to the opening paragraph and offer a reminder that this coverage is not exhaustive of all possible themes loosely embraced by the terms personality, individual differences and sport. For example, there is the extensive literature dealing with positive mental states and physical exercise (see Chapter 4). From the days of Homer and the early pan-Hellenic games, the association between the healthy body and the healthy mind has been fertile ground for speculation and supposition. The ancient Greeks regarded the development of mental and physical prowess as inseparable in the pursuit of personal excellence, a sentiment which is still unreservedly supported by a great many sport scientists. The relationship between physical activity and mental health, and the impact of exercise on psychological well-being, is not dealt with here but is covered in the latter part of Chapter 5. To summarize briefly, the message which sport psychologists often like to convey remains a positive one, sometimes excessively positive, namely that physical activity is positively associated with mental health (Morgan and Goldston, 1987). Without doubt, physical activity can promote mental health but certain qualifications must apply. For example, this is true only when exercise is kept within limits and when the reasons why people exercise are intrinsically healthy to begin with. Once more, the movement has been away from simple and sovereign answers and towards an appreciation that the questions themselves are complex, never mind the answers. This has to be a far more healthy and respectful approach with which to move the subject forwards.

Measuring Personality: The Trait Approach

As already mentioned, sport psychologists over the years have maintained a keen interest in psychological profiling and have been naturally drawn to the quantification of personality variables. This is understandable in many ways. As competitive sport itself revolves around the measurement and reward of individual differences in performance it is no surprise to find that many sport scientists are likewise drawn, whether consciously or subconsciously, to quantifying not sporting but psychological differences. The research is often looked at in terms of three primary areas: first, the search for the 'winning profile'; second, a comparison between athletes and non-athletes; and third, quantifying differences in the personalities of athletes either competing in different sports or playing in different positions.

To begin to gain some appreciation of the extent of this literature then you are recommended to turn either to one of the numerous reviews of personality research in sport (Martens, 1975; Morgan, 1980a, 1980b; Fisher, 1984; Vealey, 1989, 1992; Cox, 1990; Vanden Auweele *et al.*, 1993), or simply to flick through an inventory describing the vast array of available sport psychology tests and measures (Ostrow, 1990). With regard to the literature reviews which are available, few irrefutable conclusions can be drawn as to the relationship between personality and sport performance. Given the sheer numbers of published articles, the inconclusive nature of the evidence is disappointing to say the least. However, the findings are entirely predictable when set in the context of similar endeavours in other branches of psychology. One example which immediately springs to mind is occupational psychology and its long term concern with leadership.

Stogdill (Bass, 1981) was able to draw on well over 100 studies in the last of his now famous reviews of leadership trait research; what was his principal conclusion as to what makes a leader? It was essentially that the search for a leader profile was not a profitable exercise because in practice, effective leadership involves a complex interplay between numerous environmental factors and specific personality dimensions. Social and organizational psychologists from the 1970s onwards had generally reached consensus that the trait approach *per se* was never going to unlock the door to understanding leadership processes, and that contingency models represented the only productive way forward. These contingency models are underpinned by the belief that success depends on an interaction between personal characteristics and environmental demands. The earliest contingency models attempted to measure personality variables and then define those situations within which individuals with certain characteristics would be the most effective leaders. To authors such as Fiedler (Bryman, 1986), the leader must change the circumstances to suit their preferred style. Here, personality (and in this case the score on Fiedler's least preferred co-worker scale) is taken as stable and unchanging and therefore it is the environment which must be altered to suit the individual. Such models are now increasingly in the minority; instead leaders and managers are advised how to change their leadership styles to meet changing demands. The implicit approach to personality which underpins latter-day models, such as those advanced by Vroom and Yetton, Hersey and Blanchard and House (see Greenberg and Baron, 1993) now assumes 'personality' to be far more fluid and subject to change over time and place. Management and leadership in sport are considered in greater detail in Chapter 7 but the important lesson to be learnt here is that it took a considerable shift in perspective to move the research forward in a more meaningful direction. This shift not only encompassed the leadership process itself but more importantly involved a radical reassessment of the underlying and implicit model of personality, a model which was found to be too simplistic and too static.

Returning our focus to sport psychology, it has certainly begun to travel down this road but still has some way to go. It is now generally recognized that irrespective of how personality itself is conceptualized, an interactional approach is the only sensible way to proceed in order to consider how personality relates to performance in particular contexts (Vealey, 1992). However, despite an increasing acceptance of alternative approaches, it is not clear that sport psychology is yet able to accommodate comfortably more dynamic models of personality itself. There is an acceptance that situations change and hence demands made on the individual change but there is still resistance in certain quarters to the idea that people themselves change fundamentally across time and place. It is to be hoped that barriers will come down over coming years, but certainly a trait mentality has become so firmly entrenched within sport psychology that this may well be a long and arduous campaign.

Measuring Global Traits

Looking back over the history of sport psychology, the search for the personality profile of the champion athlete has continued enthusiastically at least since the 1930s, albeit with somewhat less zeal over the last 15 years. It was in the late 1960s and early 1970s that this research reached its zenith, and the most influential writers at that time were undoubtedly Thomas Tutko and Bruce Ogilvie of San José State College in the USA, encapsulated in their highly popular and controversial book, *Problem Athletes and How to Handle Them* (1966). Their work centred around the development of a personality inventory for athletes known as the Athletic Motivation Inventory (AMI). From a review of existing studies, and reportedly drawing on existing inventories including Cattell's 16 PF, Ogilvie (1968) maintained that certain characteristics were associated with success in sport. These characteristics included drive, determination, leadership, aggressiveness, guilt proneness, emotional control, self-confidence, conscientiousness, mental toughness, trust and coachability. Having established this list of desirable traits, the AMI was produced and the rest, as they say, if not science is certainly history.

The AMI was subsequently made available to coaches who were given freedom to administer the test to their charges without the requirement of professional supervision. Coaches were then required to send completed forms back to the Institute for the Study of Athletic Motivation at San José where they were charged a fee to have the tests scored. A player profile was finally returned to the coach, for s/he to do with whatsoever s/he desired. In terms of the code by which professional psychologists operate, such procedures could be described as unethical (Rushall, 1973), and the indiscretion is made worse by the fact that there exists no published evidence to validate the inventory or link any of the traits to successful performance. Over the years it is estimated that the AMI has been administered to over 75,000 children and adults across the USA (Gill, 1986). How the test scores may have been used or misused, and the untold damage which could have been wrought by untrained coaches, can only be guessed at. It could be argued that this work was very significant in raising the profile of sport psychology within the sport community but whether this was always in a positive direction is doubtful. At the same time, research of this nature hammered a wedge between applied sport psychologists and their more research oriented colleagues, a rift which remains evident to this day (see Chapter 1).

This was not an auspicious starting point to trait research in the new era of sport psychology. Since that time more rigorous attempts have been made by sport psychologists to seek out winning traits using existing and well validated psychological inventories, and often working strictly according to scientific methods. Prominent amongst the tests and inventories which have been used are Cattell's 16 PF and Eysenck's EPI (or Eysenck Personality Inventory). One large scale study which is often cited used the 16 PF to compare approximately 1500 young students, approximately half of whom were actively involved in sport (Schurr *et al.*, 1977). Each subject completed the 16 PF (the dependent variable), with student year, type of sport, level of success and sport involvement as the main independent variables. A complex set of results and analyses emerged, with few clear cut conclusions. However, those who took part in team sports tended to be less independent, self-sufficient and stress-free than those participating in individual sports. In addition, certain athletes in certain sports scored higher on extroversion, independence and lower on anxiety, although the caveats and inconsistencies ensured that no general profile could be established to distinguish those who took part in sport from those who did not. Other authors have been less circumspect in describing the relationship between personality traits and sport. According to Hans Eysenck, 'extroverts and high psychoticism scorers are more likely to take up sports and excel in them, because their low arousal levels lead them to seek sensory stimulation . . . and they are more tolerant of the pain associated with sport' (Eysenck *et al.*, 1982: 8). Such gross generalizations do not stand close scrutiny. By way of example, Sack (1975) found that middle and long distance runners, athletes who routinely take themselves to the limits of physical endurance, were actually more introverted, and Geron *et al.* (1986), in a review of personality differences across various sports, found track and field sprinters to be among the most anxious, emotionally disturbed and tense.

Taken as a whole, the results from these inventories have been far from impressive, although research continues to this day. Fortunately, these endeavours are now being supplemented by the development of psychological inventories geared specifically towards sport-related psychological skills, and not personality traits as such. Two recent examples are the Psychological Skills Inventory for Sport (PSIS) (Mahoney *et al.*, 1987), and the 56 item Sport-Related Psychological Skills Questionnaire (SPSQ) (Nelson and Hardy, 1990). The former measures six 'metacognitive skills' (anxiety control, concentration, confidence, mental preparation, motivation and team orientation), and the latter measures seven (imaginal skills, mental preparation, self-efficacy, cognitive anxiety, concentration skill, relaxation skill and motivation skill). Applied sport psychologists often deal directly with all these skills in the course of their work, and for them to have access to questionnaires with which to assess clients' strengths and weaknesses in terms of these dimensions would seem eminently sensible. The validation process for both the PSIS and the SPSQ remains very much in its infancy but it is to be hoped that development work on these questionnaires continues, and at a healthy distance from the wider discussion of trait theory in sport.

Returning to the questions posed much earlier (in terms of personality traits, do athletes differ from non-athletes? Do competitors in different sports differ? Do winners differ from losers?) the answers are far from equivocal. Supporters of the trait approach would argue that there is some evidence to suggest first, that athletes may be less anxious and more extroverted (Sack, 1975; Morgan, 1980b; Eysenck *et al.*, 1982), second, that specific personality types can be shown to cluster in particular sports and in particular positions within sports (Schurr *et al.*, 1977), but finally, that when comparing those who succeed in their chosen sport and those who do not, even supporters of the trait approach would be hard pressed to find consistent evidence of any differences. From a coaching perspective this last finding is the most notable; sport psychology has not been able to come close to providing a personality formula to predict sporting success (Vealey, 1992).

One further issue is worthy of mention here, namely causality. Irrespective of the size of differences, if athletes and non-athletes differ along certain personality dimensions, were these differences present before the athletes took up the sport or did they develop through the experience of sport? This is a fascinating issue for a host of reasons, some specific to the practice of sport psychology, others concerning methodology, others with a bearing on personality theory as a whole. If personality dimensions do not change substantially over time then this enables us to lay down parameters as to an athlete's likely response in different situations. Consequently the task of the sport psychologist in predicting and controlling performance becomes that much more straightforward, and trait theorists can feel more comfortable with the major psychological constructs (first-order traits) which they regard as forming the core of personality. However, if personality is seen as inherently more dynamic, changing across time and circumstance, then the task of performance prediction is made doubly difficult for sport psychologists working in the field, and at the same time the fundamental tenet of trait theory is attacked.

The more positive side to this coin, from the perspective of sport psychology, is that it then becomes possible to consider how sport and physical exercise may facilitate personal growth and development, a philosophy which underpins the use of physical exercise in promoting psychological well-being. What does available evidence suggest is true? Unfortunately, as you may have guessed, no hard and fast conclusions can be reached and support can be found for either argument. On the one hand, longitudinal research based on the administration of personality inventories at various stages during an athlete's career have found little evidence of substantial shifts in general personality characteristics (Gabler, 1976; Folkins and Sime, 1981; Eysenck *et al.*, 1982). On the other hand, the sport and exercise psychology literature is peppered with examples showing how exercise can affect specific personality dimensions (Biddle and Mutrie, 1991), thus demonstrating personality change in response to sport. There is a need to resolve this contradiction. It could well be that sport in itself is not the crucial variable here but rather it is the associated changes in lifestyle which come about through a healthy involvement in a sport or recreation which make a far greater impact on our psyche. This issue is explored further in other chapters in relation to participation motivation (Chapters 5, 7 and 8) and psychophysiological changes (Chapter 9). Notwithstanding this discussion, this seems to be one of those occasions where more research is urgently required. In the words of Diamant *et al.* (1991: 232),

> The studies . . . suggest a link between low trait anxiety and a cool detachment and athletic success. They do not, however, answer the question of whether athletes succeed because of personality variables, or whether athletic participation and success contribute to changes in personality traits over time. This would be a fruitful area for longitudinal studies of personality traits and athletic success.

Gender

Biographical variables (for example ethnic origin and socio-economic class) do not feature significantly in the sport psychology literature, except as examples of factors which may influence sport participation rates (Greendorfer, 1987). The only biographical variable which has generated interest is gender, and here the interest has a life span which goes back only as far as the birth of the women's movement in the 1970s. In this respect the history of sport psychology parallels that of psychology as a whole. Sport psychology has not been immune from the androcentrism or male bias which has characterized so much of psychology's past (Russo and Denmark, 1987). This chauvinism reflects either in research focusing exclusively on male subjects, or on work which tends to disregard sex differences. With this in mind it is an interesting experience to scan the most popular sport psychology texts, even those dating from the 1980s. With few exceptions, references to gender, sex or women are rare, and where they do appear, they tend to cluster in books either written or edited by sport psychologists who are women. Williams (1980), in a review of existing material, found little evidence to suggest significant differences based on biological sex. However, as Diane Gill (1992) points out, when discussing the relationship between gender and sport, biological sex is less significant than the individual's sex role orientation, or psychological sex, and this becomes a much more fruitful launching pad for enquiry.

Sex role orientation refers not to the biology of sex but to the social psychology of sex roles, as originally outlined by Bem (1974) and measured by her Bem Sex Role Inventory (BSRI), and later taken up by Spence and Helmreich (1978) with their Personal Attributes Questionnaire (PAQ). Each scale measures two personality characteristics, masculinity and femininity. Contrary to what many believe, these are not related or opposite sides of the same coin; instead they are independent dimensions of personality. In the past, scores from these scales have been used routinely to categorize both men and women as either masculine (low feminine; high masculine scores), feminine (high feminine; low masculine scores), androgynous (high feminine; high masculine scores) or undifferentiated (low feminine; low masculine scores).

Herein lay yet another opportunity to pigeonhole sportsmen and women, and as you may expect, sport psychologists were not slow off the mark to recognize the research opportunities which could follow. Studies comparing the sex role orientations of men and women between sports (for example, Wrisberg *et al.*, 1988), in and out of sport (Helmreich and Spence, 1977), or in terms of specific sports-relevant characteristics (Anderson and Williams, 1987) followed. This work demonstrated that those who succeeded in sport tended to endorse masculine or androgynous traits, and that feminine traits were often associated with poor motivation in sport and high levels of competitive anxiety.

As Gill (1992: 146) rightly points out, this work continued despite the ongoing debate within psychology as to whether or not it is legitimate first to use scores derived from masculinity and femininity scales to categorize people (rather than place along an ordinal scale), or second, to combine masculinity and femininity scores (Archer, 1989; Ballard-Reich and Etton, 1992). Unquestionably, it is the case that success in sport is associated with competitiveness and instrumental behaviour for both men and women. In turn, instrumentality is often associated with masculinity and expressiveness with femininity. However, there is then no necessity to slide into a discussion of competitive sport in relation to sex role orientation (masculinity/femininity) as if this were some type of first-order or source trait from which competitiveness (the second-order trait) derives. In addition, there is a need to take into account recent discussion of gender schema (Bem, 1985), which argues that our scores on sex role inventories do not sex type us as such but are best interpreted as indicators of the significance of sex typing to our world view. Those with high scores on either masculinity or femininity are more likely to make reference to schema (cognitive sets or frameworks) which include a gender component, and this in turn may influence their willingness to take up certain sports, or to sex type sports in general. In reality this almost invariably means classifying competitive sports as masculine (Matteo, 1988; Kane and Snyder, 1989), with few exceptions such as dance, synchronized swimming and aerobics labelled as feminine sports.

Taking these recent theoretical developments into account it remains true that competitive sport sits most easily alongside the traditional masculine stereotype. Men run towards their stereotype whereas women are more likely to experience sex role conflict if they feel that their behaviour in a sporting context goes against what their culture or society dictates to be appropriate for their sex (Butt, 1987). However, this is only the beginning of the story, for any review of work in this area must recognize that sex role stereotypes are not fixed but will change over time and place. For example, in western societies there has traditionally been a reluctance for many women to take up field events in athletics, events such as the shot-put and discus. Culturally these pursuits were seen as 'unfeminine'. In former Soviet bloc states this was rarely a problem, as those cultures had historically valued the manual work which women carried out, most especially as part of the rural economy, and many of the body traits associated with athletic strength were not seen as incongruent with 'being a woman'.

Similarly, stereotypes change over time. Up until recent years in the United Kingdom it would have been exceptional to see women lifting weights in a gym, or taking part in many sports which were traditionally seen as male preserves, for example rugby or boxing. There have been changes in patterns of sports activity, and these changes in behaviour can be very revealing of fundamental shifts in sex role stereotypes. Within the psychology of gender it is argued that the traditional stereotype of the woman as carer and provider is gradually being replaced by the 'superwoman' ideal and especially among the younger population. Where in the past, working women may have experienced low self-esteem because they were working against their stereotype, now women are expected to accommodate multiple roles encompassing all aspects of their lives. This shift has its positive side, in allowing women greater freedom of choice and expression but it also has its down side. For example, the increase in eating disorders, including anorexia and bulimia nervosa, has been linked to women's need to strive for the superwoman ideal, to be masculine yet feminine, thin yet curvaceous, nurturant yet independent, instrumental yet expressive. In turn, women's relationship with sport and exercise then becomes a fascinating new arena for research (Davis and Cowles, 1991), asking basic questions such as why do men and women choose to exercise in the first place, and what benefits do they derive?

This research is looking towards the future. The traditional literature which exists on gender in sport psychology has tended to concentrate on the more established issue of sex role conflict (Cann, 1991), widening into a more general discussion of female (but usually not male) sexuality in sport (Mechikoff, 1987). The arguments here are well rehearsed, and are couched in terms of the traditional stereotypes as already outlined. The literature has tended to concentrate on the process of sport socialization during childhood and adolescence (Greendorfer, 1992), and demonstrates that despite starting on a generally level playing field in early childhood, for a whole host of reasons, girls move away from sport as they approach adolescence but boys' enthusiasm grows (van Wersch *et al.*, 1992). Again, whether these patterns will change over coming years remains to be seen but this is clearly a fascinating area of research, and one which is likely to become increasingly salient to a great many fields within psychology in the years to come.

Competitive Anxiety

Any discussion of personality traits in sport could not ignore one particular trait which has occupied more time than any other, competitive anxiety. Time and again, the sport psychology literature returns to a preoccupation with competitive anxiety, that is the response of the individual to sporting occasions, and perhaps most significantly, the big sporting occasion. Helping athletes deal with pressure has become the bread and butter of many professional sport psychologists. Given this expanding market, together with widespread interest within sport, it should come as no surprise to find that a considerable number of inventories have been developed and adapted for use within sport (Ostrow, 1990). It could be argued that these scales do not measure a personality trait as defined by traditionalists such as Cattell or Eysenck, given that an individual's response to competition can depend so much on context. Nevertheless, the underlying assumption appears to be that it is possible to quantify, and then predict, a particular response set and this pattern of response remains constant over time. Therefore, even when describing the distinction between 'trait' anxiety (i.e. the more enduring predisposition to respond to stress) and 'state' anxiety (i.e. the immediate response to stressors), the individual's inherent predisposition to respond remains firmly in view (see Chapter 4 for further discussion).

It is also interesting to note that the majority of sport psychology texts choose to describe the literature on anxiety and its measurement apart from that dealing with personality. Why this is the case is not immediately obvious. Certainly, the sheer volume of work devoted exclusively to stress, anxiety and arousal cannot be denied, but at the same time, to adopt a stance where these are regarded as distinct and separate from other cognitive processes may not necessarily be always healthy.

Making a choice between the scales and inventories on offer is not an easy task. The list of available anxiety measures is considerable but in practice the number of scales which sport psychologists routinely use is quite small. Presently, the scale which enjoys greatest popularity is the second version of the Competitive State Anxiety Inventory, or CSAI-2 (Martens *et al.*, 1990; see Figure 2.1).

The history of the CSAI-2 provides us with a fascinating insight into the evolution of anxiety research over the years. It represents one occasion where there has been a genuine cross-fertilization of ideas between clinical and sport psychology. At the same time it also highlights the problems which sport psychology still encounters in the wake of its historically close ties with trait theory. According to Martens *et al.* (1990), the story began in earnest in 1966. It was then that Charles Spielberger first addressed a fundamental problem with existing anxiety scales which tried to measure anxiety without ever genuinely pinning down or defining the concept itself. In response, he argued that it was necessary to make a distinction between momentary anxiety states ('subjective, consciously perceived feelings of tension') and more permanent anxiety traits ('a motive or acquired behavioural disposition'), later referred to as A-state and A-trait respectively. By 1970, Spielberger had formalized his ideas with the development of scales dedicated to measuring state and trait anxiety, respectively known, not surprisingly, as the Trait Anxiety Inventory (TAI) and the State Anxiety Inventory (SAI), often combined into a 40-item Likert scale known and widely respected across psychology as the STAI or State-Trait Anxiety Inventory (Spielberger, 1983; Spielberger, 1989).

During the time that Spielberger was developing his general measure of state-trait anxiety, there was a growing recognition across psychology that anxiety was yet more complicated. Not only must general anxiety measures incorporate both traits (dispositions) and states (outcomes) but they must also take into account the specific stimuli that provoke anxiety. This recognition encouraged sport psychologists to develop anxiety questionnaires which were tailored specially to sport, one of the earliest and most popular being Marten's Sport Competition Anxiety Test (SCAT), also referred to as the Illinois Competition Questionnaire. This 15-item scale did not set out to encompass both state and trait anxiety; instead it was described as 'a sport-specific A-trait inventory' (Martens *et al.*, 1990), designed to measure trait anxiety in competitive situations. With reference back to Spielberger's earlier distinction between A-state and A-trait, it is not clear whether it is appropriate to classify SCAT as a trait or a state measure, given that respondents are asked to recall momentary states immediately prior to competition (e.g. 'Before I compete I am nervous'). This confusion also reveals itself in the literature relating to SCAT. On some occasions the scale has been correlated with other A-trait measures (for example Ostrow and Ziegler, 1978), but Martens also claims that it has been cited as a predictor of A-state in 30 published studies (Martens *et al.*, 1990: 81). What this means for the measure itself, or indeed for the distinction between, and definition of, A-trait (perhaps as a cognitive set), and A-state (as either an affective or behavioural response) has inevitably been a source of controversy (Endler, 1977), and doubtless will continue to be such.

Make no mistake, this is not easy territory to chart, and particularly for those coming to the material as outsiders. There remain so many fundamental questions which have yet to be resolved that attempts to quantify concepts such as 'anxiety', when we are still not sure just what this term actually means (see Chapter 4), can seem rather

Figure 2.1: CSAI-2 (*Illinois Self Evaluation Questionnaire*)

Name: _____ Sex: M F Date: _____

Directions: A number of statements which athletes have used to describe their feelings before competition are given below. Read each statement and then circle the appropriate number to the right of the statement to indicate *how you feel right now* — at this moment. There are no right or wrong answers. Do *not* spend too much time on any one statement, but choose the answer which describes your feelings *right now*.

		Not At All	Somewhat	Moderately So	Very much So
1	I am concerned about this competition	1	2	3	4
2	I feel nervous	1	2	3	4
3	I feel at ease	1	2	3	4
4	I have self-doubts	1	2	3	4
5	I feel jittery	1	2	3	4
6	I feel comfortable	1	2	3	4
7	I am concerned that I may not do as well in this competition as I could	1	2	3	4
8	My body feels tense	1	2	3	4
9	I feel self-confident	1	2	3	4
10	I am concerned about losing	1	2	3	4
11	I feel tense in my stomach	1	2	3	4
12	I feel secure	1	2	3	4
13	I am concerned about choking under pressure	1	2	3	4
14	My body feels relaxed	1	2	3	4
15	I'm confident I can meet the challenge	1	2	3	4
16	I'm concerned about performing poorly	1	2	3	4
17	My heart is racing	1	2	3	4
18	I'm confident about performing well	1	2	3	4
19	I'm concerned about reaching my goal	1	2	3	4
20	I feel my stomach sinking	1	2	3	4
21	I feel mentally relaxed	1	2	3	4
22	I'm concerned that others will be disappointed with my performance	1	2	3	4
23	My hands are clammy	1	2	3	4
24	I'm confident because I mentally picture myself reaching my goal	1	2	3	4
25	I'm concerned I won't be able to concentrate	1	2	3	4
26	My body feels tight	1	2	3	4
27	I'm confident of coming through under pressure	1	2	3	4

(Reprinted with kind permission of the publishers from Martens *et al.* (1990: 177)

premature at times, but the development of research instruments has nevertheless proceeded rapidly. Moving on from SCAT, as a very active participator in the ongoing debate on stress, arousal and anxiety in sport, Rainer Martens recognized that any measure of sport anxiety must take due regard of its multidimensional nature. This includes not only the distinction between underlying predispositions (A-trait), and behaviour and emotion in the here-and-now (A-state), but also the two types of anxiety which sport psychologists routinely describe and all too conveniently dichotomize, namely cognitive anxiety (negative thoughts, worry) and somatic anxiety (physiological response). As applied sport psychologists are primarily concerned with athletes' response to competition itself, Martens' focus of attention quite naturally concentrated on the here-and-now of anxiety, that is A-state. This process of debate, distinction and selection laid the groundwork for the development of first the CSAI and more recently, the CSAI-2 (Martens *et al.*, 1990), otherwise known to respondents as the Illinois Self-Evaluation Questionnaire. (The alternative title is used on the form itself to reduce response bias but whether the actual title is important given the transparency of test items in this and similar self report scales is debatable [Williams and Krane, 1989].)

The CSAI-2 is described as a sport specific measure of multidimensional A-state, and certainly represents the best validated psychometric instrument with which to quantify competitive anxiety. The scale has been developed through five versions, with Form E the latest and most refined. The 27-item scale is divided into three subscales each comprising nine items. These are cognitive A-state (e.g. 'I am concerned about this competition'; 'I have self doubts'), somatic A-state (e.g. 'I feel tense in my stomach'; 'My body feels tight') and state self-confidence (e.g. 'I'm confident I can meet the challenge'; 'I feel comfortable'). The scale is recommended to be administered within an hour of competition, and is presented in full here as well as in the author's recent book, together with an array of norm tables (Martens *et al.*, 1990). In terms of research, the scale has enjoyed widespread popularity, regardless of the perennial problem of how to overcome social desirability of response. In its favour, the subscales of the CSAI-2 do appear to tap different dimensions of anxiety, for example, cognitive anxiety has been shown to remain elevated for several days before competition while somatic anxiety tends to rise quickly in the few hours before the event itself (Parfitt *et al.*, 1990).

Despite the best efforts of researchers working in this area, the changes in anxiety which occur during competition itself remain something of a mystery. Some athletes, and particularly élite competitors, report that their A-state drops quickly, while others find it more difficult to 'come down', but questions such as who, why or how remain unanswered (Martens *et al.*, 1990: 204–6). For this reason, if no other, precompetition measures of A-state remain poor predictors of performance. This is an important issue which cannot be sidestepped. From a practical point of view, if anxiety measures cannot be used to predict an individual's performance then why spend so much time tracking and measuring anxiety prior to competition itself? From a theoretical point of view, what does this tell us about our knowledge of competition anxiety? Sadly, once more it demonstrates not the extent but the limit of our understanding of the relationship between cognition, physiological state, affective state and behaviour in real life situations.

Achievement Motivation, Competitiveness and Self-Confidence

While anxiety has been the focus of a great deal of attention this is not to say that other areas have been ignored completely. Three are of particular note, achievement motivation, competitiveness and self-confidence. Together with competition anxiety, these seem to form a cluster of core psychological constructs which intuitively would seem to be most relevant to our understanding of sport performance. With regard to achievement motivation and competitiveness, recent advances have been predicated upon the interest originally stimulated by the Atkinson (formerly McClelland–Atkinson) model of achievement motivation, a model which has long been held in high esteem within sport psychology (see Gill, 1986). Atkinson's nAch or the need to achieve was originally taken to be a composite made up of two independent factors, the motive to achieve success (M_s) and the motive to avoid failure (M_{af}), mediated by the probability of success (P_s) and the value attached to success, otherwise known as incentive value of success ($1-P_s$) (which is hence inversely related to the probability of success). This relationship is normally represented by the following formula:

$$nAch = (M_s-M_{af}) \times (P_s \times [1-P_s])$$

Without exploring the considerable subtleties of this model in any depth, the single most important message to come through is that high achievers will be drawn towards competition and difficult yet realizable challenges, whereas low achievers will try to avoid personal challenges, for example by playing only inferior opponents or they will set unattainable goals where failure is a high probability and thus does not present a personal threat. In terms of applied sport psychology, this motivational model can often be very revealing of problems, particularly those afflicting young athletes. One simple way in which to present this material to coaches and athletes is to talk about a number of basic categories or types, as shown in Figure 2.2.

A further research area to emerge from work with nAch has been dealing with risk taking in sport. High achievers are prepared to face challenges and to take risks, and so it should come as little surprise to find that a literature has developed dealing with sensation seeking, and in particular using Zuckerman's sensation seeking scale (Zuckerman, 1979). Predictably, this research has confirmed that sensation seekers predominate in high risk sports (for example, Rowland *et al.*, 1986; Ewart and Hammenhurst, 1989).

The risk taking research has provided strong support for Atkinson's model. Unfortunately, the same cannot be said for research relating to other dimensions, and it would be fair to say that nAch is still not a reliable predictor of performance in sport. Instead, what this work reveals yet again is just how difficult it is actually to apply any theory concerned with personality to the complexities of real world situations, where a host of intervening variables contrive to defy our best attempts at prediction and control. The inability of the model to predict performance has led to many refinements and elaborations, including the incorporation of additional factors such as fear of success (especially among women, and based on the early and perhaps now dated work of Horner, 1972), inhibitions/motivations associated with future aspirations in the sport, and the impact of extrinsic motivators over and above intrinsic dispositions. Despite these complexities, and including acceptance of the role which the situation plays in determining nAch, the fundamental goal of many working in this area is still to categorize athletes into one of a number of types. For this reason, this work is included here as an elaboration upon a trait approach, although clearly one which embraces considerable cognitive complexity.

As should be obvious, the task of measurement is not straightforward and there have been many scales used in conjunction with this work (Fineman, 1977). Perhaps surprisingly, the most popular is the Thematic Apperception Test or TAT (Murray, 1938). The TAT is a projective, open ended test involving subjective interpretations of a series of pictures, and within psychology as a whole it has been more commonly

Figure 2.2: How much do you want to win?

Being as truthful with yourself as possible, on a scale from 0 to 10, how would rate your interest in winning or need for achievement?
(0 = no interest; 5 = moderate interest; 10 = crucial)?

_____ out of 10.

Now in terms of your fear of failure, how would you rate your fear of losing or failing?
(0 = fear not important; 5 = moderately important; 10 = crucial)?

_____ out of 10.

TYPE wF   **Low** interest in winning; **High** fear of failing
Things are often left unfinished or you lose interest in activities. You will avoid genuine competition whenever possible but enjoy playing against someone who you know you can beat easily and impress.

TYPE wf   **Low** interest in winning; **Low** fear of failing

You aren't really bothered about competition and can't really understand why people get so worked up about winning and losing. After all, it's only a game!

TYPE Wf   **High** interest in winning; **Low** fear of failing

You really enjoy competition, especially when you are presented with a real challenge. You are always well motivated and enjoy taking risks. You love to win but don't lose much sleep if you don't always succeed. There's always next time!

TYPE WF   **High** interest in winning; **High** fear of failing

You enjoy competitive situations and take personal responsibility for what happens around you. You sometimes find failure hard to take. It raises self-doubt and lowers your confidence. You can sometimes come across as a bad sport and as unwilling to take risks, perhaps with a superficial air of arrogance. You often feel that you haven't played to your potential.

associated with clinical settings than the world of sport. More recently, the Work and Family Orientation Questionnaire (WOFO) (Spence and Helmreich, 1978) has been found useful insofar as it considers achievement motivation as being multidimensional, involving four domains (namely mastery, competitiveness, work and personal unconcern). Of these four areas, competitiveness has been singled out for the closest attention within sport. Diane Gill has built on the WOFO to produce a sport-specific measure, known originally as the Competitiveness Inventory, more recently as the Sport Orientation Questionnaire or SOQ (Gill and Deeter, 1988). This contains three subscales, competitiveness, win orientation and personal goal orientation, with athletes not surprisingly scoring higher on competitiveness (defined as the desire to strive for success in competitive sport situations) than non-athletes.

Susan Harter's work on competence motivation has also found a comfortable niche here, considering achievement motivation within the context of experiences of success and failure. If mastery attempts are rewarding then the positive emotions which are aroused will encourage future attempts, and a 'success circle' will develop. Once more, this work does not consider motivation as a unitary concept. Instead, Harter's Perceived Competence Scale (Harter, 1982) operates in relation to three separate life domains, social, cognitive and physical.

As regards developing a need for achievement, Harter's work on perceived competence has close ties with Bandura's theory of self-efficacy (Bandura, 1982). Bandura's basic argument is that success breeds self-efficacy and self-confidence, and hence future success. In a similar vein, Deci (Vallerand *et al.*, 1987) has introduced cognitive evaluation theory to the sport world. Intrinsic motivation is said to be enhanced when the individual feels in control of his/her environment and when he/she feels competent at the task at hand. At the same time, external rewards may detract from intrinsic motivation, although research findings in this area are far from cut and dried (Weiss and Chaumeton, 1992). Yet another literature has also developed dealing specifically with the construct of self-confidence in sport, centring around the work of Robin Vealey (Vealey, 1986).

By this stage, it should be apparent that there are a great many research enterprises under way in this general area, and looking past their surface structures, and most especially the terminology which is used, there is considerable common ground. Unfortunately, attempts to chart this common ground are few and far between, but the scope for model building has to be considerable. Despite these shortcomings, in terms of a movement away from traditional trait theory, these approaches represent a significant step forward. They have naturally evolved from their trait roots in order to explain sport performance better, and in so doing they now raise fundamental questions as to the efficacy of a trait theory of personality. These more cognitive models are able to accept that individuals may be driven by different priorities and may view the world uniquely, and certainly that traits are not common to all people at all times. If there continues to be an interest in categorization in sport psychology then it is these models which are most likely to produce coherent answers.

The State of the Traits: Mood State and POMS

The relative lack of success experienced by trait research could have led to a wholesale movement away from quantitative methods and towards alternative approaches. This revolution did not take place. Instead, as can be seen from the earlier discussion of competitive anxiety, over time the emphasis inexorably shifted towards a consideration of temporary states and fluctuations in personality, with a particular emphasis on mood state. Against this climate, it is fascinating to look at a particular research tool which was used primarily within the trait tradition but which more latterly has moved closer to its true home as a measure of mood state, namely the Profile of Mood States or POMS questionnaire. The POMS questionnaire was first developed by McNair, Lorr and Droppelman (1972:5) as 'a rapid, economical method of identifying and assessing transient, fluctuating affective states', primarily for the clinical assessment of psychiatric patients. Within sport psychology, almost from its first appearance POMS's place in the history of the subject was guaranteed by the wholehearted, enthusiastic and uncritical support it received. Over the years, POMS has been used extensively by both academics and practitioners alike (see Cockerill *et al.*, 1991; Vanden Auweele *et al.*, 1993), part of its attraction being the beguiling simplicity of the approach—although this is increasingly seen more as a weakness than a strength (Silva *et al.*, 1985).

The POMS questionnaire is normally presented as a 65-item checklist. In response to each item or word (for example, sluggish, relaxed, blue, grouchy) subjects are required to indicate how they feel on a five point scale from 'not at all' to 'extremely'. Item scores are then summed and mood state is then described in terms of six independent dimensions, namely tension–anxiety, depression–dejection, anger–hostility, vigour–activity, fatigue–inertia and confusion–bewilderment. These independent dimensions are also routinely aggregated to produce a global measure of total mood disturbance which is obtained by subtracting the one positive factor (vigour) from the five negative factors, and adding a constant of 100. Within sport psychology, POMS is associated most strongly with the work of one person, William P. Morgan. From the early 1970s, Morgan had spotted the potential of POMS in sport. In 1972, Morgan and Costill first argued that a particular pattern of scores on these subscales was related to above average athletic performance. Specifically, low scores on tension, depression, anger, fatigue and confusion, together with a high score on vigour was regarded as indicative of superior performance. This pattern became known as the 'Iceberg Profile', which is the shape produced when scores on each mood state are plotted in turn to make up a line graph. Morgan, in the best tradition of trait theorists at that time, subsequently used POMS alongside a host of other standard measures (including the State-Trait Anxiety Inventory, STAI; the Minnesota Multi-Phasic Personality Inventory, MMPI; the Depression Adjective Checklist; the Somatic Perception Questionnaire; and the Eysenck Personality Inventory, EPI) in order to compare above and below average athletes. On the basis of this work, POMS was heralded as a reliable predictor of athletic success and, alongside the STAI and the EPI, later became the pitprop of Morgan's Mental Health Model (Morgan, 1985), the fundamental tenet of which being that positive mental health correlates positively with athletic success.

While POMS continued to stand as the most strongly supported predictor of athletic success, it did not take long for commentators to begin to ask critical questions about the existing literature. First and foremost, they asked if it was valid to use a measure of temporary mood state to draw fundamental distinctions between individuals, and beyond this, to argue that élite performers consistently have mood profiles which are more positive than less successful athletes. The answer to these questions has to be no. By their very nature and definition, moods are not stable dimensions of personality; they are not traits, they are transitory, affective states. At various times over the last 20 years this simple fact has often been forgotten. Bearing this in mind, the administration of the questionnaire also becomes very important. Four instruction sets have been used with POMS (for example, How have you been feeling over the past week, including today? How do you feel right now?) It should come as little surprise to learn that POMS is at its most accurate as a predictor of athletic performance when instructions refer to the here and now and when it is administered as close to competition as possible. It is in these circumstances that the scale is being used for its true purpose, to measure transitory mood state. Unfortunately, instructions and timing of POMS in relation to actual performance varies considerably between studies, and equally important, detail of how the POMS was administered is not always made available. In addition, the scale has been criticized insofar as it is used to derive criterion group mean scores, rather than as an individual diagnostic tool. Recent authors including Prapavessis *et al.* (1992) point out that mean scores can easily disguise the fact that many athletes perform very successfully in the absence of an Iceberg Profile, and argue that the POMS is used appropriately only with individuals and not groups (Cockerill *et al.*, 1991). Other critics have attacked the presentation of mood states as a line graph (thus assuming continuity between discontinuous variables), the rationale for only dealing with six mood states, for then deriving a total mood disturbance score from independent mood states, and the construct validity of the questionnaire itself (Scott, 1992). This welter of criticism has encouraged recent researchers to use the POMS somewhat more judiciously. Quite rightly, POMS research has not been abandoned completely for it remains a useful device in repeated measures experimental designs, for example charting shifts in individual mood states during training and prior to competition, and picking up signs of staleness and fatigue (Veale, 1991). Rare attempts have been made to use alternative mood state questionnaires, the most notable being the Eight State Questionnaire (Institute for Personality and Ability Testing, 1979; Silva and Hardy, 1986), although alternatives to POMS remain overshadowed in the popular sport psychology literature.

Whichever mood state questionnaire is employed, to use that scale to measure a pseudo-trait called mood state or mood disturbance is, quite simply, asking for trouble. As to why so many authors have followed this dubious route, then clearly the prominence of trait approaches in sport psychology must play a significant role, and once more, the problems and paradoxes which accompany the adoption of this simple and sovereign approach to personality make for a salutory lesson. It is to be hoped that that particular lesson has now been well and truly learnt.

The Way Forward

As you will now appreciate, sport psychology and trait theories go back a long way and it is a relationship which has witnessed many trials and tribulations over the years. It is doubtful if the marriage will ever end in divorce, nor would a complete separation necessarily be a happy outcome for either party given their mutual interests and priorities. However, it is certainly true that a little distance would give each some welcome breathing space, particularly the younger partner, sport psychology. There now appears to be a recognition that the relationship should be different and more open, and that alternatives can be legitimately explored. For example, going right back to basics, what is meant by the term personality itself has to be the subject of closer scrutiny within sport psychology, and this critical evaluation must translate into research practice. Even as early as the mid-1970s, the inadequacies of a simple trait model were being discussed. Influential authors such as Rainer Martens openly adopted an interactional approach at this time. He maintained that in sport, as elsewhere, the environment plays an equal or even greater role alongside intrapersonal variables, a sentiment encapsulated in Kurt Lewin's now famous formula, $B = f(P,E)$, or behaviour (B) represents a function of personality (P) and the environment (E).

Recent commentators likewise extol the advantages of adopting an interactional perspective, and more significantly go on to raise serious question marks against the use of trait measures even within an interactional framework. Despite the difficulties which he himself encountered with the use of POMS, by 1980 William Morgan had also seen the writing on the wall (Morgan, 1980a, 1980b). He believed it was possible to divide sport psychologists into three camps, those who remained credulous as to the value of personality testing in sport, those who had become increasingly sceptical and who now regarded psychological profiling as unprofitable; and those, including himself, who recognized the limitations of trait research but who could still see some possibilities for relating specific personality dimensions to sport performance. The majority of sport psychologists, even at that time, would have fallen into the latter two categories, with the last category being the safest option, what could unkindly be called the liberal position of compromise.

Despite the temptation of fence sitting, there was a growing awareness from that time that things must change. In her extensive review of the 'personology' literature relating to sport, Robin Vealey (1989) found that since 1974, over half of all research could be described as adopting an interactional approach, and within this approach itself, the shift was definitely away from trait measurement and towards what she describes as cognitive approaches, a broad church encompassing many perspectives concerning how individuals respond to and interpret sporting situations.

Whether the death knell for pure trait research has been rung, or ever will sound, is questionable but certainly the tide is running strongly against this type of research in sport psychology. Criticisms are well summarized by Richard Cox (1990: 23–6). He maintains that the approach has never come to terms with a number of fundamental problems, including the essentially atheoretical nature of the majority of trait research, the demarcation of independent variables in experimental design, poorly defined dependent variables, inadequate sampling procedures and the use of unrepresentative samples, a failure to take into account situational variables, a failure to use multivariate statistics in conjunction with multivariate experimental designs, the use of correlational designs to imply causality, a failure to account for faking and response distortion in questionnaires, and finally reliance on first order or source traits rather than second order or surface traits.

Despite the inadequacies of previous research, Cox still shies away from arguing for a major paradigm shift. Instead, the call is for greater experimental rigour, that is the same but better, for rebellion not revolution. Whether such changes really strike to the heart of the issue, namely the efficacy of a trait theory of personality, must remain a matter for conjecture. There has been so much investment in personality research linked tightly to the notion of enduring traits that reticence to start with a new and more dynamic model of personality is understandable. The debate as to how much of personality is permanent and how much is subject to change manifests itself vividly in the knots in which we become tied when trying to distinguish between what is a state and what is a trait, between the cognitive and the somatic, and between mood state and personality. Trait theory, even when embedded in an interactional approach, may never provide a model of personality which is sufficiently dynamic to be able to accommodate these psychological/cognitive structures, nor can it ever provide genuine insight into individual motivations and perceptions. Within psychology as a whole, Kelly's personal construct theory or PCT (Kelly, 1955) has become widely recognized and respected as an approach which allows us to consider individual priorities and world views, and to deal with change. For whatever reason, sport psychologists have been reluctant to turn to PCT and to use repertory grid techniques to understand athletes, either in experimental or more applied settings. In both, the potential of PCT would appear to be immense, and this would be a profitable way forward for both pure and applied sport psychologists.

Another alternative is not to abandon traits completely but to set our sights lower, to pursue Morgan's third compromise position and not to attempt to grapple with the nature of personality. Instead we must adopt a very pragmatic, even atheoretical, approach and work with psychological skills which we can identify as salient to sport, and which, through experience alone, we know are important to quantify in order to facilitate meaningful intervention programmes. Here it may be possible to talk of more rigorous research but of the same genre. Such research will only ever take us so far. It will help us deal with immediate problems in terms of psychological sport skills but it is increasingly obvious that it will never help us develop understanding of more basic psychological processes. Here there is a need to sever links with traditional approaches and take stock of our existing knowledge base. Nowhere is this more obvious than in relation to work on achievement motivation which in turn relates intimately to the work on competitive anxiety. Overviewing this literature, it is apparent that there is a real danger of sport psychologists reinventing the wheel not once but several times over. It is not immediately obvious where it is possible to draw lines of demarcation between concepts such as achievement motivation, self-efficacy, perceived competence, competitiveness, self-confidence, or even competitive anxiety. That is not to say that each is synonymous. They are not, but equally they are not independent and cannot be regarded as having a life of their own. This proliferation of terms to describe overlapping psychological constructs may be yet another throwback to the early dependence on trait theory. A 'trait mentality' would create a predisposition to pigeonhole, to create convenient boxes and labels for 'things' when in reality these categories are not discrete but are inputs, products and processes woven together into an intricate psychological tapestry. One task for the future remains the development of psychological models which can accommodate these disparate research trends. It is interesting to see these models now beginning to appear in the literature, one example being the integrated model of sport motivation proposed recently by Weiss and Chaumeton (1992), another being the expectancy-value model of motivation as proposed by Eccles (Eccles and Harold, 1991). By their very nature, and specifically their complexity, these models defy comprehensive empirical testing, yet heuristically we would argue that they represent the only way forward. There could be interesting times ahead for sport psychology.

References

ANDERSON, M. B. and WILLIAMS, J. M. (1987) 'Gender role and sport competition anxiety: A re-examination', *Research Quarterly for Exercise and Sport*, 58, pp. 52–6.
ARCHER, J. (1989) 'The relationship between gender role measures: A review', *British Journal of Social Psychology*, 28, pp. 173–84.
BALLARD-REICH, D. and ETTON, M. (1992) 'Gender orientation and the Bem Sex Role Inventory: A psychological construct revisited', *Sex Roles*, 27, 5/6, pp. 291–306.
BANDURA, A. (1982) 'Self-efficacy mechanism in human agency', *American Psychologist*, 37, pp. 122–47.
BASS, B. M. (1981) *Stogdill's Handbook of Leadership*, New York: Free Press.
BEM, S. L. (1974) 'The measurement of psychological androgyny', *Journal of Consulting and Clinical Psychology*, 42, pp. 155–62.
BEM, S. L. (1985) 'Androgyny and gender schema theory: A conceptual and empirical integration', in SONDEREGGER, T. B. (Ed.) *Nebraska Symposium on Motivation (1984): Psychology and Gender*, Lincoln, NB: University of Nebraska Press, pp. 179–226.
BIDDLE, S. and MUTRIE, N. (1991) *Psychology of Physical Activity and Exercise*, London: Springer-Verlag.
BRYMAN, A. (1986) *Leadership and Organizations*, London: Routledge and Kegan Paul.
BUTT, D. S. (1987) *The Psychology of Sport: The Behavior, Motivation, Personality and Performance of Athletes*, New York: Van Nostrand Reinhold.

CANN, A. (1991) 'Gender expectations and sport participation', in DIAMANT, L. (Ed.) *Psychology of Sports, Exercise and Fitness*, New York: Hemisphere, pp. 187–214.

COCKERILL, I. M., NEVILL, A. M. and LYONS, N. (1991) 'Modelling mood states in athletic performance', *Journal of Sports Sciences*, 9, pp. 205–12.

COX, R. H. (1990) *Sport Psychology: Concepts and Applications*, Dubuque, IW: Wm C. Brown.

DAVIS, C. and COWLES, M. (1991) 'Body image and exercise: A study of relationships and comparisons between physically active men and women', *Sex Roles*, 25, 1/2, pp. 33–44.

DIAMANT, L., BYRD, J. H. and HIMELEIN, M. J. (1991) 'Personality traits and athletic performance', in DIAMANT, L. (Ed.) *Mind-Body Maturity: Psychological Approaches to Sports, Exercise and Fitness*, New York: Hemisphere, pp. 227–36.

ECCLES, J. S. and HAROLD, R. D. (1991) 'Gender differences in sport involvement: Applying the Eccles' expectancy-value model', *Journal of Applied Sport Psychology*, 3, 1, pp. 7–35.

ENDLER, N. S. (1977) 'The interaction model of anxiety: Some possible implications', in LANDERS, D. M. and CHRISTINA, R. W. (Eds) *Psychology of Motor Behavior and Sport*, Champaign, IL: Human Kinetics, pp. 332–51.

EWART, A. and HAMMENHURST, S. (1989) 'Testing the adventure model: Empirical support for a model of risk recreation participation', *Journal of Leisure Research*, 21, 2, pp. 124–39.

EYSENCK, H. J., NIAS, D. K. B. and COX, D. N. (1982) 'Sport and personality', *Advances in Behavioral Research and Therapy*, 4, 1, pp. 1–56.

FINEMAN, S. (1977) 'The achievement motive construct and its measurement: Where are we now?', *British Journal of Psychology*, 68, pp. 1–22.

FISHER, A. C. (1984) 'New directions in sports personality research', in SILVA, V. M. and WEINBERG, R. S. (Eds) *Psychological Foundations in Sport*, Champaign, IL: Human Kinetics, pp. 70–80.

FOLKINS, C. H. and SIME, W. E. (1981) 'Physical fitness training and mental health', *American Psychologist*, 36, pp. 373–89.

GABLER, H. (1976) 'Development of personality traits in top-level sport performers', *Sportwissenschaft*, 6, pp. 247–76.

GERON, D., FURST, P. and ROTSTEIN, P. (1986) 'Personality of athletes participating in various sports', *International Journal of Sport Psychology*, 17, pp. 120–35.

GILL, D. L. (1986) *Psychological Dynamics of Sport*, Champaign, IL: Human Kinetics.

GILL, D. L. (1992) 'Gender and sport behavior', in HORN, T. S. (Ed.), *Advances in Sport Psychology*, Champaign, IL: Human Kinetics, pp. 143–60.

GILL, D. L. and DEETER, T. E. (1988) 'Development of the Sport Orientation Questionnaire', *Research Quarterly for Exercise and Sport*, 59, pp. 191–202.

GREENBERG, J. and BARON, R. A. (1993) *Behavior in Organizations*, 4th edn, Boston: Allyn and Bacon.

GREENDORFER, S. L. (1987) 'Psycho-social correlates of organized physical activity', *Journal of Physical Education, Recreation and Dance*, 58, 7, pp. 59–64.

GREENDORFER, S. L. (1992) 'Sport socialization', in HORN, T. S. (Ed.), *Advances in Sport Psychology*, Champaign, IL: Human Kinetics, pp. 201–18.

GRIFFITH, C. R. (1928) *Psychology and Athletics*, New York: Scribners.

HARTER, S. (1982) 'Effectance motivation reconsidered: Towards a developmental model', *Human Development*, 21, pp. 34–64.

HELMREICH, R. L. and SPENCE, J. T. (1977) 'Sex roles and achievement', in CHRISTINA, R. W. and LANDERS, D. M. (Eds) *Psychology of Motor Behavior and Sport*, Champaign, IL: Human Kinetics, pp. 33–46.

HORNER, M. S. (1972) 'Toward an understanding of achievement-related conflicts in women', *Journal of Social Issues*, 28, pp. 157–76.

INSTITUTE FOR PERSONALITY AND ABILITY TESTING (1979) *Eight State Questionnaire*, Champaign, IL: IPAT.

KANE, M. J. and SNYDER, E. (1989) 'Sport typing: The social containment of women', *Arena Review*, 13, pp. 77–96.

KELLY, G. A. (1955) *The Psychology of Personal Constructs*, Vol. 1, New York: Norton.

McNAIR, D. M., LORR, M. and DROPPELMAN, L. F. (1972) *Profile of Mood States Manual*, San Diego, CA: Educational and Industrial Testing Service.

MADDI, S. (1976) *Personality Theories: A Comparative Analysis*, Homewood, IL: The Dorsey Press.

MAHONEY, M. J., GABRIEL, T. J. and PERKINS, T. S. (1987) 'Psychological skills and exceptional athletic performance', *The Sport Psychologist*, 1, pp. 181–99.

MARTENS, R. (1975) 'The paradigmatic crisis in American sport personology', *Sportwissenschaft*, 1, pp. 9–24.

MARTENS, R., VEALEY, R. S. and BURTON, D. (1990) *Competitive Anxiety in Sport*, Champaign, IL: Human Kinetics.

MATTEO, S. (1988) 'The effect of gender-schematic processing on decisions about sex-inappropriate sport behavior', *Sex Roles*, 18, pp. 41–58.

MECHIKOFF, R. A. (1987) *Sport Psychology for Women*, New York: Harper and Row.

MISCHEL, W. (1971) *Introduction to Personality*, New York: Holt.

MISCHEL, W. (1979) 'On the interface of cognition and personality: Beyond the person-situation debate', *American Psychologist*, 34, pp. 740–54.

MORGAN, W. P. (1980a) 'Sport personology: The credulous–sceptical argument', in STRAUB, W. (Ed.) *Sport Psychology: An Analysis of Athlete Behavior*, Ithaca, NY: Mouvement Press, pp. 330–9.

MORGAN, W. P. (1980b) 'The trait psychology controversy', *Research Quarterly for Exercise and Sport*, 51, pp. 50–76.

MORGAN, W. P. (1985) 'Affective beneficence of vigorous physical activity', *Medicine and Science in Sport and Exercise*, 17, pp. 94–100.

MORGAN, W. P. and COSTILL, D. L. (1972) 'Psychological characteristics of the marathon runner', *Journal of Sports Medicine and Physical Fitness*, 12, pp. 42–6.

MORGAN, W. P. and GOLDSTON, S. E. (1987) 'Summary', in MORGAN, W. P. and GOLDSTON, S. E. (Eds) *Exercise and Mental Health*, Washington, DC: Hemisphere, pp. 155–60.

MURRAY, H. A. (1938) *Explorations in Personality*, New York: Oxford University Press.

NELSON, D. and HARDY, L. (1990) 'The development of an empirically validated tool for measuring psychological skill in sport', *Journal of Sports Sciences*, 8, p. 71.

OGILVIE, B. C. (1968) 'Psychological consistencies within the personality of high level performers', *Journal of the American Medical Association*, 205, pp. 780–6.

OGILVIE, B. C. and TUTKO, T. (1966) *Problem Athletes and How to Handle Them*, London: Pelham Books.

OSTROW, A. C. (1990) *Directory of Psychological Tests in the Sport and Exercise Sciences*, Morgantown, WV: Fitness Information Technology.

OSTROW, A. C. and ZIEGLER, S. G. (1978) 'Psychometric properties of the Sport Competition Anxiety test', in KERR, B. (Ed.) *Human Performance and Behavior*, Calgary, Alberta: University of Calgary, pp. 139–42.

PARFITT, C. G., JONES, J. G. and HARDY, L. (1990) 'Multidimensional anxiety and performance', in JONES, J. G. and HARDY, L. (Eds) *Stress and Performance in Sport*, London: John Wiley and Sons, pp. 43–80.

PATMORE, A. (1986) *Sportsmen Under Stress*, London: Stanley Paul.

PRAPAVESSIS, H., BERGER, B. and GROVE, R. J. (1992) 'The relationship of training and pre-competition mood states to swimming performance: An exploratory investigation', *The Australian Journal of Science and Medicine in Sport*, 17, pp. 364–74.

ROWLAND, G. L., FRANKEN, R. E. and HARRISON, K. (1986) 'Sensation seeking and participation in sporting activities', *Journal of Sport Psychology*, 8, pp. 212–20.

RUSHALL, B. S. (1973) 'The status of personality research and application in sports and physical education', *Journal of Sports Medicine and Physical Fitness*, 13, pp. 281–90.

RUSSO, N. F. and DENMARK, F. L. (1987) 'Contributions of women to psychology', *Annual Review of Psychology*, 38, pp. 279–98.

SACK, H. G. (1975) *Sport Participation and Personality (Sportliche Betatigung und Personlichkeit)*, Ahrensburg: Czwalina.

SCHURR, K. T., ASHLEY, M. A. and JOY, K. L. (1977) 'A multivariate analysis of male athletic characteristics: Sport type and success', *Multivariate Experimental Clinical Research*, 3, pp. 53–68.

SCOTT, D. A. (1992) *Mood State, Personality Dimensions and Performance in an Elite Swimming Squad*, unpublished MSc thesis, School of Psychology, Queen's University of Belfast.

SILVA, J. M. and HARDY, C. J. (1986) 'Discriminating contestants at the United States Olympic marathon trials as a function of precompetitive affect', *International Journal of Sport Psychology*, 17, pp. 100–109.

SILVA, J. M., SHULTZ, B. B., HASLAM, R. W., MARTIN, M. P. and MURRAY, D. F. (1985) 'Discriminating characteristics of contestants at the United States wrestling trials', *International Journal of Sport Psychology*, 16, pp. 79–102.

SPENCE, J. T. and HELMREICH, R. L. (1978) *Masculinity and Femininity*, Austin, TX: University of Texas Press.

SPIELBERGER, C. D. (1983) *Manual for the State-Trait Anxiety Inventory* (revised), Palo Alto, CA: Consulting Psychologists Press.

SPIELBERGER, C. D. (1989) 'Stress and anxiety in sports', in SPIELBERGER, C. D. (Ed.) *Anxiety in Sports: An International Perspective*, New York: Hemisphere, pp. 3–18.

VALLERAND, R. J., DECI, E. L. and RYAN, R. M. (1987) 'Intrinsic motivation in sport', in PANDOLF, K. B. (Ed.) *Exercise and Sport Sciences Reviews*, Vol. 15, New York: Macmillan, pp. 48–57.

VANDEN AUWEELE, Y., DE CUYPER, B., VAN MELE, V. and RZEWNICKI, R. (1993) 'Elite performance and personality: From description and prediction to diagnosis and intervention', in SINGER, R. N. *et al.* (Eds) *Handbook of Research on Sport Psychology*, New York: Macmillan, pp. 257–80.

VAN WERSCH, A., TREW, K. and TURNER, I. (1992) 'Post-primary school pupils' interest in physical education: Age and gender differences', *British Journal of Educational Psychology*, 62, pp. 56–72.

VEALE, D. M. V. (1991) 'Psychological aspects of staleness and dependence on exercise', *International Journal of Sports Medicine*, 12 (Supplement), pp. 19–22.

VEALEY, R. S. (1986) 'Conceptualization of sport confidence and competitive orientation: Preliminary investigation and instrument development', *Journal of Sport Psychology*, 8, pp. 221–46.

VEALEY, R. S. (1989) 'Sport personology: A paradigmatic and methodological analysis', *Journal of Sport and Exercise Psychology*, 11, pp. 216–35.

VEALEY, R. S. (1992) 'Personality and sport: A comprehensive view', in HORN, T. S. (Ed.) *Advances in Sport Psychology*, Champaign, IL: Human Kinetics, pp. 25–59.

WEISS, M. R. and CHAUMETON, N. (1992) 'Motivational orientations in sport', in HORN, T. S. (Ed.) *Advances in Sport Psychology*, Champaign, IL: Human Kinetics, pp. 61–100.

WILLIAMS, J. M. (1980) 'Personality characteristics of the successful female athlete', in STRAUB, W. F. (Ed.) *Sport Psychology: An Analysis of Athlete Behavior*, Ithaca, NY: Mouvement Publications, pp. 74–98.

WILLIAMS, J. M. and KRANE, V. (1989) 'Response distortion on self-report questionnaires with female collegiate golfers', *The Sport Psychologist*, 3, pp. 211–18.

WRISBERG, C. A., DRAPER, M. V. and EVERETT, J. J. (1988) 'Sex role orientations of male and female collegiate athletes from selected individual and team sports', *Sex Roles*, 19, pp. 81–90.

ZUCKERMAN, M. (1979) *Sensation Seeking: Beyond the Optimal Level of Arousal*, Hillsdale, NJ: Lawrence Erlbaum.

Further Reading

COCKERILL, I. M., NEVILL, A. M. and LYONS, N. (1991) 'Modelling mood states in athletic performance', *Journal of Sports Sciences*, 9, pp. 205–12.

DIAMANT, L., BYRD, J. H. and HIMELEIN, M. J. (1991) 'Personality traits and athletic performance', in DIAMANT, L. (Ed.) *Mind-Body Maturity: Psychological Approaches to Sports, Exercise and Fitness*, New York: Hemisphere, pp. 227–36.

ECCLES, J. S. and HAROLD, R. D. (1991) 'Gender differences in sport involvement: Applying the Eccles' expectancy-value model', *Journal of Applied Sport Psychology*, 3, 1, pp. 7–35.

GERON, D., FURST, P. and ROTSTEIN, P. (1986) 'Personality of athletes participating in various sports', *International Journal of Sport Psychology*, 17, pp. 120–35.

GILL, D. L. (1992) 'Gender and sport behavior', in HORN, T. S. (Ed.), *Advances in Sport Psychology*, Champaign, IL: Human Kinetics, pp. 143–60.

MARTENS, R., VEALEY, R. S. and BURTON, D. (1990) *Competitive Anxiety in Sport*, Champaign, IL: Human Kinetics.

OSTROW, A. C. (1990) *Directory of Psychological Tests in the Sport and Exercise Sciences*, Morgantown, WV: Fitness Information Technology.

PARFITT, C. G., JONES, J. G. and HARDY, L. (1990) 'Multidimensional anxiety and performance', in JONES, J. G. and HARDY, L. (Eds) *Stress and Performance in Sport*, London: John Wiley and Sons, pp. 43–80.

SPIELBERGER, C. D. (1989) 'Stress and anxiety in sports', in SPIELBERGER, C. D. (Ed.) *Anxiety in Sports: An International Perspective*, New York: Hemisphere, pp. 3–18.

VEALEY, R. S. (1992) 'Personality and sport: A comprehensive view', in HORN, T. S. (Ed.) *Advances in Sport Psychology*, Champaign, IL: Human Kinetics, pp. 25–59.

Chapter 3

Exercising Your Mind

(Cognitive Psychology)

Introduction

Since the late 1960s, cognitive psychology has come to be one of the major driving forces within the discipline as a whole. From the point of view of sports science, since the mid-1970s its influence in the field of motor behaviour has also been significant. 'Cognitive psychology refers to all processes by which the sensory input is transformed, reduced, elaborated, stored, recovered and used' (Neisser, 1967), and psychologists working in this tradition have long been interested in topics such as perception, memory, decision making, attention, language and problem solving. The dominant paradigm which has emerged is that based on information processing and indeed, in many people's eyes, cognitive psychology has become synonymous with this approach. Within sport, much of the early research on human movement, conducted under the rubric of motor learning and motor control (see Chapter 5), likewise utilized an information processing paradigm. As such, these areas of motor behaviour are well rooted in cognitive psychology and deal specifically with problems surrounding the acquisition and control of movement skills, for example perception, memory and attention. However, as Sanford (1985: 1) points out 'this is not to say that cognitive psychologists are not concerned with the emotions or motivation but rather to say that these issues have been less well treated in cognitive psychology than cognition itself'.

During the 1970s and 1980s sport psychology became identifiable as a separate subdiscipline, primarily concerned with the application of psychological principles to sport and physical activity. It was not by chance that a great deal of the work conducted in the sports domain became known as cognitive sports psychology, given that it placed great emphasis on how an athlete's cognitions and emotions affected his or her performance. According to Williams and Straub (1986: 5), by the early 1980s 'sport psychology began to reflect a more cognitive focus by devoting increasing attention to athletes' thoughts and images'. They go on to state that the 'growth of cognitive sport psychology has also led to a renewed interest in visualization . . . consequently, imagery and cognitive interventions have become an integral part of most mental training programs'. This somewhat idiosyncratic interpretation of the core of cognitive psychology may be at odds with accepted definitions yet it strikes close to popular notions of what the subject matter of 'applied sport psychology' is perceived to be about (Williams, 1986), and herein lies a fundamental problem which will be explored later in this chapter.

This chapter will initially outline the existing sports research on motor behaviour which falls under a broad information processing label. This will necessarily involve a consideration of the relationship between this work and that carried out in psychology and the related fields of linguistics, ergonomics and computer science. At the same time, it is inevitable that the relationship between pure and applied research must be evaluated to add another controversial dimension to the framework. Looking towards the future, we will also identify more positive developments within sport and exercise psychology, developments which reveal genuine attempts to bring contemporary thinking in cognitive psychology to bear on the world of sport. However we will begin by placing this work in its historical context.

A Historical Perspective

The story really begins early this century at a time when modern day psychology struggled to emerge from the conflicts which existed between behaviourist and cognitive traditions. Sanford (1985) has argued that the dominance of behaviourism during the infancy of psychology severely retarded any fledgeling interest in cognition because researchers became so preoccupied with the mechanics of experimentation that they lost sight of the mechanics of thought and action. However, things changed dramatically with the advent of World War II. War brought with it rapid technological advances and created a pressing need for properly trained personnel. This in turn provided opportunities for expansion in so many areas of applied psychology. One of the main concerns for the armed forces on both sides of the Atlantic was man–machine interaction, to ensure that new machines were designed to suit human operator characteristics rather than trying to fit the person to the machine. Psychologists became increasingly involved with exploring aspects of the human operator, including factors such as memory load, attentional capacity and cognitive strategies while others focused on the man–machine interaction in terms of exploring compatibility of visual/auditory displays and the effect of control systems on performance. (A further area of research was concerned with the design of training methods and programs; the impact of these on motor skill acquisition is discussed in Chapter 5.)

Implicit in this work was an acceptance of a model of the person as information processor. Yet at the same time as cognition was regarded as being of central concern, so too there was a perceived need to understand movement insofar as operators had to produce movements to operate the machines. Therefore, although movement control *per se* was not a major feature of research, a number of studies did explore movement problems, for example human movement control in tracking and steering tasks, the effect of movement feedback on control tasks, and the effect of the arrangement of instruments on hand–eye coordination. In the years following World War II, these combined areas of psychological research became known either as human factors, engineering psychology or ergonomics and they certainly played their part in the development of modern day cognitive psychology.

Other influences were also significant, for example those derived from information theory and from computer science. The communications industry expanded exponentially between 1939 and 1945, and one of the major offshoots was information theory, a mathematical treatment of the information content of signals which presented the human operator as a processor of information, or a special kind of communication channel. This model later translated into the field of perception through signal detection theory, an approach still frequently outlined in introductory textbooks on motor behaviour and often used to explain the many demands placed on a performer's perceptual mechanism in sporting situations (for example Magill, 1989). A second development arising from the growth of communications technology was a concern with information flow. The introduction of flow charts, with their familiar boxes and arrows, subsequently became familiar in psychologists' descriptive models of how the human brain processes information. Broadbent (1958) is often regarded as one of the first psychologists to produce an information processing model of the human brain, including the idea that information is passed from one stage to the next with each stage responsible for transforming the information in some way. It is noteworthy that perceptual–motor skills were among the earliest research topics conducted within this framework and the still popular and widespread use of the information processing paradigm is very evident in textbooks dealing with the psychology of motor behaviour today.

As information theory was developing so rapid advances were being made in a particular branch of engineering known as cybernetics. This deals with the study of control systems, and in particular with the theory and design of systems which are able to modify their own behaviour. An everyday example of such a system would be a thermostat which has the goal of keeping room temperature constant and therefore monitors conditions and controls temperature through continual feedback to the mechanism itself. Thus the concept of goal or intention, which had been unpalatable to many psychologists working in the behaviourist tradition, again became acceptable when related to causal explanations of behaviour, and particularly when viewing the human being as a cybernetic machine. Cybernetic constructs also transferred readily into the literature on motor behaviour, with Bernstein (1967) standing out as a key figure with regard to the use of cybernetics to explain human motor control. A final area of influence in the development of cognitive psychology was that of computer science. Through wartime efforts to break codes and to calculate missile trajectories there slowly evolved the digital computer, a rule governed system and the cornerstone of artificial intelligence or AI. According to an AI viewpoint, the human brain is analogous to a computer and hence human cognition should be expressable in computer language. This approach has been influential from that time to the present day, and has led to the development of many offshoots, including work on neural networks.

This brief history of cognitive psychology shows that by the early 1960s experimental psychology was being subjected to numerous influences from both inside and outside the discipline. Ulric Neisser's (1967) seminal text *Cognitive Psychology* is typically regarded as marking the birthplace of cognitive psychology itself (despite the fact that a book by the same title was published in New York by T.V. Moore in 1939). Nevertheless, it was Neisser who gave the field a specific identity by drawing together much of the experimental work conducted in the post-war years. While many cognitive psychologists of this era utilized movement as a means of studying stimulus or retention effects it was not until a decade later, in the late 1970s, that researchers became interested in understanding and exploring movement control in its own right. A much more recent development within sport psychology itself is the growing interest in how cognitive processes influence performance, and vice versa. Much of this work has emanated from the field of psychophysiology with modern contributions coming mainly in the form of increased sophistication of instrumentation and new research techniques (see Chapter 9). According to Fuchs and Zaichkowsky (1980) typical measures taken by sport psychology researchers include electrical signals from the body, such as muscle activity (electromyography, EMG), heart function (electrocardiogram, ECG), brain waves (electroencephalography, EEG), skin conductivity, core and peripheral temperature, blood pressure and blood flow. It is believed that these and other physiological measures, either separately or together, provide correlates of psychological states such as attention, motivation, anxiety, stress, relaxation, aggression, fear and anger. Current research into the interrelationship between psychological and physiological events in sport psychology focuses on both the interaction between the two and on the regulation by the individual of physiological events, for instance heart rate and muscle tension through psychological manipulations or interventions (see Chapters 4 and 9). In this chapter we will concentrate our attention on the impact of some cognitive theories of psychological states and also interventions such as imagery and thought control which have a deliberately cognitive focus.

The Information Processing Approach

Traditionally, one of the purposes served by information processing models was to examine the limitations of the human performer in terms of perception, memory, decision making, feedback and attention. However, a fundamental concern of theorists with an interest in movement behaviour was to understand the capacities and mechanisms underlying movement itself. According to Welford (1976: 2), who was one of the most prolific of all researchers in the area of skilled performance, 'all action is the result of a complex computation based on data from many sources — not only from the eyes and ears, but from postures, environmental sources, and the results of past actions and future aims'. Taking this view, it is not the movement itself which is of primary interest but the various steps and stages which are involved in translating input stimulus information into output, in the form of an action response. A key method of measurement which is relied upon when working within this approach is that of reaction time. It is accepted that each of the mental operations performed on any given stimulus will take a certain amount of time and the amount of processing will therefore be reflected in how long a person takes to react (that is the time between the presentation of a stimulus and the start of a response). A diagram of the information processing model is presented in Figure 3.1 and each of its main stages will then be outlined briefly in relation to existing research on motor behaviour.

The sense organs appear at the input stage of the model and these include the five familiar sensory receptors, the eyes, ears, nose, skin, tongue, as well as the less familiar proprioceptors (for example, the muscle and joint receptors) and the vestibular apparatus adjoining the inner ear which together are responsible for sensing movements and body position. A sport performer's sense organs are continually bombarded with stimulus information from the environment but not all of this information is likely to be salient at any one time. For example, a footballer playing outdoors on a grass pitch will have many different environmental cues available, such as visual information about the positions of teammates, opponents, ball, pitch markings; auditory information from teammates, coaches or spectators; tactile information from contact with other players or the ball; kinaesthetic information (body-awareness) from proprioceptors and vestibular apparatus regarding positions and movements of body and limbs as s/he runs over uneven ground,

Figure 3.1: *Hypothetical* **Representation** *of the Information Processing System*

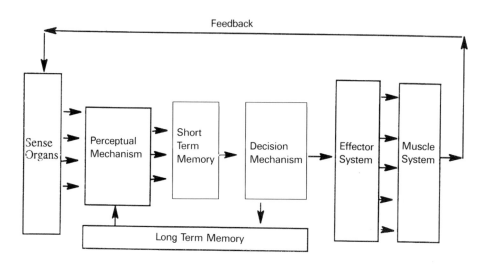

Source: Adapted from Welford (1968)

keeping balance, while attempting to kick, pass or tackle an opponent. All of this information is subjected to a pre-attentive analysis which the performer conducts by comparing incoming information to knowledge available to her or him in memory about similar situations or events. According to Lindsay and Norman (1977) previous experience has an important role to play in establishing the pertinence value of incoming information. The more familiar the person is with a situation and thus the higher the pertinence value, the more likely it is that s/he will process such information automatically and without conscious control. As a result of this process the stimulus information transmitted to the perceptual mechanism for detection is usually drastically reduced, with the remainder of the stimulus information being stored in memory for future reference (Norman, 1976). At this early stage of the process it is not thought that much meaning is attached to the pre-processed information; in fact meaning is only attached when the information makes contact with previously stored knowledge in memory.

The information now arrives at the perceptual mechanism and it is here that further meaning is acquired within the context of the current situation, and the person then begins to interpret the environment. For example, a surfer must 'read' the situation quickly in order to establish which stimulus cues are most relevant to him or her with regard to making the best possible decision. The perceptual system is thought to function as a kind of filter which allows meaningless information to be filtered away allowing the performer to attend selectively to the most pertinent information. This information is then forwarded to short term memory for further processing. Simultaneously, information from the long term store is also advanced to the short term store to enable the individual to have readily available all relevant information. For example, a netball player might recall that when faced with a similar situation in a previous game she used a particular technique effectively. For this reason the short term memory has more recently been referred to as working memory due to the amount of processing that actually occurs at that site. In fact, the working memory is responsible for receiving all of the information from the perceptual mechanism and from the long term store and then organizing it for appropriate decisions or further storage. Singer (1980) outlines three functions of the short term store. First it provides the performer with a 'working memory' to process current information. Second it is largely responsible for the cognitive processes of thinking, problem solving and decision making, and third it combines both of the above functions and decides which information will then be forwarded to long term storage for future referral.

Despite the many functions of this system the short term store does have limitations which have been well documented. Originally Miller (1956) proposed that the amount of information which can possibly be stored is limited to 'seven plus or minus two' items or chunks of information. Obviously, the size of an item or chunk will largely depend on experience or familiarity with the information. For example, it has been shown that there are considerable differences in the amount of information which experts and novices in various sports can pick up at a single glance. One explanation for this superiority in recall of experts over novices is that the experts' knowledge of the structured game situations allows them to chunk the information into meaningful units whereas the novice presented with similar information attempts to recall each individual item and therefore reaches the limit of his or her short term store very quickly.

The next stage of processing in the original Welford (1968) model is known as translation and, as you would expect, refers to the translation of perception into action. More recently, this phase is typically referred to as response selection or more specifically motor program selection, implying the selection of an already formulated response from memory. During this phase the performer must select the most appropriate response from the many possibilities available to him or her. For example, a soccer player may decide that he needs to pass the ball to a teammate who is in a better position than he is but the question is, how does he select the most appropriate action? Classical explanations of this phenomenon invoked the use of a motor program, a predetermined set of neural commands which are structured before a movement begins and which controls the execution of each particular movement. In explaining how a soccer player selects a specific technique it would be argued that he simply calls up one motor program from his memory stores. However, this somewhat rigid definition and explanation of the use of motor programs was later modified in favour of a more flexible and abstract notion of generalized motor programs and schema (Schmidt, 1975; also see Chapter 5). Adopting this latter approach it is suggested that rather than calling up a specific motor program from a central store, the performer calls upon an abstract programming rule which is applied to the specifics of a given situation in terms of the task requirements, the initial starting conditions of the individual, the repertoire of similar response, and the expected sensory consequences of the action. It is during the decision making process that a phenomenon entitled the Psychological Refractory Period (PRP) sometimes occurs. According to Welford (1952) there is only a 'single channel' through which all information must pass and this sometimes means that delays in processing will occur if there is more than one stimulus to be processed. Support for the PRP has been found in experiments where subjects are presented initially with one stimulus (S_1) to which they have been instructed to respond (R_1) as quickly as possible, but during processing of this stimulus the subject is then presented with a second stimulus (S_2) to which they must also respond (R_2). Typically, the second stimulus (S_2) will have to wait until the first stimulus (S_1) has been processed which causes a longer reaction time to (S_2) than if it had occurred alone. This delay in reacting to (S_2) is known as the PRP and is a common phenomenon in sport, for example when a player sells a dummy or fake. Take the situation where a basketball player may fake (S_1) a jump-shot but she remains firmly on the ground. Meanwhile her opponent jumps (R_1) to try to block the faked shot. Once the opponent has begun her movement the player can then dribble the ball past the airborne defender (S_2), by which time the defender realizes that she must quickly respond to the actual play (R_2). Despite the application of the concept to sport and its intuitive appeal, to date there has been little field testing of PRP in sport itself and most of the findings tend to come from more mainstream psychological experiments.

The final phase of processing is concerned with response execution or effector control and this involves two processes, planning and specifying motor program parameters. Generally speaking, planning can be thought of as the temporal ordering of a sequence of actions. For example, in order to execute a lay-up in basketball the performer must dribble the ball in towards the basket, take two steps with the ball being scooped up to shooting position and then lay the ball up against the backboard and (hopefully) score a basket. If this temporal order of operations is not evident then the overall action will not be recognizable as a lay-up, the action itself being defined by the temporal order of individual elements. The same may be said for many actions in sport, for example serving a tennis ball, performing a handspring vault, executing a gybe turn in sailing, or kicking a conversion in rugby. Parameter specification is the term used to refer to the addition of context-dependent and task-dependent information as part of a motor program. Returning to our hypothetical soccer player this would refer to him applying the appropriate force, speed, and direction to his chosen method of passing the ball.

Welford's model also includes a number of feedback loops whereby information is fed back into the system both during the course of movement and after actions have been completed. During movement production the performer is receiving intrinsic feedback in the form of sensory information, for example proprioceptors indicate body and limb locations and the speed/direction of movements. A performer is sometimes able to use this type of feedback, at a subconscious level, to control ongoing movement; again keep our soccer player in mind. He may be running over uneven or wet ground and may have to correct his stride momentarily to ensure he does not slip or fall. A performer also receives extrinsic feedback about the consequences of his or her actions on the environment. The player can see and hear that he made a good contact with the ball and passed it successfully to his teammate. This type of information is useful in terms of planning or modifying future responses; the player may decide that he should have chosen an alternative means of passing the ball (he should have selected a different motor program). An additional form of feedback often available to performers is known as augmented feedback. This is usually defined as information about response characteristics which is provided by another person or device. Here a performer may be given instructions from the coach about what to do on future attempts or s/he may be shown a video replay and given advice as to how to improve. Figure 3.1 includes numerous feedback loops and many more loops can also be added at different stages in the process. Feedback is essential to the entire system if learning is to take place and performers are to benefit from previous experiences. Feedback information about perceptual information, movement decisions, selected motor programs and program execution is all fed back into the memory systems to enable performers to establish a reference of correctness for various movements and thereby assist in the regulation of future actions. Feedback also serves a purpose in the conscious evaluation of performance when athletes attempt to provide reasons for performance outcome. Such causal attributions can make a significant impact on subsequent motivation (see Chapter 6).

As this outline of Welford's (1968) model indicates, motor behaviour research has often tended to do little more than replicate work in mainstream human experimental and cognitive psychology. The model itself and each of its stages have received considerable research interest from both pure and applied academics within motor behaviour, and the model is frequently outlined and explained in both textbooks on motor learning and control, as well as in more applied books directed at teachers or coaches. The basic model has also served as a starting point for more sophisticated information processing models or integrative models which incorporate cybernetics.

This is clearly an area which is experiencing great change at the present time, and our presentation of movement research in relation to cognition could not hope to be exhaustive. For example, noteworthy contributions have also been provided in areas including perception, short term motor memory, response selection, response programming, feedback and attention. For those interested in pursuing this topic further, good overviews have been provided by Magill (1989) and Schmidt (1991). However, before moving on, we last turn our attention to a particular topic which has generated considerable attention particularly within sport psychology, and that topic is attention itself.

Attention

The psychology of attention has enjoyed a long history, from the day that William James (1890: 403–4) first defined it as 'the taking possession by the mind, in clear and vivid form of one out of what seems to be several possible objects or trains of thought. It implies withdrawal from some things in order to deal effectively with others.' The concept itself forms an intricate part of information processing models although it has been researched and discussed under a variety of different headings and within a number of theoretical frameworks (for a review see Abernethy, 1993). In this section we will review and explain the concept of attention as it has developed within cognitive psychology but we also outline work in social psychology and psychophysiology as it relates to our understanding of the attentional processes of athletes.

In the previous outline of the information processing model, several references were made to the fact that performers selectively choose some informational cues over and above other stimuli at the input stage of processing. This phenomenon is commonly referred to as selective attention and was first studied by an English psychologist by the name of Cherry (1953). Cherry's work demonstrated that subjects tended to reduce the amount of stimulus information presented to them and selectively attended to just one item or message at a time. This finding led to several theories being proposed to account for the phenomenon, each with the common notion that a bottleneck or filter occurred somewhere in the early stages of processing. In sport, selective attention can be seen to function at any time when a player screens out irrelevant stimulus information and focuses solely on selected cues. For example, a hockey goalkeeper attends to the penetrating play by the opposition's forwards but 'gates out' the movements of players who are in less threatening positions; the volleyball player blocking a dig focuses solely on the shot rather than being distracted by movements of other players on court; the doubles partner in badminton selectively attends to the server while ignoring the sights and sounds of other players or spectators. Given the speed of so many sports the whole process of selective attention becomes fascinating as performers are continually faced with situations which involve extremely hefty time constraints. A number of sport psychologists have focused their research efforts on examining the role of selective attention in developing anticipation in fast-ball sports. In general, this work suggests that selective attention can be improved through practice and experience, with more mature performers from a variety of sports including basketball, volleyball, tennis, badminton, and hockey all showing an ability to focus on selected relevant information very quickly and being able to process this information accurately before making rapid and correct decisions.

In addition to considering attention as a selective process, psychologists have focused on our ability to attend to more than one thing at a time in some circumstances. For example, a soccer player is described as having good vision when simultaneously he can dribble the ball, read the defensive pattern, spot holes in the defence, indicate to a teammate where to receive the ball and accurately pass the ball. However, we are also all too familiar with instances where we have difficulty doing two things at once, such as throwing a ball with the right hand while accurately catching a ball with the left hand (or in the reputed case of former US President and American football player Gerald Ford, chewing gum and walking at the same time). Various capacity theories have been proposed to account for situations where information processing space appears to become either limited or more flexible, in some cases allowing for the performance of two tasks simultaneously while in other situations prohibiting this. Kahneman (1973) proposed that there is a single pool of attention available which can be allocated flexibly as required to any number of tasks. No decrements in performance will occur providing the total capacity is not exceeded. More recent theoretical developments suggest multiple resources or several pools of attention each with their own limited capacity. Within this theory it is possible to perform more than one task if the separate tasks require different attentional resources. If the demand for resources overlaps then performance will be affected if any given pool of attention reaches its limit. For example, if two tasks both involve the same output resources (perhaps limb coordination) there is an increased likelihood that there will be resource limitations.

It has been suggested that one difference between novices and experienced performers in sport is in the type of attentional processing conducted. During the early stages of skill acquisition it is thought that attention involves controlled processing, a slow and cumbersome method which requires conscious effort to all details in order to make decisions. The role of a teacher or coach in these early stages would be to help the player realize which information is more pertinent and relevant to effective decision making. The novice's attentional capacity may also be greatly limited by the nature of this cumbersome control processing with much attention being allocated to motor output (the actual mechanics of throwing, catching, dribbling, running etc.) leaving fewer resources for reading the play and making decisions. As a performer gains experience and improves in terms of skill acquisition then it is thought that attention involves more automatic processing, a fast and effortless procedure not under conscious control.

Motor response elements in particular are thought to be performed under this type of subconscious control, freeing attentional resources to be allocated to evaluating the opposition's strategies and planning future responses.

In addition to the notions of selective attention and attentional capacity the third aspect of attention considered within the information processing framework involves the concept of arousal or alertness (see Chapter 4). The phenomenon of attentional narrowing as a result of increased emotional arousal was first brought to light in the work of Easterbrook (1959). Easterbrook maintained that in normal (non-threatening) situations the performer uses as many cues (or stimuli) as are available to her or him, selectively attending to the most relevant information. As arousal increases (which will happen as an event increases in importance) so attention narrows making the selection process to relevant information even more effective. However, if arousal continues to increase beyond an optimal level then the performer is in danger of narrowing attention to a point where some relevant information is discarded along with irrelevant cues — the blinkers come on. Sport offers many examples of situations where players who have become overaroused fail to see teammates who are in good receiving positions, or who fail to see the positions of defence players and barge through them, or they fail to see easy scoring opportunities. A sport psychologist by the name of Dan Landers has conducted some research into Easterbrook's notions in the sports context and has found considerable support for the suggestion that increased emotional arousal results in a deterioration of performance due to increased attentional narrowing (Landers, 1981).

The concepts of selective attention, capacity limitations and arousal effects form the main basis for understanding attention from within an information processing perspective. However, as indicated earlier, to gain a true picture of attentional issues in sport we need to also consider the impact of other related fields of study. Social psychologists have offered explanations for attentional losses through the distraction theories of Wine (1971), Sarason (1972) and Carver and Scheier (1981). Basically, these theories suggest that cognitive worry, in particular negative thoughts about oneself and one's performance (self-doubts), can cause such a distraction that the performer's attention is diverted to task irrelevant cues, including negative thoughts, rather than task relevant information. A related idea emerges in the work of Baumeister (1984) who suggests that the competitive nature of most sports encourages individuals to focus on 'trying hard'. In actual fact, by 'trying hard' performers may disrupt the natural automatic processing of information which should be taking place (if the performer is not a novice) and therefore forces the system into a type of controlled processing. By consciously trying to control an automatic process the outcome in terms of performance can be disrupted. These suggestions have been supported in a number of studies examining the effects of consciously focusing attention on motor performance (see Boutcher, 1992).

Another suggestion emanating from the social psychological perspective is that of individual differences in attentional style and the notion that individual performers may have a tendency to adopt an attentional style which either helps or hinders their performance. Much of the research work currently being conducted into attentional processes and sporting performance is along these lines, very often using Nideffer's (1976) Test of Attentional and Interpersonal Style or TAIS (Short Version) as a self-report measure of attentional style. The short form is a 12-item scale which yields six subscale measures for attentional strengths (broad–external, broad–internal, and narrow effective focuses) and potential weaknesses (external overload, internal overload, and errors of underinclusion). According to Nideffer (1976) attentional demands fall along two dimensions, breadth (either broad or narrow) and direction (internal or external).

Breadth refers to the number or range of possible stimuli to be attended. A broad focus would be required by the yachtsman jockeying for position at the start of a race whereas a narrow focus would be required by the snooker player executing a pot. Direction refers to whether the focus is directed internally to the performer's thoughts, feelings and body sensations, or externally to stimuli in the environment. Nideffer (1976) argues that individuals exhibit a natural tendency to function within a restricted range along each of these two dimensions and this then gives us one of four distinct attentional styles, namely broad–external, narrow–external, broad–internal and narrow–internal. Problems may then arise if an individual has a predisposition to function within a style that is incompatible with the demands of a particular sporting circumstance. For example, a player in a physical contact sport who favours a narrow–internal attentional style may be at a distinct disadvantage in comparison with someone who naturally attends to the broad–external requirements of many ball games. Conversely, an individual with a tendency to rely on a broad–external style may have difficulty coping with the narrow–external demands of a golf swing or the throw of a dart. Nideffer also acknowledges that the competitive and sometimes stressful nature of many sporting events may also contribute to attentional style mismatches. He too uses Easterbrook's notion of attentional narrowing to explain the effects of overarousal on the inability to shift attentional style with the demands of the situation. Much research is currently being conducted into the effects of attentional style on sporting performance but the results are somewhat equivocal. Support for the notion that individual styles, as measured by TAIS, affect performance has been found in basketball, swimming, diving, golf, shooting, cricket, baseball and softball batting whereas no relationship was found in studies conducted on the sports of gymnastics, surfing, archery and tennis. Most arguments centre not on the underlying principles but on the sensitivity of TAIS as an appropriate instrument, and time is now being spent trying to devise sport-specific versions of TAIS.

Finally, to conclude this discussion of attention it is appropriate to consider the impact of psychophysiological accounts of attentional processes, and the impact which they have made on cognitive sport psychology. The main thrust of psychophysiological accounts of cognition has been in relation to the concept of left brain/right brain functions. The idea that the different brain hemispheres may have different cognitive functions seemed to open a whole new window of research opportunity for cognitive psychologists. Numerous studies within human experimental psychology have indicated that left and right brain hemispheres process information differently. The left hemisphere is seen as largely responsible for verbal, linguistic and analytical processing whereas the right hemisphere is reponsible for spatial orientation and holistic interpretation. In the psychophysiological examination of attentional processes, the most common techniques appear to be either electroencephalogram (EEG) recordings of general cortical activity (obtained through scalp electrodes), or evoked response potentials of the brain's response to specific stimuli, or heart rate responses. In sport psychology, one of the few studies to examine attention with regard to psychophysiological processes was conducted by Hatfield, Landers and Ray in 1984. Subjects were élite rifle shooters and measurements of alpha brain waves were taken during the last few seconds prior to them pulling the rifle trigger. Results showed increased relaxation in the left-brain sites and this was interpreted by the investigators as indicating a conscious control of attentional processes possibly by reducing those cognitions which were unrelated to task performance. Studies like this may suggest that it is possible for performers to suppress negative self-talk and focus on task relevant cues, although clearly more work needs to be carried out before firm conclusions can be drawn. This appears to be an exciting area for future development.

Various theories and perspectives of attention have been presented here in an effort to provide the reader with a general overview of attention in sport. Within sport psychology as a whole it is evident that researchers and practitioners are increasingly dipping or buying into more than one perspective and we are currently witnessing attempts to synthesize the various perspectives into a unified model (see Boutcher, 1992). These approaches are to be commended and will almost inevitably serve to emphasize the multidimensional nature of attention.

Cognitive Styles

The previous topics have definable precedents within disciplines other than sport psychology. The work on cognitive styles tends to be different in this respect as it represents a topic made by, and exclusively for, sport psychology. Within the sport psychology literature the topic sits easily. However, whether it would stand close scrutiny in the wider context of human experimental psychology as a whole remains a matter for debate. Individual differences have preoccupied sport psychologists almost from the time the subject first came into existence (see Chapter 2). It should therefore come as little surprise to find that the idea of individual and identifiable cognitive styles or strategies has long interested sport psychologists and especially those with a primary interest in skill acquisition. Singer (1988), for example, has suggested that learners impose some kind of structure on movement information so that movements can be learned more efficiently. In particular, he has attempted to relate hypothesized information processing mechanisms with a learner's ability to cognitively process information appropriately. Ultimately this is linked with his or her capacity to employ a particular strategy to assist in the learning process. Accordingly, learner strategies include any self-initiated or externally imposed way of directing information which will lead to appropriate decisions regarding movement outcomes. For example, Singer suggests that strategies such as the use of verbal rehearsal, coding, chunking and imagery which facilitate recall and recognition of action, can either be taught or self-initiated. Other developmental psychologists, such as Bruner (see Bruner *et al.*, 1966) assert that strategy choice is partially determined by the situation. Therefore, according to Singer teachers of motor skills should initially teach a variety of strategies and then provide a variety of experiences in order that learners can learn to problem solve and choose the right strategy to match the situation.

A related area of research which has interested a group of Canadian sport psychologists (Allard and colleagues) is exploring differences in the knowledge structures or cognitive styles of novice and skilled performers. This work has somewhat tenuous links with research by several cognitive psychologists involving tasks with more easily recognizable cognitive components, including chess, bridge and physics problem solving (see Allard and Burnett, 1985). Expert and novice differences in knowledge representation have been well documented in these areas, both in terms of the amount and type of information, as well as in terms of processing capacity and ability to perform the task. In many respects, the idea of knowledge representation is very similar to Singer's earlier notion of cognitive strategies. Basically, both views assume that the differences between the novice and the expert lie in how the individual uses the information available to him/her rather than in terms of some underlying differences in the 'hardware' of the central nervous system. In fact, a number of studies examining the 'hardware' issue have found no differences between novice and expert sports performers in terms of dynamic visual acuity, simple visual reaction time and coincident timing. Allard's work shows that expert players in a variety of sports show superiority in the recall of game-structured information and that expert players make use of advanced visual cues to predict where a ball should be caught or struck. It has also been found that élite players make more accurate decisions about appropriate movements. Moreover, differences have also been found to exist between expert performers in different sports. For example, Allard reports that volleyball players tend to excel in a cognitive strategy of 'detecting' information, that is, they can very rapidly decide on what information is available to them. In contrast, expert basketball and hockey players tended to be poorer at rapid detection but showed a tendency to 'chunk' information meaningfully to make appropriate decisions about program action.

A number of sport psychologists have also examined accounts of athletes' individually expressed cognitive styles. In particular, the attentional strategies of associative and dissociative thinking have been examined by Morgan (1978), in relation to long-distance running. It has been suggested that individuals adopting an associative style tend to focus on the internal sensory feedback available within the body regarding the state of physiological demands being made. Such associative thinking may manifest itself in self-talk concerned with controlling breathing or foot stride and is thought to help the athlete cope with stressful or painful conditions by offering constructive suggestions about strategies to adopt. On the other hand, dissociative thinking is defined as an attentional style in which the performer directs the focus of attention away from sensory feedback available to him/her. Instead, the performer focuses on many different external events in an effort to take their mind off the pain. The small amount of research conducted into these different attentional strategies suggests that an associative style is possibly the more effective and some recent research provides evidence that athletes can be taught to adopt this internal focus through training. The benefit of adopting this strategy is thought to arise from the protection it provides the athlete in immediately alerting him/her to potential danger signals or injuries.

Cognitive Psychology and Applied Sport Psychology

The previous research mentioned in this chapter (with the possible exception of the last section on cognitive styles) would sit easily alongside theoretical developments across psychology. At this juncture it would be tempting to draw a convenient line under the literature and pretend that sport science and sport psychology has drawn selectively and prudently on available material from within cognitively related fields in order systematically to develop an understanding of motor performance. This is true but at the same time it only tells us one half of the story. The other half concerns the various attempts which have been made to use the term 'cognitive' to embrace a hotchpotch of topics, all loosely concerned with how athletes think and feel about their sport, and to use this material to inform a wide range of intervention strategies. In this section we will therefore review this material, warts and all, and consider some of the issues which arise when theory and practice clash heads in the arena of sport.

Since the early 1980s there has been pressure from within sport psychology, often North American sport psychology, to use the term cognitive psychology as a generic label to apply to any situation where an athlete's thoughts and feelings are under scrutiny. For example, 'cognitive' techniques and strategies are advocated for coping with competitive stress, and a good many of the techniques which deal predominantly with somatic (that is bodily) relaxation skills (through breathing and muscle relaxation exercises) are covered primarily in Chapter 4 on clinical psychology in sport. However, there are other techniques which place their emphasis not on how the body can influence the mind but on how the mind can influence the body and these are reviewed separately below. Often the links with cognitive psychology are tenuous, but at least the nature of these connections can be explored in the context of a chapter on cognition. Purists may question the scientific or even ethical validity of some of these techniques but practising sport psychologists would counter by citing the evidence which shows that, for whatever reason, they have been proved effective where it really matters, in changing sport behaviour (Greenspan and Feltz, 1989). There is an adage used in sport psychology which warns against indiscriminate intervention, 'If it isn't broken, don't fix it!' To this could be added, 'If it works, use it!' Very much in this spirit, the following section presents a number of popular cognitive intervention strategies and shows, wherever possible, their links with work conducted within the cognitive domain.

Cognitive-Behavioural Intervention Packages

Traditional behaviour modification techniques seek to change behaviour by amending the environment in systematic ways. However, there have been claims that it is not the environmental events themselves which are of primary importance in behaviour change but the individual's perception of those events (Mahoney, 1974; Meichenbaum, 1977). Cognitive coping strategies may be amended by conventional behaviour modification but involvement of the individual in expressing his or her own thoughts and feelings has been held to increase the efficacy of treatment. Meichenbaum's Stress-Inoculation Training (SIT) is one of a range of stress management packages advocated as useful to coaches and athletes for reducing stress and enhancing performance (Meichenbaum, 1977). Other popular programmes include Smith's Cognitive-Affective Stress Management or SMT (Smith, 1980) and Suinn's programme of Anxiety Management Training or AMT (Suinn, 1972). SIT and SMT have been adapted or developed specifically for use in sport and both outline essentially the same four stage process shown in the following list:

Cognitive-Behavioural Programs

The following four phases are common to cognitive-behavioural programs such as Meichenbaum's (1977) SIT or Smith's (1980) SMT:

1   *An educational phase* during which athletes explore the stress reaction itself, including antecedents of stress, nature of stressors, own reactions and consequences of action.

2 *An introduction to coping skills for handling stress.* This includes relaxation training and the use of cognitive skills such as effective self-instruction to prepare for stress, confront and handle it and face the possibility of being overcome by it.

3 *A practice phase.* SIT encourages supervised practice in coping in increasingly stressful situations, e.g., practice, game-like practice and games. SMT introduces an 'induced affect' as a major factor: the athlete imagines distressing situations which generate high levels of emotional arousal and is then required to use the coping skills learned in the previous phase to 'turn off' the affective response.

4 *An evaluation component.* This stage is included to assess the effectiveness of the programme in meeting individual needs.

Bandura (1977) claimed that beliefs about our own ability can influence success or failure in a task, and in this vein, both SIT and SMT appear to be aimed at changing the athlete's beliefs about his or her own ability. Similar programmes have been used in clinical contexts to help people overcome fear and anxiety, anger and pain. However, Meichenbaum (1977) himself has pointed out that such programmes run the risk of ending in failure. The greatest support for the use of these programmes in sport comes from evaluations of group studies, from popular sport specific magazines and from the anecdotal evidence included in popular self-help manuals. There have also been a few empirical studies which have attempted to assess the effectiveness of one or both of SIT and SMT. Three of these studies (Ziegler *et al.*, 1982; Mace and Carroll, 1985; Crocker *et al.*, 1988) claim to have found support for the effectiveness of these cognitive–behavioural techniques but methodological problems in the design of the studies would suggest caution with too literal an interpretation of results. Furthermore, the dearth of empirical evidence in this area has been commented on by a number of other authors, and there is a need for further genuine evaluation before definitive conclusions can be reached.

Imagery and Visualization

Imagery has been defined as 'all those quasi-sensory and quasi-perceptual experiences of which we are self-consciously aware and which exist for us in the absence of those stimulus conditions that are known to produce their genuine sensory or perceptual counterparts' (Richardson, 1969: 2–3). In other words when we imagine ourselves performing an action in the absence of physical practice we are said to be using imagery. Many self-help manuals for coaches and athletes (for example Terry, 1989) currently advocate the use of imagery for a wide variety of purposes including skill acquisition, skill maintenance, competition preparation and arousal control. Empirical investigations of imagery have tended to focus on the role of mental practice in skill acquisition, the role of imagery as a pre-competition cognitive 'psyching-up' strategy and comparisons in the use of imagery by successful and unsuccessful athletes. A number of these studies also explore the various variables thought to mediate imagery effects (for a comprehensive review of these studies see Murphy and Jowdy, 1992).

Findings from a well-established research base in psychology, in general, and sport psychology, in particular, attest to the effectiveness of imagery in enhancing skill acquisition and in acting as an effective psyching-up strategy. The bulk of research evidence suggests that the effects are more significant for cognitive tasks than for motor tasks. Where comparisons have been made between successful and less successful competitors it has been suggested that the former claim to use imagery more than unsuccessful athletes. However, despite these apparently supportive findings the extant research has not been without criticism. In particular, much of the work conducted within sport psychology has been accused of being methodologically flawed and lacking a coherent theoretical framework to explain imagery effects. Although suggestions for improvement in both these areas have been made, ironically research efforts have tended to lag behind actual practice of interventions and practical guidelines for imagery use in sport. The following is an example of an exercise used by the authors to assist golfers in developing the vividness and the controllability of their images.

Imagery in Practice

Image vividness: Golf scene — Imagine yourself walking out of the locker room and up to the first tee on a warm summer day. Be aware of the heat of the sun on your face as you leave the shade of the building. Take a deep breath and smell the freshly mown grass. As you walk towards the tee, notice the feel of the ground. Is it hard or soft? Rough or smooth? Now look around the tee area. Look at the other people present, their bags and trolleys. In your mind's eye create an image of the first tee. Become aware of the white competition markers. Notice the box and read the par, distance and stroke index. Now see yourself stepping up to tee off. Feel the heat of the sun on your back as you bend down to tee up the ball. Hear the other people around you gradually becoming quiet. Finally, focus on the feelings you have just prior to teeing off.

Image vividness: Success scene — Recall as vividly as possible a time when you performed very well on the golf course. Picture how you looked when you were playing well. Notice any differences in how you looked when you played well as opposed to when you play poorly. You walk differently, carrying your head and shoulders differently. When a golfer is confident on the inside, it shows on the outside. Try to get as clear a picture as possible of what you looked like when you were playing well. Listen in your mind to the sounds you hear when you are playing well, particularly the internal dialogue you have with yourself. There is often an internal silence that accompanies your best performances. Listen to it. What is your internal dialogue like? Recreate all the sounds as vividly as possible. Now, recreate clearly in your mind all the bodily sensations you have when playing well. How do your feet and hands feel? Do you have a feeling of quickness, looseness, speed or intensity in your body? Often, your clubs have a distinctive feel when playing well. How does your club feel on a drive, a chip, a putt? Focus on the bodily sensations that are associated with playing well. Finally, focus on the feelings you have as you are playing well.

Image control: Error correction — Imagine yourself working on a particular aspect of your game which has given trouble in the past. Take careful notice of what you were doing wrong. Now imagine yourself performing that shot perfectly. See and feel your movements and watch the ball go exactly where you want it to go. Now do the same thing, this time thinking about a competitive tournament situation in which you have had trouble in the past, for example putting to win the game, falling behind early, teeing off under pressure after a disastrous hole. Put yourself in this situation and then see yourself staying calm and hitting a successful shot.

Image control: Stress inoculation — Most golfers have problems with tensing up, becoming angry, losing concentration or losing confidence. Picture yourself in a situation that usually brings out one of these emotions. It might be missing an easy putt, going out of bounds and dropping a shot etc. Recreate the situation and especially the feelings that accompany that situation. For example, feel the anxiety experienced when putting under pressure at an important stage of the game, but use one of the stress management techniques learned, e.g., centring, positive talk, imagery etc. Feel the tension drain out of your body and focus on what you need to do to sink the putt. Again the focus should be on controlling what you see, hear and feel in your imagery.

The two most common theoretical explanations for how imagery works in sport have relied on either psychoneuromuscular theory or symbolic learning theory. In explaining the psychoneuromuscular theory Schmidt (1988) elaborated a view first put forward by Jacobson (the founder of autogenic training — see Chapter 4) in the 1930s. He believed that mental rehearsal of a motor task is the equivalent of actually performing the appropriate motor program but with the 'gain' turned down on the associated neuro-muscular activity. Mental rehearsal is usually associated with internal imaging, where the person imagines himself or herself performing the task 'from inside' rather than as an external observer. In the latter case neural activity tends to be totally visual rather than visual and kinaesthetic. Feltz and Landers (1983) concluded in their review of mental rehearsal that there was no solid evidence which linked internal imaging and associated neural activity with improved performance, and they thought it more likely that minute innovations concurrent with mental practice were general throughout the whole limb or even the whole body.

The symbolic learning theory, as originally proposed by Sackett (1935), claims that imagery effects occur due to the learner or performer cognitively rehearsing the task which in turn assists in memorizing the task. A number of investigations have supported this notion in relation to cognitive rather than motor components of performance (see Murphy and Jowdy, 1992). Tulving and Donaldson (1972) suggested that the strong effects of mental practice in verbal learning may reflect two distinct functions. The first is a maintenance function which allows material to be kept in some memory store to prevent decay, and the second is an elaborative function which extends and embellishes memory by activating an associative network thus integrating new and existing information. In a similar vein, Feltz and Landers (1983) proposed that mental practice may allow the learner to develop a rough schema of the cognitive elements of the task which, with physical practice and associated feedback, leads to a fuller, elaborated schema of the task's cognitive elements. Another suggestion is that mental practice may be effective in the earlier, cognitive, stages of learning, when the learner is attempting to understand the demands of the new task, but is less likely to be beneficial for the practice of high-level skills.

Murphy and Jowdy (1992) recently suggest both these theories have limited scope in that they merely provide plausible explanations for some of the findings within mental practice literature but make little impact in explaining either how images develop in the first place or their causal effects on performance. It is in this area of theory development that sport psychologists may gain by integrating their work with that of other psychologists who have proposed alternative theories to explain imagery processes. Examples of these include Paivio's (1971) and Kosslyn's (1981) information-processing based model, Lang's (1979) psychophysiological information-processing theory and

Ashen's (1984) triple code model. These models together attempt to integrate stimulus (image) characteristics with both the meaning of images for individuals and with response characteristics. Through their foundation in cognitive information processing psychology, they also attempt to address issues concerning the effects of imagery on attention, arousal, emotional states and cognitive states (for example dealing with self-efficacy and causal attributions). Much more research needs to be conducted which is theory driven and which will address many of the issues currently arising from the widespread use of imagery interventions prior to their proper investigation. At the same time it is important to recognize that within cognitive psychology as a whole, a growing realization of the limitations of cognitive models based solely on artificial intelligence has paved the way for growing interest in imagery research. These recent developments should not be ignored by those continuing to research and apply imagery techniques in the context of sport.

The Inner Game

At first glance, one popular approach to improving sporting performance which appears to be above all else psychological is that of the Inner Game. Inner Game was a expression 'coined' (some would say in more senses than one!) by Gallwey in the 1970s, and has been the basis for a considerable number of popular sport psychology books by Gallwey focusing on games including golf, skiing and tennis. Gallwey claimed that the most formidable opponent a performer in sport must face is inside his or her own head. Inner Game is essentially a conflict between two selves, Self 1 and Self 2. These are conceptualized as having quite different characteristics. Self 1 is conscious, self-conscious and linguistic. It is the 'thinking' self which evaluates, analyses and criticizes performance and it may be responsible for inappropriate responses or it may motivate the athlete towards counterproductive actions. Self 2, on the other hand, is described as unconscious and computer-like, the 'doing' self which deals most effectively with visual and spatial information. The self-analysis and self-criticism of an athlete during performance is a function of Self 1 and is symptomatic of the conflict between the two selves. Self 1 can express itself linguistically and, therefore, usually gains control but this control may be inappropriate. According to Gallwey it is not necessary to analyse why doubts, fears and lapses in concentration occur but to recognize their intrusion which directs attention away from the more relevant visual and spatial elements of the task. The Inner Game is directed toward allocating the resources of the two selves to the functions in which each is more competent so that they can operate in harmony and therefore produce optimal performance.

Inner Game Techniques

Gallwey (1974) advocates a variety of approaches to enhance harmony between Self 1 and Self 2. The following skills provide some examples of the unique Inner Game approach.

Awareness/skills programmes — The essence of awareness skills is to observe current action 'as it is', non-judgementally. The usual way of approaching skill learning is to analyse current performance critically and instruct oneself verbally to change. Gallwey instead advocates becoming attuned to the *feeling* of movement, the person is simply encouraged to focus on differences in *feel* between what the body is doing during the performance of various actions.

Trust skills — Gallwey claims that 'trusting and letting go' is probably one of the most difficult lessons to be learned in the Inner Game. In essence, he is talking about letting go of Self 1 control because the doubt in yourself generated by an overly analytic Self 1 is counter-productive to developing focused attention on current action. The idea is that once a performer has learned to perform with a certain amount of skill, s/he needs to rely on a type of *automatic* attentional process whereby the subconscious and visual Self 2 is allowed to direct the movement without unnecessary interference from the conscious and analytic Self 1.

Imagery skills — In order to break away from the usual way of learning which is to verbally instruct yourself to do certain things, Gallwey claims that we need to ask ourselves to change using programming methods involving image and feel. Rather than giving yourself a list of self-instructions (often including highly critical statements about your own self-worth as a sports performer) you should encourage Self 2 control by imagining both visually and kinaesthetically the desired action or path of the ball to the target.

To the layperson, these topics appear 'psychological' but Gallwey himself never made an attempt to appeal to formal psychological evidence in order to support his views. However, in his defence it would be fair to say that psychologists who are unfamiliar with the Inner Game may still find that some of Gallwey's statements have a familiar ring. He claims, for instance, that minimizing both internal and external comments which take into account how well or badly one has done in the immediate or more distant past (Self 1 activity) allows the focus of attention to shift to the information needed by Self 2 to correct errors and perform better. There seems to be a clear relationship here with the cognitive concepts of information overload (Welford, 1976), attentional shifting (Nideffer, 1976) and cue utilization (Easterbrook, 1959). Unfortunately, we could find no research which specifically links these concepts with the Inner Game notion.

However, hemispheric differentiation is one important area in which there have been attempts to link empirical evidence from formal psychological studies with the Asian philosophies, on which the Inner Game is based (Blakeslee, 1980). There seems to be a fairly close correspondence between the cognitive functions attributed to the left hemisphere (verbal and analytical) and Gallwey's critical Self 1. His spatially competent, non-linguistic, 'doing' Self 2 appears comparable with the functions of the right hemisphere (spatial and holistic). Gallwey's recommendations that mantras such as 'bounce-hit' in tennis, or singing while skiing, should be used as distractors which decrease Self 1 interference and allow Self 2 to proceed with those tasks in which it has more competence. This instruction could be interpreted reasonably as an attempt to occupy the capacity of the left hemisphere rather than allowing it to direct those movements which are more effectively coordinated by the right hemisphere.

Inner Game techniques may well be successful in teaching us how to use appropriate cognitive strategies in specific situations and Gallwey's concepts are now commercialized not only in sport but also in management and a range of other human activities. It is not surprising that a number of psychologists (Blakeslee, 1980; Hall, 1982) have proposed a relationship between the Inner Game and hemispheric specialization. This may be plausible enough but we have been unable to trace any published research which seeks to substantiate this relationship empirically. Clearly this is yet another area where there is tremendous scope for cross-fertilization of ideas and the development of research strategies to explore these notions both within sport psychology and beyond.

The Way Forward

Cognitive psychology and sport psychology have so many common interests that there is a natural compulsion to want to sweep aside differences and encourage further interdisciplinary work. At no time has the climate been more right than at present for recognizing the need for greater tolerance of different perspectives. The information processing view of cognitive psychology which grew in popularity throughout the 1970s and became the dominant theme in motor behaviour research throughout the 1980s is currently being challenged by proponents of the ecological perspective (see Chapter 5). However, rather than adopting a hardcore 'either–or' approach there appears to be an increased willingness by theorists to at least adopt a more tolerant approach and consider alternative theoretical perspectives. Ecological psychologists refuse to 'take out loans on intelligence' in order to explain perception and action and are renowned for their insistence on the ecological validity of research. The approach which developed out of Gibson's wartime research on applied problems of aviation has taken some time to be accepted within motor behaviour research but increasing numbers of journal articles and book chapters show that the view is guaranteed a future within the motor domain. Holding (1989), in discussing future trends of motor skills research, predicts that one emerging trend will see the development of a variety of cognitive models for action and alongside these models he suggests that the ecological perspective will increase in popularity and encourage a consideration of human action within the broader context of interaction with the environment.

Another trend which this chapter has highlighted is the fact that traditionally, cognitive psychology has tended to neglect social, motivational and emotional factors of cognition. Conversely, as this chapter has illustrated, applied sport psychology has tended to focus on these very aspects of cognitive psychology, particularly in terms of performance enhancement strategies. Some of the techniques offered to coaches and athletes (e.g. imagery) have an established history within mainstream psychology whereas others (e.g. Inner Game techniques) show enormous potential for fostering links but have yet to develop in terms of an empirical base. Perhaps this is an area in which we will see some cross-fertilization of not only clinical interventions but also of research paradigms. Certainly, with the current rapid pace of development within sport psychology there is the potential and desire to investigate empirically the clinical interventions and performance enhancement techniques advocated by practitioners. Cognitive psychology too might stand to gain by considering some of these broader aspects of cognition, particularly as they relate to applied problems such as how to enhance sporting performance. As Norman (1981) has argued for cognitive psychology as a whole, perhaps there is a need for sport psychologists to pause for thought from time to time, instead of racing off in pursuit of research objectives which are often of little value or practical concern to the real world. Norman's plea is for closer links between theory and practice, between the academic and the practitioner, and between the pure and the applied in cognitive research projects. Bearing in mind the long term well-being of sport psychology, this plea should not be allowed to fall on deaf ears but should act as a clarion call for future enterprises.

References

ABERNETHY, B. (1993) 'Attention', in SINGER, R. N., MURPHEY, M. and TENNANT, L. K. (Eds.), *Handbook of Research on Sport Psychology*, New York: Macmillan, pp. 127–70.

ALLARD, F. and BURNETT, N. (1985) 'Skill in sport', *Canadian Journal of Psychology*, 39, pp. 294–312.

ASHEN, A. (1984) 'ISM: The triple code for imagery and psychophysiology', *Journal of Mental Imagery*, 8, pp. 15–42.

BANDURA, A. (1977) 'Self-efficacy: Toward a unifying theory of behavior change', *Psychological Review*, 84, pp. 191–215.

BAUMEISTER, R. F. (1984) 'Choking under pressure: Self-consciousness and paradoxical effects of incentives on skillful performance', *Journal of Personality and Social Psychology*, 46, pp. 610–20.

BERNSTEIN, N. (1967) *The Co-ordination and Regulation of Movements*, Oxford: Pergamon Press.

BLAKESLEE, T. R. (1980) *The Right Brain*, New York: Anchor-Doubleday.

BOUTCHER, S. H. (1992) 'Attention and athletic performance', in HORN, T. (Ed.) *Advances in Sport Psychology*, Champaign, IL: Human Kinetics, pp. 251–66.

BROADBENT, D. E. (1958) *Perception and Communication*, New York: Pergamon Press.

BRUNER, J. S., OLIVER, R. R. and GREENFIELD, P. M. (1966) *Studies in Cognitive Growth*, New York: Wiley.

CARVER, C. S. and SCHEIER, M. F. (1981) *Attention and Self-Regulation*, New York: Springer-Verlag.

CHERRY, E. C. (1953) 'Some experiments on the recognition of speech, with one and two ears', *Journal of the Acoustical Society of America*, 25, pp. 975–9.

CROCKER, P. R. E., ALDERMAN, R. B. and SMITH, F. M. R. (1988) 'Cognitive-affective stress management training with high performance youth volleyball players: Effects on affect, cognitions and performance', *Journal of Sport and Exercise Psychology*, 10, pp. 448–60.

EASTERBROOK, J. A. (1959) 'The effect of emotion on cue utilization and the organization of behavior', *Psychological Review*, 66, pp. 183–201.

FELTZ, D. L. and LANDERS, D. M. (1983) 'The effects of mental practice on motor skill learning and performance: A meta-analysis', *Journal of Sport Psychology*, 5, pp. 25–57.

FUCHS, C. Z. and ZAICHKOWSKY, L. (1980) 'Motor behavior research: Current developments', in ZAICHKOWSKY, L. and FUCHS, C. Z. (Eds) *The Psychology of Motor Behavior*, Ithaca, NY: Mouvement Pub, pp. 3–12.

GALLWEY, W. T. (1974) *The Inner Game of Tennis*, New York: Random House.

GREENSPAN, M. J. and FELTZ, D. L. (1989) 'Psychological interventions with athletes in competitive situations: A review', *The Sport Psychologist*, 3, pp. 219–36.

HALL, E. G. (1982) 'Hemispheric dominance: Using the right brain in sports', in ZAICHKOWSKY, L. D. and SIME, W. E. (Eds) *Stress Management for Sport*, Reston, Vancouver, BC: AAPHERD, pp. 118–35.

HATFIELD, B. D., LANDERS, D. M. and RAY, W. J. (1984) 'Cognitive processes during self-paced motor performance: An electroencephalographic profile of skilled marksmen', *Journal of Sport Psychology*, 6, pp. 42–59.

HOLDING, D. (1989) 'Final survey', in HOLDING, D. (Ed.) *Human Skills*, Chichester: John Wiley, pp. 281–92.

JAMES, W. (1890) *The Principles of Psychology*, Vol. 1, New York: Holt.

KAHNEMAN, D. (1973) *Attention and Effort*, Englewood Cliffs, NJ: Prentice-Hall.

KOSSLYN, S. M. (1981) 'The medium and the message in mental imagery', in BLOCK, N. (Ed.) *Imagery*, Cambridge, MA: MIT Press, pp. 207–58.

LANDERS, D. M. (1981) 'Arousal, attention, and skilled performance: Further considerations', *Quest*, 33, pp. 271–83.

LANG, P. J. (1979) 'A bioinformational theory of emotional imagery', *Psychophysiology*, 17, pp. 495–512.

LINDSAY, P. H. and NORMAN, D. A. (1977) *Human Information Processing: An Introduction to Psychology*, New York: Academic Press.

MACE, R. and CARROLL, R. (1985) 'The control of anxiety in sport: Stress Inoculation Training prior to abseiling', *International Journal of Sports Psychology*, 16, pp. 165–75.

MAGILL, R. A. (1989) *Motor Learning: Concepts and Applications*, 3rd edn, Dubuque, IA: Brown.

MAHONEY, M. (1974) *Cognition and Behavior Modification*, Cambridge, MA: Ballinger.

MEICHENBAUM, D. (1977) *Cognitive-Behavior Modification*, 2nd edn, New York: Plenum.

MILLER, G. A. (1956) 'The magical number seven, plus or minus two: Some limits on our capacity for processing information', *Psychological Review*, 63, pp. 81–97.

MOORE, T. V. (1939) *Cognitive Psychology*, New York: J. B. Lippincott.

MORGAN, W. (1978) 'The mind of the marathoner', *Psychology Today*, April, pp. 38–49.

MURPHY, S. M. and JOWDY, D. P. (1992) 'Imagery and mental practice', in HORN, T. (Ed.) *Advances in Sport Psychology*, Champaign, IL: Human Kinetics, pp. 221–50.

NEISSER, U. (1967) *Cognitive Psychology*, New York: Appleton-Century-Crofts.

NIDEFFER, R. (1976) 'Test of attentional and interpersonal style', *Journal of Personality and Social Psychology*, 34, pp. 394–404.

NORMAN, D. A. (1976) *Memory and Attention*, New York: John Wiley.

NORMAN, D. A. (1981) 'Twelve issues for cognitive science', in NORMAN, D. A. (Ed.) *Perspectives in Cognitive Science*, Hillsdale, NJ: Lawrence Erlbaum, pp. 265–95.

PAIVIO, A. (1971) *Imagery and Verbal Processes*, New York: Holt, Rinehart and Winston.

RICHARDSON, A. (1969) *Mental Imagery*, New York: Springer.

SACKETT, R. S. (1935) 'The relationship between amount of symbolic rehearsal and retention of a maze habit', *Journal of General Psychology*, 13, pp. 113–28.

SANFORD, A. J. (1985) *Cognition and Cognitive Psychology*, New York: Erlbaum.

SARASON, I. G. (1972) 'Experimental approaches to test anxiety: Attention and the uses of information', in SPIELBERGER, C. D. (Ed.) *Anxiety: Current Trends in Theory and Research*, Vol. 2, New York: Academic Press, pp. 380–403.

SCHMIDT, R. A. (1975) 'A schema theory of discrete motor learning', *Psychological Review*, 82, pp. 225–60.

SCHMIDT, R. A. (1988) *Motor Control and Learning: A Behavioral Emphasis*, 2nd edn, Champaign, IL: Human Kinetics.

SCHMIDT, R. A. (1991) *Motor Learning and Performance: From Principles to Practice*, Champaign, IL: Human Kinetics.

SINGER, R. (1980) *Motor Learning and Human Performance*, 3rd edn, New York: Macmillan.

SINGER, R. N. (1988) 'Strategies and metastrategies in learning and performing self-paced athletic skills', *The Sport Psychologist*, 2, pp. 49–68.

SMITH, R. (1980) 'A cognitive-affective stress management approach to training for athletes', in NADEAU, C. H., HALLIWELL, W. R., NEWELL, K. M. and ROBERTS, G. C. (Eds) *Psychology of Motor Behavior and Sport — 1979*, Champaign, IL: Human Kinetics, pp. 54–73.

SUINN, R. (1972) 'Rehearsal training for ski racers', *Behavior Therapy*, 3, pp. 519–20.

TERRY, P. (1989) *The Winning Mind*, London: Tomsons.

TULVING, E. and DONALDSON, W. (Eds) (1972) *Organization of Memory*, New York: Academic Press.

WELFORD, A. T. (1952) 'The psychological refractory period and the timing of high-speed performance — A review and a theory', *British Journal of Psychology*, 43, pp. 2–19.

WELFORD, A. T. (1968) *Fundamentals of Skill*, London: Methuen.

WELFORD, A. T. (1976) *Skilled Performance: Perceptual and Motor Skills*, London: Scott, Foresman and Co.

WILLIAMS, J. (1986) *Applied Sport Psychology*, Palo Alto, CA: Mayfield.

WILLIAMS, J. and STRAUB, W. F. (1986) 'Sport psychology: Past, present, future', in WILLIAMS, J. (Ed.) *Applied Sport Psychology: Personal Growth to Peak Performance*, Palo Alto, CA: Mayfield, pp. 1–14.

WINE, J. (1971) 'Test anxiety and direction of attention', *Psychological Bulletin*, 76, pp. 92–104.

ZIEGLER, S. G., KLINZING, J. and WILLIAMSON, K. (1982) 'The effects of two stress management training programmes on cardiorespiratory efficiency', *Journal of Sport Psychology*, 4, pp. 280–9.

Further Reading

ABERNETHY, B. (1993) 'Attention', in SINGER, R. N., MURPHEY, M. and TENNANT, L. K. (Eds) *Handbook of Research on Sport Psychology*, New York: Macmillan, pp. 127–70.

ANDERSON, J. R. (1990) *Cognitive Psychology and its Implications*, New York: W. H. Freeman.

BOUTCHER, S. H. (1992) 'Attention and athletic performance', in HORN, T. (Ed.) *Advances in Sport Psychology*, Champaign, IL: Human Kinetics, pp. 251–66.

KELSO, J. A. S. (1982) *Human Motor Behavior: An Introduction*, Hillsdale, NJ: Erlbaum.

MAGILL, R. A. (1989) *Motor Learning: Concepts and Applications*, 3rd edn, Dubuque, IA: Brown.

MURPHY, S. M. and JOWDY, D. P. (1992) 'Imagery and mental practice', in HORN, T. (Ed.), *Advances in Sport Psychology*, Champaign, IL: Human Kinetics, pp. 221–50.

SCHMIDT, R. A. (1988) *Motor Control and Learning: A Behavioral Emphasis*, 2nd edn, Champaign, IL: Human Kinetics.

WELFORD, A. T. (1968) *Fundamentals of Skill*, London: Methuen.

Chapter 4

Helping Athletes Help Themselves
(Clinical Psychology)

Introduction

Of all professional psychologists, almost certainly those who have made the greatest contribution to applied sport psychology have been clinical psychologists. Over the years, a great many clinical psychologists have found that their professional skills have transferred easily to the world of sport. Some would argue that a distinction can and should be made between different types of clinical intervention in sport, on the one hand those who deal with serious behavioural and emotional problems amongst athletes and on the other hand those who offer advice and teach mental skills but who do not see themselves primarily as clinicians (Morris and Bull, 1991). On occasion, the latter have been categorized as educational sport psychologists (LaRose, 1988) but in practice the distinction between forms of intervention is not an easy one to make. For example, at what stage does an athlete's problem with self-belief or attention become classified as a clinical abnormality? Given that all intervention programmes are designed to effect changes and to resolve psychological problems, however trivial these may be, then within this chapter an array of interventions will be subsumed under the broad umbrella of clinical psychology.

To encompass this wide ranging material the chapter has been divided in two. The first part deals with competitive sport and the role of the sport psychologist in understanding and facilitating performance. This section begins with a general discussion of three much used and abused terms, arousal, anxiety and stress. Practical intervention strategies are next outlined, giving an indication of the sorts of techniques which professional sport psychologists regularly employ and especially in relation to stress management. To conclude, the growing literature relating mental health with exercise is presented.

Stress, Arousal and Anxiety: The Theory

The history of sport psychology from the days of Triplett to the present is littered with discussion of the relationship between arousal and performance. Since the turn of the century if not before there has been a recognition that for all sportsmen and women there is an optimal level of arousal, or zone of optimal functioning (Hanin, 1980) towards which they should strive. On so many occasions competitors fail to realize their potential not because of a lack of physical prowess but because they suffer from the effects of either over or under arousal.

Without question the debate has moved on considerably from Triplett's early work on dynamogenics (1898). However, despite (or perhaps because of) the level of sophistication and complexity of argument, it would seem that we are still a long way from producing a clear understanding of the relationship. Standing back from this literature, the joke about the tourist travelling in the west of Ireland springs to mind. Having spent several hours trying to find a small village, the visitor eventually asks a farmer for directions, only to be told, 'Sure if I was going there I wouldn't start from here.' So the quest for understanding often seems constrained from the outset by the terminology, traditions and frames of reference with which we have grown up and become familiar.

Three terms in particular have been used extensively, these being stress, arousal and anxiety. The use of these terms can cause genuine confusion to those coming to sport psychology for the first time, even for those with a background in clinical psychology. This confusion is entirely understandable given the overlap between the three. Essentially each is describing the antecedents, and sometimes precedents, both physical and mental, to a cognitive appraisal that we are about to face a situation which is uncertain or demanding. According to Jones and Hardy (1990: 8), 'Precise identification of the relationship between stress and performance has proved elusive. This elusiveness has been at least partly due to a general lack of precision in defining and distinguishing between key concepts such as arousal and anxiety.'

Overall, the actual physiological mechanisms appear to be best understood, and these are described in greater detail in Chapter 9. However, when we turn to the relationship between physiological and psychological responses then the waters become murkier. For example, imagine the situation of a young hockey player about to represent her county for the first time. On the morning of the game she may begin to worry about her performance and this fear may well reflect in physical responses such as an upset stomach and increased heart rate. These physical signals are in turn picked up by the brain, reinforcing the initial perception of fear which then exacerbates the problem even further. Even if we are able to pick up these signals, how these manifest themselves in thoughts and eventually in performance is difficult to predict but sport psychologists have set themselves the daunting task of unravelling these processes.

It is not easy to plot a straight course through the minefield of terminology which bedevils literature in this area. Almost invariably, commentators have offered definitions of stress, arousal and anxiety but then, almost as often, their discussion moves quickly on to the practicalities of measurement and intervention. This approach is very understandable given the difficulties of disentangling the three terms and the degree of overlap between each. For example, it is not clear to what extent each is being used to describe purely physiological or psychological phenomena, or whether the two are realistically inseparable. (It is significant that orthodox Cartesian ideas of dualism, or a rigid separation between the functions of the mind and the body, underpins almost all analyses. Whether such unequivocal acceptance of dualism is healthy is debatable.) By way of example, the term arousal is often used to refer to a physiological state, that is the degree of activation of the organs that are under the control of the autonomic or involuntary nervous system. Typical physiological measures of arousal include blood pressure, pulse rate, respiration rate, electrocortical activity (using an electroencephalo-graph or EEG), muscle tension (using an electromyograph or EMG), pupil dilation, hormonal secretions (e.g. adrenalin and epinephrin) and galvanic skin response. In combination these measures can provide a useful index of arousal, although single measures alone are regarded as less powerful discriminators and should be used with caution.

While these measures are designed to tap physiological reactions, Gould and Krane (1992, pp. 120–1) maintain that 'arousal is best defined as general physiological *and psychological* activation of the organism that varies on a continuum from deep sleep to intense excitement' given, they argue, that arousal involves mental activation as well as physiological activation. Other writers have also explored this relationship. For example, although the term arousal is normally used interchangeably with activation, Sanders (1983), and later Jones (1990) argue that a further distinction should be made between arousal (a response to input which energizes perceptual processes, i.e. cognition), the activation system (which governs the individual's readiness for motor response, i.e. action) and effort (the coordination of both arousal and activation systems to produce maximal performance, i.e. both cognition and action). Therefore depending on your approach, arousal can be talked about either as a somatic or bodily response, a cognitive response or both.

In a similar vein, the definition of the term stress has been troublesome, at different times referring to either the stimulus variable, a mediating variable or a response variable (Martens, 1977). To many, the term refers specifically to any external or internal situation that tends to grossly disturb homeostasis or stability (Grossman, 1984), therefore stress is a stimulus variable operating to provoke activation or arousal. To others, stress is the response itself, so according to Selye (1975, 1976), stress is to be regarded as our non-specific response to any demand made upon us. Being non-specific it thus encompasses both cognitive and somatic reactions. In addition, stress can be labelled as either positive (eustress) or negative (distress). A further line argues that stress should be used to describe the entire process which is invoked when there is a mismatch between perceived environmental demands made upon us and our ability to respond, otherwise known as our response capability. For example, McGrath (1970) describes stress in terms of four stages. Stage one is the environmental demand itself (for example a major tournament); stage two is the evaluation of that demand and our ability to respond (am I good enough to win?); stage three is the physiological and psychological outcome of that evaluation (negative thoughts and butterflies); and stage four is performance itself.

The final term to be explained is anxiety. Once more, within sport psychology it is possible to unearth a whole host of meanings and connotations which are often, but by no means always, describing both psychological and physiological processes. While the previous terms stress and arousal are both used to describe our general response processes across many situations, anxiety is often more narrowly defined in terms of the competitive stress response, that is the response of the individual to the prospect of competition (otherwise known as the yips or the jitters). Discussion almost invariably describes both a state of heightened physiological activation together with worry, concern or negative affective response, in a nutshell defined by Iso-Ahola and Hatfield (1986: 180) as, 'A state of autonomic arousal accompanied by perceptions of negative affect or emotion'.

In reality, it is this state which has been the major preoccupation of practising sport psychologists, representing as it does the endpoint or outcome of the stress process and at the same time incorporating the symptoms of activation or arousal. This interest is reflected in a very sophisticated literature dealing exclusively with competitive anxiety and a plethora of measures which are routinely used to quantify athletes' responses to competition. Anxiety is taken to be multifaceted, normally conceptualized in terms of a two-by-two taxonomy. In the words of Jones and Hardy (1990: 282), anxiety is 'a multidimensional construct which can be considered from both state and trait perspectives, each of which comprises at least two components: cognitive anxiety and somatic anxiety'. For example (and as already discussed in relation to stress and arousal), anxiety is discussed in terms of two components, cognitive anxiety (fear of failure, negative thoughts, worry) and somatic anxiety (physiological symptoms associated with arousal). In addition, following the work of Spielberger (1971), two types of anxiety are recognized — trait anxiety and state anxiety. Trait anxiety is the more enduring of the two, often described as a stable dimension of personality. It is the substrate or base level of anxiety against which environmental threats make their mark. Hence an individual with high trait anxiety will be more likely to look upon a greater number of situations as threatening and will be more prone to 'go critical' in stressful situations. State anxiety refers to a temporary condition which is produced in response to the immediate perception of threat or challenge.

These theoretical debates have led us to to a position where we can at least now appreciate the complexities of the relationship between cognitive and somatic state and performance, and how individuals respond so differently to competitive situations. For example, some may manifest primarily psychological symptoms, others physiological symptoms, others both, and others neither. Without doubt, great advances have been made in our understanding of how individuals respond to competition but it is doubtful if progress has been facilitated by wrangles over terminology. Instead it may be prudent to take the Irish farmer's advice and make a fresh start. One possibility could be to lose one or more of the terms completely, another would be to lay down lines of demarcation, so, for example, stress could be used to refer to the process in its entirety, the stressor could refer to the particular cue or stimulus which activates the system, arousal could refer specifically to physiological or somatic responses to that stimulus, and anxiety the package of psychological and physiological antecedents to these responses. This may sound tidy in theory; in practice there is still likely to be overlap given that the relationship between cognitive and somatic responses is so tangled and intimate, and also given the unchallenged philosophy of dualism which implicitly yet firmly underpins the research at present.

Certainly, the spirit of enquiry which characterizes research in this area is entirely commendable; very few stones have remained unturned in an endeavour to understand the relationship between cognitive appraisal and physical performance. The history of this literature, and significant contributions along the way reinforce this impression.

One of the earliest approaches and one which is still routinely cited in almost all texts is drive theory (Hull, 1943). According to drive theory, performance (P) is regarded as a function of habit (H) multiplied by drive strength (D), or $P = f (H \times D)$. Therefore, as drive increases so performance should improve so long as that performance is well learnt and well rehearsed, that is a dominant response. Therefore according to classical drive theory if athletes are already skilled then 'psyching up' should enhance their performance. Support for this basic assumption is, quite predictably, very scarce (Martens, 1974), and indeed the fundamental components of the equation itself continue to defy capture. For example, it is extremely difficult to classify tasks along a dominant to non-dominant continuum. This is especially true when dealing with complex motor tasks and novel situations which form the core of almost all sporting occasions.

Figure 4.1: The Inverted-U Hypothesis

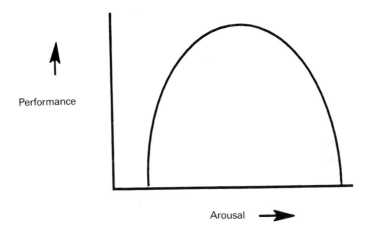

A second approach which has likewise had a very strong influence over the years, and continues to be influential, albeit against the tide of recent empirical research (Fazey and Hardy, 1988), is the inverted-U hypothesis. This has enjoyed massive popular appeal primarily because of its simplicity and perceived practical utility. In contrast to drive theory's linear relationship between arousal and performance, the inverted-U hypothesis, as derived from the Yerkes-Dodson law, predicts a curvilinear relationship between arousal and performance, as shown in Figure 4.1.

Quite simply, the hypothesis predicts that increasing arousal will lead to an increase in sporting performance but only up to an optimum point. As arousal continues beyond this point so performance will then suffer. This basic model has been the major driving force behind the majority of research dealing variously with arousal, stress, anxiety and sport since the early 1970s. Not surprisingly, during this time a considerable number of modifications and refinements had been added before the hypothesis came under more concerted attack in the late 1980s.

It is important to emphasize that the inverted-U presents a hypothesis or perhaps a model of the relationship between two variables, rather than being a genuine theory of arousal and performance (Landers, 1980). The distinction is important for the model does not attempt to explain why the relationship is as it is. This task has been left to other writers, working from a number of traditions. One branch has looked at attentional theory, as derived from Easterbrook's cue utilization theory (Landers, 1980; Nideffer, 1978; Wine, 1971). The fundamental postulate is that as arousal increases so perceptual sensitivity narrows, or, put more simply, the blinkers come on. Clearly in games involving wide vision and response to a number of cues from the environment then this blinkering will impair performance. At the same time, a moderate level of arousal may be

Figure 4.2: Oxendine's Taxonomy of Sport

Optimum Arousal	Sport
5	American football blocking; 200/400 metres race; gym exercises; weight lifting
4	Long jump; sprints/long distance; shot-put; swimming races; wrestling/judo
3	Basketball; boxing; high jump; gymnastics; soccer
2	Baseball; diving; fencing; tennis
1	Archery; bowling; golf putting/chipping; figure skating

beneficial in certain sports as it could help us to shut out unnecessary distractions and focus attention on play. Two further theories which have been brought into play, albeit selectively, are signal detection theory and information processing theory. The principal idea behind both is similar, namely that as arousal increases so the amount of neural 'noise' (the number of signals being processed by the central nervous system) increases and hence our ability to make correct decisions and choices deteriorates. According to signal detection theory, when highly aroused there will be increased neural activity which in turn will make it more likely that we will respond indiscriminately to signals from the environment. Conversely when underaroused, we are less likely to attend to the signals or cues themselves in the first place. Hence these theories attempt to provide some explanation for general predictions based on the inverted-U hypothesis but the lack of sophistication of the model and its poor predictive validity remain major problems. Indeed, most research dealing with arousal and performance has been introduced to help clarify what is now generally regarded as a deceptively simple and unidimensional model, and to help the model to accommodate conflicting and sometimes disconfirmatory previous research (Gould and Krane, 1992: 126). As early as 1970, Oxendine argued that an arousal/performance model must take into account context, namely the demands of particular sports and the tasks associated with that sport. He argued that high levels of arousal are likely to enhance performance of tasks involving gross motor skills (for example weightlifting) but impede performance involving complex motor skills, coordination, steadiness, concentration and fine movement (for example snooker or golf). However, overall it is likely that across a wide range of motor tasks, and hence sports, raising levels of arousal slightly above average will improve performance. Oxendine actually developed a taxonomy which endeavoured to place sport skills alongside relevant levels of arousal, as shown in Figure 4.2.

Predictably, empirical support for Oxendine's taxonomy has been disappointing although as a rule of thumb, or sometimes as a way of putting over a message quickly to athletes and coaches, it may be of limited benefit. In a more general way, given the lack of sophistication of the hypothesis, it is little wonder that the inverted-U has come under increasing attack. This attack has been mounted on numerous fronts, very often citing the model's lack of empirical support and poor predictive validity. In turn it has been replaced by models which are better able to accommodate complexity, ranging from the heavily theoretical to the principally practical. The former include multidimensional anxiety theory, threshold theory, catastrophe theory and reversal theory; the latter is dominated by Hanin's work on zones of optimal functioning or ZOF.

Multidimensional anxiety theory has evolved slowly over the years, representing the coming together of a number of different research traditions and including work on the inverted-U hypothesis. In some ways, it is still not clear whether or not all the approaches named above are actually multidimensional theories as sometimes the term is used to encompass a number of competing models. Recently authors including Hardy (1990) and Gould and Krane (1992) have been more specific in associating multidimensional anxiety theory closely with the work of Burton (1988) and Martens *et al.* (1990).

The theory draws upon the distinction made earlier between cognitive anxiety and somatic anxiety. It proposes that anxiety reflects in two responses, a somatic response based on the perception of physiological arousal, and a cognitive response which includes worry about performance, inability to concentrate, disrupted attention and fear of failure. The theory makes a number of specific predictions about the relationship between anxiety and performance (Martens *et al.*, 1990). First, it predicts a negative but linear relationship between cognitive state anxiety and performance but a relationship between somatic anxiety and performance which is more akin to the inverted-U. Second, it argues that somatic anxiety should decline once performance begins but that cognitive anxiety may remain high so long as fear of failure remains. Third, it maintains that cognitive anxiety will be generally stable across time whereas somatic anxiety will tend to rise dramatically prior to competition. Each of these propositions has intuitive appeal but available support remains thin on the ground (Hardy, 1990).

An even more radical attack on the inverted-U hypothesis has been offered by a number of British sport psychologists, including most notably John Fazey and Lew Hardy, and spearheaded in their BASS monograph, *The Inverted-U Hypothesis: A Catastrophe for Sport Psychology?* (1988). Their model is premised upon catastrophe theory (Thom, 1975), an approach which stands as a counterpoint to the traditional view that natural processes are characterized by slow change and gradual evolution. Rather than thinking of linear or curvilinear relationships, which imply gradual change and continuity, instead Thom maintained that in the natural and behavioural world we often witness discontinuity or catastrophe. Translating this idea to the world of sport, Hardy and Fazey argue that the effects of physiological arousal on performance may be either relatively mild or they may be catastrophic, and this depends almost entirely upon cognitive anxiety. When cognitive anxiety is low, for example during training, then an increase in arousal will normally facilitate performance. However, when cognitive anxiety is high, for example immediately prior to competition, then the dangers of increasing physiological arousal are that much more serious. The model is often described as shown in Figure 4.3, where the surface of the three dimensional model represents performance. In the background, increasing arousal leads to marginal improvements in performance within limits (the inverted-U); in the foreground, increasing arousal leads the performer over the edge of a cliff with a rapid descent and a subsequent climb back to adequate performance which is far from easy.

From the very start, Fazey and Hardy (1988) were aware of the limitations of this 'cusp catastrophe model', given that it did not take into account task difficulty nor indeed individual differences in self-confidence. Therefore the authors proposed developing a 'butterfly catastrophe model' which can deal with five dimensions, namely the effects of cognitive anxiety, physiological arousal, task difficulty and self-confidence upon performance (Fazey and Hardy: 1988: 18). In theory such a model has great appeal; in practice its complexity may defy empirical verification.

A final approach which has some similarities to catastrophe theory but which is also in an early stage of development in relation to sport is reversal theory (Smith and Apter, 1975). Kerr (1985) has used this approach to understand arousal and stress effects in

Figure 4.3: Catastrophe Model of the Effects of Anxiety upon Performance

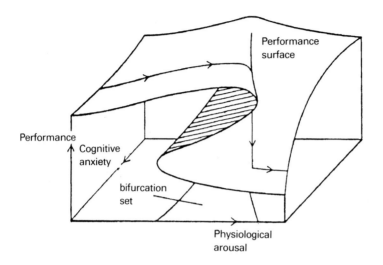

Reprinted with the kind permission of the authors from Fazey and Hardy (1988) p. 15.

sport, arguing that switching between telic (goal oriented) and paratelic (non-goal oriented) states may explain how, for example, anxiety or worry, as a telic state, may suddenly switch into excitement, the paratelic state, depending on instruction and task mastery, and this in turn will reflect in huge shifts in affective or emotional state. Working in a purely practical vein, Martens has recognized the utility of reversals for understanding how arousal can be either positive (in Seyle's terminology, eustress) or negative (distress), and how movement between the two states can be so rapid. For helping athletes understand and come to terms with their responses to competition, such an approach would seem to have considerable appeal, in some respects irrespective of existing theoretical and methodological limitations.

These approaches represent a growing recognition of the complex relationships at work, and commendable attempts to grapple with genuine, real life problems concerning the arousal/performance relationship. This is further exemplified by the recent work of Gould and Krane (1992) which takes the form of a process model of stress, describing stages from environmental demands (stage one), to the perception of threat (stage two), to responses to that threat (stage three), to performance outcomes and consequences (stage four). Along the way, numerous cognitive, somatic and environmental variables are taken into account, and the development of such process models is likely to point the way towards the future. Whether anything other than massive empirical, experimental research will ever be able to effectively test these models remains to be seen but the challenge is certainly there.

To try to translate these increasingly sophisticated approaches into practice can present real difficulties, as even Oxendine's early work demonstrated. One solution to this problem is for practitioners simply to take on board the general messages which they offer. For example, some very basic conclusions to be drawn are first, that stress and anxiety do influence performance, second that each individual will respond in a unique way to stress and anxiety, and third that this will ultimately in their performance in an idiosyncratic fashion. One approach which incorporates these three simple messages and elegantly bridges the gap between theory and practice is Hanin's Optimum Arousal Theory. Yuri Hanin is a Russian sport psychologist and, like so many former Eastern bloc sport psychologists, his primary concern is with real world application. He argues that each athlete has an arousal zone of optimal function or zone of optimum functioning (ZOF) (Hanin, 1980). According to Hanin, the individual will perform at their most efficient in a particular event when their level of arousal falls within their ZOF. The task of the sport psychologist is to come to know their athletes, help them develop self-awareness as to in what arousal state they perform best and then use techniques to move them to that state prior to competition.

In many respects this confirms the work of a great many applied sport psychologists who may sometimes use different terminology but who also try to create or recreate the circumstances where the athlete feels most at ease and comfortable with him or herself prior to and during competition. The term peak experience or peak performance is often used by applied sport psychologists to describe such circumstances

> the psychological experience that characterises an athlete's most fulfilling psycho-emotional moments while participating in sport . . . These rare moments, when the participant is performing optimally and experiencing heightened levels of awareness, offer great significance in advancing our understanding of the nature of optimal performance. (Ravizza, 1989: 9).

This state is one where performance flows completely easily and is said to be characterized by feelings of control, mastery, transcendence of self, relaxation, loss of fear and focused awareness (Garfield and Bennett, 1984). As you may expect, the phenomenon has not been the subject of close empirical investigation but as any practising sport psychologist will testify, almost all athletes are able to bring to mind a few special occasions when they experienced peak performance. As part of a programme designed to enhance self-confidence and increase self-awareness, working with the memories of these special occasions can be extremely valuable.

In drawing this section to a close, it must be readily apparent that independently, theory and practice have moved together. The implicit message which research on anxiety now carries is, 'There's nowt so queer as folk!' Therefore the wholesale use of interventions, be they relaxation or arousal techniques, will always be danger ridden so long as such approaches ignore individual differences. The simplicity of Hanin's approach belies its value and its practical utility in bringing together theory and practice and arguing that it is impossible to generalize from athlete to athlete, from sport to sport. Each athlete must be dealt with as an individual and each programme of intervention must be tailored to their personal needs. This does not deny the value of psychological profiling (see Chapter 2), but it does place considerable restrictions on what must be done with the information which is obtained. With this message firmly in mind we now turn to intervention strategies themselves.

Intervention Strategies

Before describing various techniques used by applied sport psychologists, a few matters need to be resolved. To begin, any discussion of intervention strategies almost inevitably raises ethical concerns, and it is these concerns that have been very much to the fore during the ongoing debate over the professionalization of sport psychology (Nideffer, 1986). Chartered sport psychologists in the United Kingdom must adhere to a very thorough and detailed code of conduct, as specified by the British Association of Sports and Exercise Sciences (BASES). This code of conduct covers the use of psychological tests, consent and confidentiality, research ethics and personal conduct, and the guidelines do provide very positive help to protect the counsellor and the counselled alike. However, they do not go so far as to state explicitly which types of intervention should or should not be practised. For example, should a sport psychologist encourage gifted young athletes to compete when they have indicated no desire to continue with their sport? This is one example where professional sport psychologists must tread very warily, and where individual freedom and choice should, we believe, remain sacrosanct. Therefore, the intervention strategies presented here (see also Chapters 3 and 7) must be used to help people with their sport but not to manipulate athletes against their will. This would represent an unwarranted invasion of personal freedom. Intervention should only proceed with the explicit cooperation of the athlete, in a recognition that the skills acquired will not only enhance performance but will also help the athlete to enjoy his or her sport that much more.

The popular press has occasionally portrayed sport psychologists as manipulators or puppet masters pulling the strings of their hapless victims. This representation has little bearing on the reality of modern day professional sport psychology. In most cases intervention strategies evolve through a process of negotiation and discussion between the athlete, the sport psychologist, and increasingly, the coach. Whether or not these interventions actually achieve what they set out to achieve is another matter and certainly the empirical support for any one strategy over another remains inconclusive. Nevertheless, the range of techniques which have been employed over the years is staggering, and if nothing else, reveals just how wide ranging and free-thinking applied sport psychologists have been in their quest for sporting excellence (Vealey, 1988).

What do these intervention techniques have in common? The answer is relatively little. Some focus directly on mental skills, others on physical relaxation and yet others fail to make a clear distinction. In terms of differences, according to Morris and Bull (1991: 5) the most significant relate to the timing and scope of intervention. First, there are packages dealing with lifetime skills where the aim is to develop a range of psychological skills to be used as and when necessary (for example, time management, stress management, goal setting, interpersonal skills, lifestyle management, self-confidence, relaxation techniques and imagery). Second, there is long term preparation for a specific event where a tailor-made programme is put together to build an athlete towards a goal over several years, for example the Olympic games. Third, the authors identified medium term preparation for a specific event, a programme which may be very similar to the long term but developed over the course of months or one season. Finally there is short term or crisis intervention where counselling is offered immediately in response to one issue, perhaps a physical injury or an inexplicable loss of form, or when the build up to a major competition goes awry.

Table 4.1: Intervention Packages Used in Sport

Title	Author(s)	Brief Description
Stress Inoculation Training	Meichenbaum, 1977	Four phase approach using self-talk and relaxation to cope with imagined stress
Stress Management Training	Smith, 1980	Five phase approach using self-awareness and relaxation to cope with imposed stress
Anxiety Management Training	Suinn, 1983	Relaxation training under conditions of arousal (e.g. anxiety, anger)
Visual Motor Behaviour Rehearsal	Suinn, 1984	Combination of relaxation and mental imagery techniques to desensitize athletes to stress
Seven Steps to Peak Performance	Suinn, 1985	Seven step approach including relaxation training, stress management, positive thought control, self-regulation, mental rehearsal, concentration and energy control
Psychological Skills Education Program	Boutcher and Rotella, 1987	Four phase approach for improving closed skills involving self-awareness, motivation and various interventions

In reality there would be considerable overlap between the sorts of interventions which would be offered whatever the overall timescale of the programme (Ravey and Scully, 1989), and there are also numerous examples in the literature of intervention packages which have been put together combining many of the techniques outlined below. A selection from the most popular multifaceted programmes is shown in Table 4.1.

Within these packages a great many themes are introduced. These include 'cognitive' techniques dealing with attentional style, concentration, imagery and visualization. These techniques are dealt with more thoroughly in Chapter 3, with those associated primarily with anxiety and stress management forming the main focus of this section. As to the efficacy of these techniques, then in honesty there is little evaluative research but perhaps their enduring popularity testifies to their practical efficacy if nothing else. Without doubt, the right level of muscle tension is very useful for producing optimal performance but simply to use a relaxation programme by itself is useless and may even be dysfunctional; the objective is to combine the control of stress and anxiety with the control of negative thoughts in order that athletes can reach their optimal energy zone or ZOF.

As will become evident, the overlap between these intervention strategies is often considerable, and the underlying philosophies are often remarkably similar. There is nothing weird, wonderful or mysterious about these forms of intervention; a great many simply rely upon a combination of breathing exercises and physical relaxation. In order for you to know precisely what each technique involves, and hopefully to overcome some of the mystery which surrounds these procedures along the way, a brief outline of each is presented below.

Relaxation Techniques

Self-Directed Relaxation

Self-directed relaxation aims to release tension in each of the body's major muscle groups while emphasizing slow, easy breathing, and encouraging visualization of stress flowing away from the body (see Gill, 1986). Through training it is possible to reduce gradually the time needed to achieve complete relaxation of the entire body. While initially it may take 10 minutes to work through instructions, with some practice, greater and greater relaxation should be achieved in less and less time. Over time and with practice athletes require fewer self-instructions to relax each muscle group, and the muscle groups can be slowly combined, so that eventually only a few seconds are needed to achieve full body relaxation. An example of a self-directed relaxation script follows:

> Close your eyes and adjust your body so that you are stretched out making maximum contact with the ground. Raise and lower your head to stretch your neck, making sure your head is not tilted backwards. Flatten your back and push away with your heels to stretch out your legs. Take a deep breath and let it out slowly. Feel the weight of your body on the floor, take another deep breath and let the floor support the full weight of your body.
>
> Now take a good deep breath and then slowly breathe out. Think of the word 'calm' then pause. Breathe in deeply . . . then out slowly . . . (and repeat twice).
>
> Now concentrate on your head. Feel any tension in your forehead then consciously let the tension flow away from your forehead. Feel the tension flow away to the floor and think of the word 'calm'.
>
> Feel any tension in your jaw then let the tension in these muscles flow away. Breathe in deeply . . . then breathe out slowly.
>
> Feel the relaxation in your facial muscles. Relax . . . then pause. Breathe in deeply . . . breathe out slowly (pause). Enjoy that feeling of warmth as you relax and feel calm and rested.
>
> Now feel any tension in your arms, forearms and hands then just let that tension g. and feel it flowing away. Again, breathe in deeply . . . and out slowly.
>
> Feel any tension in your hands, fingers, or arms, and then relaease the tension in these muscles. Feel the warmth as the tension flows out your body. Breathe in deeply and out slowly.
>
> Feel the relaxation in your arms and hands. Think of the word calm . . . (pause). Breathe in deeply . . . breathe out slowly (pause). Allow

yourself to drift into deeper and deeper relaxation and enjoy the feeling of warmth and calm then breathe in deeply . . . breathe out slowly.

Now focus your attention on your neck and upper back. Feel any tension in the muscles of your neck and upper back and then release the tension in these muscles. Feel the tension flow out of your body. Breathe in deeply . . . breathe out slowly. Feel the warmth and relaxation in these muscles. Feel calm and peaceful . . . (pause). Breathe in deeply . . . breathe out slowly (pause). Let yourself relax even deeper . . . and deeper . . . and deeper.

Remember your facial muscles, your arms and hand muscles, your neck and upper back muscles. Keep that feeling of warmth and relaxation. Breathe in deeply . . . breathe out slowly. Feel the warmth in all these muscles. Feel the relaxation even deeper . . . and deeper.

Now feel any tension in your lower back and stomach muscles. Focus all your attention on these muscles and get them to relax. Let yourself relax these muscles fully. Feel the tension flow away. Breathe in deeply . . . breathe out slowly. Feel the relaxation in your lower back and stomach muscles. Relax . . . (pause). Again breathe in deeply . . . breathe out slowly (pause). Think of 'calm' and relax even deeper . . . and deeper . . . and deeper.

Now feel any tension in your upper legs, both the front and back. Focus all your attention on these muscles and let them relax. Feel the muscles relax, feel the tension flow away. Breathe in deeply . . . breathe out slowly. Feel the relaxation in your upper legs. Relax . . . (pause). Breathe in deeply . . . breathe out slowly (pause). Relax even deeper . . . and deeper . . . and deeper.

Now feel any tension in your lower legs and your feet. Focus all your attention on these muscles and ask them to relax. Relax these muscles fully. Feel the tension flow away. Breathe in deeply . . . breathe out slowly. Feel the relaxation in your lower legs and feet. Relax . . . (pause). Breathe in deeply . . . breathe out slowly (pause). Relax even deeper . . . and deeper . . . and deeper.

Now relax your entire body. Relax it completely. Feel all the tension flow away from your facial muscles . . . your arms and hands . . . your neck and upper back . . . your lower back and stomach . . . your upper legs . . . and your lower legs and feet. Breathe in deeply . . . breathe out slowly. Feel the relaxation in all your body. Relax . . . (pause). Breathe in and breathe in deeply . . . breathe out slowly (pause). Relax even deeper . . . and deeper . . . and deeper.

Self-directed relaxation is especially effective for those who find it easy to focus their attention on different muscle groups and who are able to turn on and off the tension when directed to do so. Many athletes, because they are quite aware of tension and relaxation in different parts of their bodies, are readily able to do this . However, if this is difficult or the athlete is constantly distracted, s/he may be a better candidate for the more active and demanding progressive relaxation training procedure described below. Others find it helpful to combine self-directed relaxation with imagery relaxation (discussed later). For example, using this technique an athlete could be asked to imagine a broom sweeping away the tension in the appropriate muscle group, or visualize tension as autumn leaves and each breath, like a strong autumn wind, causes the tension to fall off the muscles.

Progressive Relaxation Training/Progressive Muscle Relaxation

Progressive Relaxation Training (PRT), or alternatively Progressive Muscle Relaxation (PMR) is a much more elaborate and time-consuming procedure. PRT was originally pioneered by Edmund Jacobson (1930), an American physician working in the 1920s and 1930s, but has been considerably modified over the years while retaining the vital core which is learning to feel tension in the muscles and then learning to 'let go' of this tension. You may be able to appreciate the basics by trying it yourself with the following directions.

> With your dominant arm (the one you use most often), contract your forearm and hand up toward your dominant shoulder, developing as much tension in the biceps and forearm as you possibly can. Hold this tension for about five seconds, and concentrate fully on what that tension feels like. Now bring your forearm down, and quickly and completely relax the muscles. Keep your attention focused sharply on what the relaxation feels like. Now try to relax your arm even more, letting all of the tension go. Do you feel the tension leaving your muscles?

Were you able to achieve 'deep' relaxation when you let the tension go? Probably not, unless you have already practised PRT. You can learn to achieve even deeper relaxation not only by returning the muscle to the pretensed state but by 'asking' it to relax even more. Try it this way. Imagine that the tension in the muscle is like the speedometer in a car. Maximum tension is 100; complete relaxation is 0. Now tense the arm, slowly bringing it to 50, then 75, and finally 100. Focus on the tension as you hold it for five seconds. Now release the tension quickly, trying to drop to 0 as quickly as you can. Is the muscle now fully relaxed or is it still idling at 20 or so? Can you let the rest of the tension go? Can you shut off the engine completely? When you are able to achieve this state then you have learnt how to achieve deep relaxation.

PRT is based on this principle of neuromuscular relaxation. Normally the athlete is initially taught how to tense and deeply relax 16 different muscle groups. With practice, the athlete then learns to combine the muscle groups, first into seven groups, then four, and finally the entire body at one time. The ultimate objective is to achieve complete relaxation in a few seconds — practising three times a week it is maintained that this should be possible in four to six weeks.

PRT has been recognized as helpful for athletes who have trouble achieving the right level of tension in specific muscle groups. However, when they are unable to identify specific muscle groups that are too tense, PRT is unable to do the job. In that case, using biofeedback (discussed later) may be useful. A progressive muscle relaxation script is provided below adapted from the work of Bernstein and Borkovec (1973; in Iso-Ahola and Hatfield, 1986: 256).

Progressive Muscle Relaxation Procedure
1   The athlete must lie on a mat in a comfortable environment with subdued lighting.
2   In turn, s/he is asked to asked to tense the first of 16 muscle groups (e.g. hand, upper arm, neck) for between 5 and 7 seconds, focusing on the sensation of tension.

3 The tension is released and the athlete is asked to concentrate on the feeling of deep relaxation and warmth for 30–45 seconds.

4 The same routine is followed for each muscle set, and s/he may then be asked to repeat the entire sequence.

5 Practice continues for 15–20 minutes, twice daily, gradually learning to combine the muscle groups until only four are used.

6 After sufficient practice the athlete will be able to induce relaxation without the tension phase, and finally will be able to relax simply by recalling the sensation and experience, even during competition itself.

Autogenic Training

In a great many respects, autogenic training is similar to PRT, and has enjoyed widespread popularity in sport psychology over the years. While PRT concentrates on relaxation alone, autogenic training brings in other sensations associated with the state of relaxation (for example warmth and weight), and calls for some type of self-hypnosis on the part of the athlete. The training was developed in the early 1900s by the German psychiatrist, J. H. Schultz (Schultz and Luthe, 1969). Athletes are tutored in *'Selbstentspannaug'* or self-relaxation, based on self-suggestions and imagery. This is designed to create feelings of warmth, heaviness and control in different body parts and ultimately to reach a state of mental equilibrium. While the technique has enjoyed a mixed reception in the West, it has been widely used over the years by former Eastern bloc athletes. For example, one variation was developed and widely used by Professor M. Machak of Charles University in Prague. His technique places greater emphasis on activation by tensing muscles and taking short breaths in the actual build-up to competition (Cratty and Vanek, 1970: 123). An example of one variation of an autogenic training script adapted from Cox (1990: 152) follows.

Autogenic Training Script
1 Find a comfortable position and sit or lie down but do not cross your arms or legs.

2 Close your eyes and clear your mind of worries and thoughts.

3 Concentrate on your breathing, thinking 'breath in', 'breath out', 'breath in', 'breath out' as you breathe.

4 As you continue, you will begin to feel calm and relaxed.

5 Continuing your breathing routine, systematically I want you to tighten and relax all the muscle groups in your body.

6 Starting with your right leg, tense the muscles in the leg and foot (5 secs) then relax.

7 As you relax, concentrate on how heavy and warm your leg feels.

8 Continue at your own pace to tense and relax all major muscle groups, starting with your legs and working upwards — 'tense' and 'relax', 'tense' and 'relax'.

9 Now your muscles feel heavy and warm at the same time.

10 Notice and enjoy how your hands and feet feel warm and yet your forehead feels refreshingly cool.

11   Don't forget about your breathing — 'breath in', 'breath out', 'breath in', 'breath out'.

12   You feel very calm and relaxed, each time you breathe out you breathe away worry and tension.

13   Think to yourself, 'I feel good, I feel calm and relaxed.'

Imagery Relaxation

Imagery relaxation, like imagery itself, works well for some people but is difficult for others. Essentially it involves imagining yourself in some environment or place where you have experienced feelings of relaxation and comfort. This may be a particular place at home or in the garden, or somewhere special that you remember from holidays or childhood — a warm beach with the breeze blowing off the sea, with waves gently breaking, a grassy mountainside with skylarks singing and no one else in view, or just wherever you feel good. Having located this place the athlete is ready to begin imagery relaxation, which begins in the same way as almost all imagery exercises.

Imagery Relaxation Procedure

1   Select a setting that is quiet and comfortable.

2   Be alert but not focused or overly excited about some recent event. If you are either fatigued or wound up, this atmosphere is not conducive to learning relaxation skills.

3   Create the right attitude about learning this skill. Some people find these exercises so foreign to their thinking that they fail to take them seriously. Others develop unrealistic expectations, believing that a few minutes should produce some magical change in themselves. Dispel both myths by establishing a relaxed, but serious, environment for practising the skills.

4   Find a comfortable position, preferably lying on the floor, arms to the side, feet uncrossed, and eyes closed.

5   Now think of your favourite place for relaxing — the place where you feel comfortable and safe. Take a few moments to do this.

6   Breathe in deeply and breathe out slowly, letting go of any tension in your muscles, inhaling deeply, exhaling slowly.

7   Now visualize yourself in this place; picture yourself there as vividly as you can; not only picture, but 'feel' yourself there — hear the sounds, smell the air, feel the ground, or whatever.

8   Urge yourself to notice the relaxation, to bring on the feeling of deep relaxation.

The better able the individual is to put him/herself in this place through imagery, the more relaxed s/he is likely to be, and regular practice in imagining this place without guidance will allow the athlete to create the place in their mind's eye quickly, and the individual should be able to immediately feel the associated relaxation. Athletes are encouraged to practise using the technique in their daily life, especially when confronted with stressors. Initially these should be minor stressful events, gradually increasing in seriousness as the skill develops.

Many élite sports stars have naturally used imagery without any prior training. For example, Jackie Stewart, the former world champion racing driver, evoked a special image to relax just before racing. He would sit in the car moments before the start and imagine his body inflating like a balloon. Then he would let the air out and feel himself relax. This, he contended, helped him prepare physically and mentally for the race. The keys to maximizing the potential of imagery relaxation appear to be to have a place clearly in mind with which you strongly associate feelings of relaxation; to have reasonably good imagery skills in the first place so the scene can be seen vividly in the mind's eye; and to practise the technique initially in non-stressful situations, and then gradually use it in increasingly stressful situations.

Biofeedback Relaxation

If an athlete has difficulty monitoring and adjusting the tension in his or her own body, providing supplementary feedback can help to develop such self-awareness. Biofeedback is used to accomplish this. Essentially biofeedback means direct feedback on the person's own biological responses. Many types of biofeedback are useful for learning to manage stress and tension, including pulse rate, skin temperature and electrical activity, either of the skin surface, the muscles or the brain (see Chapter 9). Pulse rate is one of the most straightforward forms of biofeedback to work with, and to begin to help develop self-awareness and control. Auditory or visual feedback on pulse can be presented without a great deal of equipment, and by working with different thoughts and images, individuals can quickly learn to exercise some control over their heart rate.

Skin temperature can be useful for indicating a general level of tension in the body. It increases when more blood flows to the skin which occurs when the muscles are relaxed, and decreases as the muscles tense up because less blood flows to the skin (thus explaining why people's hands become cold when they are stressed).

Many different methods can be used to measure the electrical activity of the skin but the most common is called galvanic skin response, or GSR. When the body is more tense the sweat glands are more active in order to dissipate the heat generated by the tensed muscles. When there is moisture on the skin, electricity flows from one point to another more readily and GSR is simply a method of measuring the ease with which a minute electrical current flows between two points on the skin. With a little practice, athletes can learn to increase or decrease the sweating on their skin by learning to relax or tense the muscles.

A further type of biofeedback measures the minute electrical activity in the muscles, and can be measured by an electromyograph. Electromyography (EMG) is especially useful for learning to relax specific muscle groups; pulse rate, skin temperature and GSR help deal with global muscular tension in the body. A more direct measure of brain activity is provided by an electroencephalogram (EEG), which records four types of brainwave including alpha waves which predominate during high excitation and beta waves which characterize relaxation. To date the use of this form of feedback in sport training has been limited but the potential would appear to be considerable.

Whichever type of biofeedback is employed, in essence each endeavours to achieve the same goal: to demonstrate to athletes that they have a degree of control over physiological response, and beyond this, they can then use this control to move towards that state which they prefer, their ZOF.

Other Relaxation Techniques

Several other popular, and sometimes costly, techniques are used to achieve a reduction in stress or to induce relaxation. Meditation techniques including Zen meditation, hatha yoga, and transcendental meditation are all intended initially to 'quiet the mind'. A common ingredient in all these forms of meditation is an emphasis on quiet concentration, relaxation and breathing control, and indeed all these procedures have been found to be effective in diffusing global muscle tension, although their impact on fine motor skills is less noticeable (Layman, 1980).

Hypnosis is another widely used relaxation technique, a technique which has been shrouded, unnecessarily, in a cloak of mysticism. Despite the longstanding debate within psychology as to the significance and meaning of hypnotism, at the very least hypnosis appears to move an individual through a state of relaxation to a state where he or she is more open to suggestion. Without question those who have been hypnotized are more suggestible but rarely will they comply with requests other than those towards which they were already inclined. Hypnosis is a cooperative venture between the hypnotist and the person being hypnotized and contrary to popular belief, a person cannot be hypnotized against his or her will. When people cooperate fully with the verbal suggestions of a hypnotist, they may discover things about themselves and experience things of which they were previously unaware. This occurs because the hypnotist helps them focus intensely on something that they may not have been willing to focus on previously.

Hypnosis, as a relaxation technique and as a means of developing self-belief, has been found to be very effective, but its use generally is questionable simply because responsibility and control moves from the athlete to another person. One of the main objectives of relaxation techniques is for the athlete to develop control and awareness, and eventually even to make a sport psychologist completely redundant!

Centring

Centring or refocusing are terms used within applied sport psychology to refer to many different techniques for quickly regaining concentration during competition (see Nideffer, 1992). They are simple and immediate relaxation techniques which, with practice, may enable the individual to counteract quickly and simply some of the changes associated with loss of control. The goal is simple: to reach the point whereby in the space of a single breath, you can bring your level of arousal to any point you choose. All that is required is a few seconds to 'calm yourself down' to a point where you regain the capacity to assess the situation accurately and then direct your concentration in appropriate ways. An example of a centring routine follows.

A Centring Routine

1 Stand with feet slightly apart and knees slightly bent. Weight evenly balanced between your two feet. The bend in the knees is important and should result in you being able to feel the tension in the muscles in the calves and thighs. The flexing counteracts a natural tendency to brace and lock knees when you become over aroused.

2 Now consciously relax your neck and shoulder muscles. Check this by making slight movements with your head, shoulders and arms (see that they are loose and relaxed).

3 Your mouth should hang open slightly to reduce tension in jaw muscles.

4 Breathe in from your diaphragm and down to your abdomen. Breathe in slowly and, as you do, attend to two cues. First, notice that you extend your stomach as you breathe. Next, consciously maintain relaxation in chest and shoulders. This helps you avoid allowing your chest to expand and shoulders to rise. It also counters a tendency to brace your neck and shoulder muscles.

5 As you breathe out slowly, attend to the feelings in your abdomen and notice your stomach muscles relaxing. Consciously let your knees bend slightly, attending to increased feelings of heaviness as your body presses down towards the ground. The exhalation counteracts the natural lifting associated with breathing in and the body does begin to feel more steady.

6 As you have attended to the relaxing physical cues you have simultaneously stopped attending to the things that were causing you to lose control. Now you should have recovered enough composure to deal in a constructive way with the situation.

Psyching Up!

The techniques described so far have all dealt with relaxation. In the light of the earlier discussion of stress and arousal it should be readily apparent that for many individuals these techniques will be just as dangerous as those commonly employed for 'psyching up' players. Each has the potential to either move the performer to or from their ZOF, and so each must be used with caution. It is interesting to note that almost all sport psychology texts deal with relaxation, concentration and attentional control yet surprisingly few offer advice on psyching up. Almost certainly this imbalance reflects on the amount of time which sport psychologists have had to spend persuading over-enthusiastic coaches to pull back. The tales of coaches' pre-game antics in sports such as American football, rugby, weightlifting and basketball are legion. Undoubtedly, the coach's own anxiety about presenting a team which is lacklustre plays a significant part here, as does the need to stimulate analgesia (i.e. increased tolerance for pain) amongst individuals engaged in what may be painful and demanding physical contact. However, the untold harm which may have been inflicted by untutored if well-meaning coaches is alarming. The use of pre-match talks, notices or posters displaying simple but eye-catching messages, noise and a wide range of pre-competition rituals (from the New Zealand All Blacks' haka to game simulations) can all be used to heighten arousal, and for specific events involving gross motor skills, such psyche-up strategies have been found to be effective (Weinberg and Jackson, 1985). However, the skill of pepping-up an undermotivated team or individual remains an idiosyncratic art rather than a precise science. That elusive characteristic, charisma, coupled with genuine commitment to the cause each play a vital role.

Exercise and Mental Health

Although this book is about sport, it would be difficult to leave out the literature dealing with exercise and mental health from a chapter focusing on clinical psychology, and particularly as so many sports are based upon feats of physical endurance and fitness. Over recent years a growing literature has charted the relationship between exercise and mental health (Hatfield, 1991; Willis and Campbell, 1992; Berger and McInman, 1993). The traditional and popular message to emerge from this literature is that, when kept within healthy limits, a strong and positive relationship often exists between physical and mental well-being, confirming the 'feel good' effect noted by regular exercisers (Carmack and Martens, 1979). This belief is further substantiated by numerous studies which have considered the effects of enforced exercise regimes on mental health (Plante and Rodin, 1990). The most positive effects have been found with regard to alleviating depression (North *et al.*, 1990) and relieving tension and stress (Norris *et al.*, 1990).

When taken as a whole, this literature demonstrates the positive psychological benefits which can accrue from taking up exercise, for women as well as men (Berger, 1984). Other research demonstrates that amongst the population as a whole, physical activity correlates positively with good mental health (Stephens, 1988), independent of measures of physical health. While research evidence continues to accumulate, it would still be true that many theoretical issues remain unresolved (Dunn and Dishman, 1991), and including the most basic, why should the relationship be as it is, and beyond this, what mechanisms are at work and what is the direction of causality? For example, are those with poor mental health less inclined to exercise, or has the lack of exercise exacerbated their condition? Until such issues are tackled head-on then it is unlikely that genuine progress can be made in our understanding of the relationship between physical activity and mental health (see also Chapter 9).

At the same time, while exercise may promote the 'feel good' factor, there is a down side which cannot be ignored. For example, withdrawal from exercise has been shown to have deleterious psychological effects, and athletes who have been used to maintaining high levels of exercise will often suffer when denied the opportunity, for whatever reason (Morris *et al.*, 1990).

Many explanations have been offered to interpret this finding (see Chapter 9). One is the 'opiate connection' where it is argued that the release of endorphins may be responsible for runner's high as well as exercise addiction in general. Later writers agree that the evidence for a straightforward opiate addiction is equivocal; instead it is argued that the relationship should be viewed in a broader psychosocial context (Dunn and

Dishman, 1991), where exercise, lifestyle, stress and self-concept all appear to be intricately related. Consequently it is now generally accepted that unitary biological or social explanations are inadequate; instead a complex interaction is at work but the mechanisms which determine this interaction are still ill-defined. Biddle and Mutrie (1991: 197) summarize the current position very well:

> Exercise has been associated with changes in both the central nervous system and the sympathetic nervous system, with improved self-esteem and feelings of mastery, and with increased work capacity. In addition it has been suggested that exercise may be beneficial because it distracts people from other aspects of life, or that becoming addicted to exercise may provide psychological strength . . . It is suggested that the mechanisms are likely to operate in a synergistic way; it is also possible that different mechanisms will explain different aspects of psychological effects noted. For example, there may be mainly a biochemical explanation for exercise alleviating depression, but a physiological reason why exercise is associated with feeling less tense.

Clearly the possibilities for further research are immense, and at the same time, the effects of numerous factors in determining this relationship cannot be ignored. One example is gender where the costs of exercise, both psychologically and physiologically, would appear to be potentially that much higher for women. For example, highly trained women athletes show a greater incidence of menstrual irregularities. Wolman and Harries (1989) noted that amongst a sample of élite women athletes, over half suffered from either amenorrhoea (i.e. fewer than one period in the previous six months) or oligomenorrhoea (a menstrual cycle lasting longer than 35 days), and this was particularly prevalent amongst gymnasts, runners and cyclists. These problems have been attributed to intensity of training and diet, although sports performance itself has been shown to be relatively unaffected by the menstrual cycle *per se* (Brooks-Gunn and Matthews, 1979).

Turning to the psychological problems encountered by women in sport, here research dealing with attitudes to physical education, participation motivation in sport and sex role identity are all relevant (Colley, 1986), and most obviously and immediately, sex role conflict. This conflict is very much a woman's problem in relation to sport and exercise (Cann, 1991). From an early age boys are encouraged to be sportsmanlike (Bryson, 1987) but for girls, and particularly adolescents, the contradiction between success in sport and the maintenance of the traditional female sex role can become more and more problematic (van Wersch *et al.*, 1992) To use a sporting analogy, men run towards their traditional stereotype but women run away from theirs. The sport psychology and sociology literature dealing with such matters is plentiful, and this demonstrates, for example, that sportswomen do have to wrestle, more or less successfully, with sex role conflict (Anthrop and Allison, 1983), that women do generally exhibit less self-confidence as regards to physical activity (Lirgg, 1991), and also that the sex role orientation of women athletes may be different from women as a whole. For example, fewer women in sport are sex typed in the feminine direction, and more are classifiable as androgynous (Gentry and Doering, 1979).

A more recent literature, tying in with work on body image and eating disorders has looked at the relationship between physical exercise and eating disorders, for both men and women but especially women (Thompson, 1993). While the results are far from conclusive (Pruitt *et al.*, 1991), the dangers of women using exercise to chase after the elusive superwoman ideal have been revealed (Davis, 1992), and such findings should not be ignored in the clamour to extol the positive benefits of exercise.

The Way Forward

Make no mistake, the role for clinical intervention in sport is enormous, whether dealing with stress management, confidence building, or more serious psychological disorders. Both in the UK and the US separate sport psychology divisions have been set up specifically for clinicians, and their contribution is genuinely welcomed. Given the practical orientation of the subject, and the healthy scepticism of the sporting community, it is not surprising that clinical psychologists with particular types of clinical orientation are seen as especially useful. For example, a cognitive–behavioural approach, stressing the relationship between thought and action, is likely to be more acceptable in the field than is a psychoanalytic or Freudian perspective. Nevertheless, irrespective of their approach, the contribution made by clinical psychologists has been considerable, and it is likely to remain so for the foreseeable future. As the pressures to succeed in sport increase so the pressure on sport psychologists to help athletes cope with pressure will inevitably grow. Clinical psychologists are uniquely placed for dealing with these problems but this does not exclude others with a more basic psychological training from also entering the field.

To conclude this section, a final word on the work of applied sport psychologists may be in order. The story of the relationship between pure and applied research in this particular field is a fascinating and in a perverse way, also a highly amusing one. 'Academic' sport psychologists have maintained a polite distance from practitioners over the years, and have often been quick to pour scorn on the unscientific way in which applied sport psychologists go about achieving results. Whether it be through the use of transcendental meditation, hypnosis, deep breathing exercises, imagery, or whatever, the guiding principle has been, if it works, use it, and a great many satisfied customers would testify that these interventions have had some positive effect. From the other side of the fence, the theoretical and methodological dilemmas which academic sport psychologists have wrestled with over the years have been phenomenal. No stone has been left unturned in an attempt to define and comprehend the role played by stress, anxiety and arousal in sport. For those who have fought these terminological battles it must be quite galling to see the direction in which research is inexorably heading. That is, the development of increasingly multifaceted models of stress, anxiety and arousal which first find it more and more difficult to disentangle the three terms, and second, make it almost impossible to establish any nomothetic laws or generalities as to their effect on performance. All that can be said with any certainty is that each individual responds in an idiosyncratic way to the pressures of sport, and hence all interventions must be individually tailored to individual needs.

Paradoxically, this conclusion therefore endorses the work of most applied sport psychologists who have set such great store by the one-to-one relationship between the client and the practitioner, and who have employed this philosophy so effectively over the years. In the light of this natural merger, how the relationship between theory and practice is handled over the next few years should make for fascinating viewing. Clearly it is no longer appropriate simply to dismiss applied work as unscientific. The healthier alternative is to carry out much more systematic appraisals and evaluations of those practical interventions which have a proven track record in the field, and from this evaluation (based on scientific methods and involving proper manipulations and controls) to identify just why it is that some are successful while others are not. This may be one route through which to establish a genuinely symbiotic relationship between pure and applied sport psychology, one where both will benefit in the long run.

References

ANTHROP, J. and ALLISON, M. T. (1983) 'Role conflict and the high school female athlete', *Research Quarterly for Exercise and Sport*, 54, pp. 104–11.

BERGER, B. G. (1984) 'Running away from anxiety and depression: A female as well as a male race', in SACHS, M. L. and BUFFONE, G. W. (Eds), *Running as Therapy: An Integrated Approach*, Lincoln, NB: University of Nebraska Press, pp. 23–62.

BERGER, B. G. and MCINMAN, A. (1993) 'Exercise and the quality of life', in SINGER, R. N. *et al.* (Eds) *Handbook of Research on Sport Psychology*, New York: Macmillan, pp. 729–60.

BERNSTEIN, D. A. and BORKOVEC, T. D. (1973) *Progressive Relaxation: A Training Manual for the Helping Professional*, Champaign, IL: Research Press.

BIDDLE, S. and MUTRIE, N. (1991) *Psychology of Physical Activity and Exercise*, London: Springer-Verlag.

BOUTCHER, S. H. and ROTELLA, R. J. (1987) 'A psychological skills educational program for closed skill performance enhancement', *The Sport Psychologist*, 1, pp. 127–37.

BROOKS-GUNN, J. and MATTHEWS, W. S. (1979) *He and She: How Children Develop Their Sex-Role Identity*, Englewood Cliffs, NJ: Spectrum.

BRYSON, L. (1987) 'Sport and the maintenance of masculine hegemony', *Women's Studies International Forum*, 10, 4, pp. 349–60.

BURTON, D. (1988) 'Do anxious swimmers swim slower?: Re-examining the elusive anxiety-performance relationship', *Journal of Sport and Exercise Psychology*, 10, pp. 45–61.

CANN, A. (1991) 'Gender expectations and sports participation', in DIAMANT, L. (Ed.) *Psychology of Sports, Exercise and Fitness: Social and Personal Issues*, New York: Hemisphere, pp. 187–214.

CARMACK, M. A. and MARTENS, R. (1979) 'Measuring commitment to running: A survey of runners' attitudes and mental states', *Journal of Sport Psychology*, 1, pp. 25–42.

COLLEY, A. M. (1986) 'Sex roles in leisure and sport', in HARGREAVES, D. J. and COLLEY, A. M. (Eds) *The Psychology of Sex Roles*, London: Harper and Row, pp. 233–49.

COX, R. H. (1990) *Sport Psychology: Concepts and Applications*, 2nd edn, Dubuque, IA: Wm C. Brown.

CRATTY, B. J. and VANEK, M. (1970) *Psychology and the Superior Athlete*, London: Macmillan.

DAVIS, C. (1992) 'Body image, dieting behaviours, and personality factors: A study of high performance female athletes', *International Journal of Sport Psychology*, 23, pp. 179–92.

DIAMANT, L., BYRD, J. H. and HIMELEIN, M. J. (1991) 'Personality traits and athletic performance', in DIAMANT, L. (Ed.) *Mind-Body Maturity: Psychological Approaches to Sports, Exercise and Fitness*, New York: Hemisphere, pp. 227–36.

DUNN, A. L. and DISHMAN, R. K. (1991) 'Exercise and the neurobiology of depression', *Exercise and Sport Sciences Reviews*, 19, pp. 41–98.

FAZEY, J. and HARDY, L. (1988) *The Inverted-U Hypothesis: A Catastrophe for Sport Psychology?*, Monograph no. 1, Leeds: British Association for Sports Sciences.

GARFIELD, C. A. and BENNETT, H. Z. (1984) *Peak Performance: Mental Training Techniques of the World's Greatest Athletes*, Los Angeles, CA: T. P. Tarcher.

GENTRY, J. W. and DOERING, M. (1979). 'Sex role orientation and leisure', *Journal of Leisure Research*, 11, pp. 102–11.

GILL, D. L. (1986) *Psychological Dimensions of Sport*, Champaign, IL: Human Kinetics.

GOULD, D. and KRANE, V. (1992) 'The arousal-performance relationship: Current status and future directions', in HORN, T. S. (Ed.) *Advances in Sport Psychology*, Champaign, IL: Human Kinetics, pp. 119–41.

GROSSMAN, A. (1984) 'Endorphins and exercise', *Clinical Cardiology*, 7, pp. 255–60.

HANIN, Y. L. (1980) 'A study of anxiety in sports', in STRAUB, W. F. (Ed.) *Sport Psychology: An Analysis of Athlete Behavior*, Ithaca, NY, Mouvement Press, pp. 236–49.

HARDY, L. (1990) 'A catastrophe model of performance in sport', in JONES, J. G. and HARDY, L. (Eds) *Stress and Performance in Sport*, Chichester: John Wiley and Sons, pp. 81–106.

HATFIELD, B. D. (1991) 'Exercise and mental health: The mechanisms of exercise-induced psychological states', in DIAMANT, L. (Ed.), *Psychology of Sports, Exercise and Fitness*, New York: Hemisphere, pp. 17–49.

HULL, C. L. (1943) *Principles of Behavior*, New York: Appleton-Century-Crofts.

ISO-AHOLA, S. E. and HATFIELD, B. (1986) *Psychology of Sports: A Social Psychological Approach*, Dubuque, IA: Wm C. Brown.

JACOBSON, E. (1930) *Progressive Relaxation*, Chicago: University of Chicago Press.

JONES, J. G. (1990) 'A cognitive perspective on the processes underlying the relationship between stress and performance in sport', in JONES, J. G. and HARDY, L. (Eds) *Stress and Performance in Sport*, Chichester: John Wiley and Sons, pp. 17–42.

JONES, J. G. and HARDY, L. (Eds) (1990) *Stress and Performance in Sport*, Chichester: John Wiley and Sons.

KERR, J. H. (1985) 'The experience of arousal: A new basis for studying arousal effects in sport', *Journal of Sports Sciences*, 3, pp. 169–79.

LANDERS, D. M. (1980) 'The arousal-performance relationship revisited', *Research Quarterly for Exercise and Sport*, 51, pp. 77–90.

LAROSE, B. (1988) 'What can the sport psychology consultant learn from the educational consultant?', *The Sport Psychologist*, 2, pp. 141–53.

LAYMAN, E. M. (1980) 'Meditation and sport performance', in STRAUB, W. F. (Ed.) *Sport Psychology: An Analysis of Athlete Behavior*, Ithaca, NY: Mouvement Publications.

LEON, G. (1984) 'Anorexia nervosa and sports activities', *Behavior Therapist*, 7, 1, pp. 9–10.

LIRGG, C. D. (1991) 'Gender differences in self-confidence in physical activity: A meta-analysis of recent studies', *Journal of Sport and Exercise Psychology*, 8, pp. 294–310.

MCGRATH, J. E. (Ed.) (1970) *Social and Psychological Factors in Stress*, New York: Holt, Rinehart and Winston.

MARTENS, R. (1974) 'Arousal and motor performance', in WILMORE, J. H. (Ed.) *Exercise and Sport Sciences Review*, Volume 2, New York: Academic Press, pp. 155–88.

MARTENS, R. (1977) *Sport Competition Anxiety Test*, Champaign, IL: Human Kinetics.

MARTENS, R., VEALEY, R. S. and BURTON, D. (1990) *Competitive Anxiety in Sport*, Champaign, IL: Human Kinetics.

MEICHENBAUM, D. (1977) *Stress Inoculation Training*, New York: Pergamon Press.

MORRIS, T. and BULL, S. J. (1991) *Mental Training in Sport: An Overview*, Monograph no. 3, Leeds: British Association for Sports Sciences.

MORRIS, M., STEINBERG, H., SYKES, E. A. and SALMON, P. (1990) 'Effects of temporary withdrawal from regular running', *Journal of Psychosomatic Research*, 34, 5, 493–500.

NIDEFFER, R. M. (1978) *Attention Control Training*, New York: Wyden Books.

NIDEFFER, R. M. (1986) 'Current concerns in sport psychology', in SILVA, J. M. and WEINBERG, R. S. (Eds) *Psychological Foundations of Sport*, Champaign, IL: Human Kinetics.

NIDEFFER, R. M. (1992) *Psyched to Win*, Champaign, IL: Leisure Press.

NORRIS, R., CARROLL, D. and COCHRANE, R. (1990) 'The effects of aerobic and anaerobic training on fitness, blood pressure and psychological stress and well-being', *Journal of Psychosomatic Research*, 34, 367–75.

NORTH, T. C., McCULLAGH, P., and VU TRAN, Z. (1990) 'Effect of exercise on depression', *Exercise and Sport Sciences Reviews*, 18, pp. 379–416.

OXENDINE, J. B. (1970) 'Emotional arousal and motor performance', *Quest*, 13, pp. 23–30.

PLANTE, T. G. and RODIN, J. (1990) 'Physical fitness and enhanced psychological health', *Current Psychology: Research and Reviews*, 9, 1, pp. 1–22.

PRUITT, J. A., KAPPIUS, R. V. and IMM, P. S. (1991) 'Sports, exercise and eating disorders', in DIAMANT, L. (Ed.) *Psychology of Sports, Exercise and Fitness*, New York: Hemisphere.

RAVEY, J. and SCULLY, D. (1989) 'Cognitive psychology of sport', in KREMER, J. and CRAWFORD, W. (Eds) *The Psychology of Sport: Theory and Practice*. Leicester: British Psychological Society.

RAVIZZA, K. (1989) 'Applying sport psychology', in KREMER, J. and CRAWFORD, W. (Eds) *The Psychology of Sport: Theory and Practice*, Leicester: British Psychological Society.

SANDERS, A. F. (1983) 'Towards a model of stress and human performance', *Acta Psychologica*, 53, pp. 64–97.

SCHULTZ, J. H. and LUTHE, W. (1969) *Autogenic Therapy, Volume 1: Autogenic Methods*, New York: Grune and Stratton.

SELYE, H. (1975) *Stress Without Distress*, New York: New American Library.

SELYE, H. (1976) *The Stress of Life*, New York: McGraw-Hill.

SMITH, R. E. (1980) 'A cognitive-affective approach to stress management training for athletes', in NADEAU, C. H. *et al.* (Eds) *Psychology of Motor Behavior and Sport: 1979*, Champaign, IL: Human Kinetics.

SMITH, K. C. P. and APTER, M. J. (1975) *A Theory of Psychological Reversals*, Chippenham: Picton Press.

SPIELBERGER, C. D. (1971) 'Trait-state anxiety and motor behavior', *Journal of Motor Behavior*, 3, pp. 265–79.

STEPHENS, T. (1988). 'Physical activity and mental health in the United States and Canada: Evidence from four population surveys', *Preventive Medicine*, 17, pp. 35–47.

SUINN, R. (1983) *Manual: Anxiety Measurement Training*, Fort Collins, CO: Rocky Mountain Behavioral Sciences Institute.

SUINN, R. (1984) 'Visual motor behavior rehearsal: The basic technique', *Scandinavian Journal of Behaviour Therapy*, 13, pp. 131–42.

SUINN, R. (1985) *The Seven Steps to Peak Performance: Manual for Mental Training for Athletes*, Fort Collins, CO: Colorado State University, Dept. of Psychology.

THOM, R. (1975) *Structural Stability and Morphogenesis*, New York: Benjamin-Addison-Wesley.

THOMPSON, R. A. (1993) *Helping Athletes with Eating Disorders*, Champaign, IL: Human Kinetics.

TRIPLETT, N. (1898) 'The dynamogenic factors in pacemaking and competition', *American Journal of Psychology*, 9, pp. 505–23.

VAN WERSCH, A., TREW, K. and TURNER, I. (1992) 'Post-primary school pupils' interest in physical education: Age and gender differences', *British Journal of Educational Psychology*, 62, pp. 56–72.

VEALEY, R. S. (1988) 'Future directions in psychological skills training', *The Sport Psychologist*, 2, pp. 318–36.

WEINBERG, R. and JACKSON, A. (1985) 'The effects of specific vs. non-specific mental preparation strategies on strength and endurance performance', *International Journal of Sport Psychology*, 8, pp. 175–80.

WILLIS, J. D. and CAMPBELL, L. F. (1992) *Exercise Psychology*, Champaign, IL: Human Kinetics.

WINE, J. D. (1971) 'Test anxiety and direction of attention', *Psychological Bulletin*, 76, pp. 92–104.

WOLMAN, R. L. and HARRIES, M. G. (1989) 'Menstrual abnormalities in élite athletes', *Clinical Sports Medicine*, 1, pp. 95–100.

Further Reading

BERGER, B. G. and McINMAN, A. (1993) 'Exercise and the quality of life', in SINGER, R. N. *et al* (Eds) *Handbook of Research on Sport Psychology*, New York: Macmillan, pp. 729–60.

BIDDLE S. and MUTRIE, N. (1991) *Psychology of Physical Activity and Exercise*, London: Springer-Verlag.

DIAMANT, L., BYRD, J. H. and HIMELEIN, M. J. (1991) 'Personality traits and athletic performance', in DIAMANT, L. (Ed.) *Mind-Body Maturity: Psychological Approaches to Sports, Exercise and Fitness*, New York: Hemisphere, pp. 227–36.

FAZEY, J. and HARDY, L. (1988) *The Inverted-U Hypothesis: A Catastrophe for Sport Psychology?*, Monograph no. 1, Leeds: British Association for Sports Sciences.

GOULD, D. and KRANE, V. (1992) 'The arousal-performance relationship: Current status and future directions', in HORN, T. S. (Ed.) *Advances in Sport Psychology*, Champaign, IL: Human Kinetics, pp. 119–41.

HACKFORT, D. and SPIELBERGER, C. D. (Eds) (1989) *Anxiety in Sports: An International Perspective*, New York: Hemisphere.

JONES, J. G. and HARDY, L. (Eds) (1990) *Stress and Performance in Sport*, Chichester: John Wiley and Sons.

MARTENS, R., VEALEY, R. S. and BURTON, D. (1990) *Competitive Anxiety in Sport*, Champaign, IL: Human Kinetics.

MORGAN, W. P. and GOLDSTON, S. E. (1987) *Exercise and Mental Health*, Washington, DC: Hemisphere.

MORRIS, T. and BULL, S. J. (1991) *Mental Training in Sport: An Overview*, Monograph no. 3, Leeds: British Association for Sports Sciences.

WILLIS, J. D. and CAMPBELL, L. F. (1992) *Exercise Psychology*, Champaign, IL: Human Kinetics.

Chapter 5

Moving in Sport

(Motor Behaviour)

Introduction

Perhaps taking Robert Frost's tongue-in-cheek maxim that 'Good fences make good neighbours' too literally, it seems that psychologists often feel compelled to draw convenient boundaries around various aspects of human behaviour in their pursuit of understanding. The study of motor behaviour is no exception and is usually identified as behaviour concerned exclusively with movement. Human movement can take many forms and is fundamental to every moment of our daily lives. These movements are of general interest to psychology but of particular concern to sport psychologists are those often complex, critical and intricate movements which we perform when we participate in sport. Historically, the area of study constituting motor behaviour has divided into at least three, and possibly four, recognizable subareas of study. Motor learning is concerned with the factors that influence learning and the learning process. Motor control focuses on how movements are coordinated and controlled, and motor development deals with changes in movement competencies throughout life.

To add confusion to anyone confronting this literature for the first time, in Europe the term sport psychology has often been used as a description of research carried out in these three areas, sometimes but not always including other applied research in social and cognitive areas of psychology. This is not the case in the USA, where sport psychology has evolved to a position where it is recognized as a distinct area of study, set apart from motor skills.

When reading this chapter it is important to recognize the framework for discussion which is being used and the assumptions underpinning this framework. In the first place, we will be assuming a distinction between movements which are taken to be learned and movements which are regarded as being in some way genetically defined. Although this distinction could be a topic for lengthy debate, for the sake of convenience it will be the former, learned behaviour, which forms the focus of this chapter while the latter, comprising fundamental movement patterns, is covered in Chapter 8 as part of developmental psychology. In addition, to conform to the framework of the book as a whole, coverage of the development of motor skills through the stages of life is also given greater prominence in Chapter 8, while the acquisition and understanding of these skills (motor learning and motor control), without reference to specific developmental milestones, is focused on here. In any discussion of motor learning and motor control it must be appreciated that there is considerable overlap between the two. Learning, control and performance of skilled motor behaviour form a Gestalt and indeed most recent research on motor skills reflects a fusion of these traditionally separate areas. However, one area of work which we omit in this analysis is the contribution to motor behaviour from the field of neurophysiology. While we acknowledge the significance of neuro-physiological knowledge in developing many psychological theories we are also cognizant of the many difficulties to be encountered in attempting to integrate psychological and neurophysiological research (see Bunge, 1990). Given the scope of this book and the limitations of reviewing major areas of influence, it was felt that the most appropriate focus of this chapter should be the traditional behavioural work made popular by motor behaviour researchers originating from the fields of psychology and physical education.

For so many chapters in this book, general psychology students will be encountering research that is new. This may not always be true of material in this chapter given the historically close links between motor skills and psychology. However, in order to provide a comprehensive account of the psychology of sport and exercise it would be impossible to leave aside this vital work. With the current interest in multidisciplinary and interdisciplinary research, in many respects this field provides a shining example of a subject which has developed and matured over the years through an integration and assimilation of contributions from many fields. Psychologists, sport scientists, physiologists, animal behaviourists, anatomists and neurophysiologists have each made, and continue to make, important and complementary contributions to our knowledge base. Holding (1989) sees the future of the subject as moving in two directions, the first dealing with motor skills *per se*, the other with cognitive models of action control. It is to be hoped that his prediction is not too accurate and that the history of integration is not superseded by separation. Whatever direction the subject follows throughout the 1990s it should be in a continuing spirit of academic cooperation, cross fertilization and, above all, openness and academic freedom.

A Historical Perspective

Most reviews and textbooks on motor skills locate the origins of the field in the mid to late nineteenth century. Welford (1968) cites the work of the astronomer, Bessel, whom he credits with having conducted the earliest investigation on individual differences in motor skill as long ago as 1820. Bessel was interested in discovering why some astronomers were more accurate than others in estimating the movement times of stars. However, the work of Bryan and Harter (1899) on learning Morse code, and Woodworth's (1899) analysis of arm and hand movements are much more frequently recognized as launching pads for the field of motor learning. These researchers, working as experimental psychologists, were interested in understanding the fundamental principles of learning and the general characteristics of learning curves. To answer their questions, they turned to an analysis of complex movements, such as typing and telegraphy.

According to Schmidt (1988), work on the neural control of movement commenced at the same time but there was little contact between researchers from experimental psychology and those with roots in neurophysiology. One such neurophysiologist was Jackson whose research in the 1870s is cited as providing an early insight into the contribution of the cerebral cortex to the control of human movements. At the same time, the discovery by Fritsch and Hitzig (1870) that the brain was electrically excitable led to many researchers adopting electrophysiological recording techniques to study neural control of movements. A key figure in this early motor control research was Sir Charles Sherrington. He was principally concerned with the contribution of reflexes and the role of sensory receptors in the control of movement, and his work is still held in high regard to this day (see Schmidt, 1988).

According to Schmidt, research tended to progress steadily if not spectacularly during the early decades of this century, with notable contributions from, predictably, the ubiquitous Coleman Griffith. However, it was during the war years, between 1939 and 1945, that the sheer volume of motor learning research increased dramatically, with efforts directed at first, using motor learning tasks within personnel selection and second, considering individual differences and abilities, including most significantly the work of E.A. Fleishman. Unfortunately, these selection programmes were not always successful. Attention therefore switched to motor training (for example, to improve high-speed and high-precision performance of pilots), including methods of teaching and practising motor skills, the transfer of training from one skill to another, knowledge of results and the retention of motor skills. This work was greatly influenced by, and interacted with, other ongoing work in psychology, resulting in the rapid transfer of general theories of learning to motor skills research. One influential approach to emerge at this time proposed that the brain could be considered as analogous to a computer where information is received, processed and finally manifested in various movement forms. The information processing approach soon became an integral part of cognitive psychology as a whole (see Chapter 3) and it also continued to influence research on motor behaviour greatly.

Towards the end of this post-war era, in the 1960s, research on motor behaviour declined within experimental psychology. However, a new direction emerged when psychologists such as F. M. Henry, A. W. Hubbard and A. T. Slater-Hammel provided the necessary leadership for continuing motor behaviour research within physical education and kinesiology as opposed to mainstream psychology. If there was a time when psychology and motor skills drifted apart then this was it. During this period research on motor control continued in apparent isolation from the work being conducted within psychology on motor learning. Nevertheless, developments were also taking place which had later significance in drawing the two areas together. For example, Merton's (1953) work on muscle-spindle mechanisms which integrated neurophysiological investigation with the measurement of the actual movements.

More recently, motor behaviour research has concentrated on theory development and at this time psychology and motor skills have worked closely in tandem. Traditionally, the influence of experimental psychology had resulted in motor skills research being conducted within a stimulus–response (S–R) or behaviourist framework. However, with the introduction of the cybernetic approach with its information processing models the emphasis shifted towards investigating the underlying processes of movement control. Research topics included short term motor memory, feedback and knowledge of results, as well as continuing investigation into, for example, individual differences and transfer of training. Against a backcloth and awareness of current trends in cognitive psychology, theories were tailored specifically to explain and interpret motor learning, rather than simply borrowing general learning theories and applying them indiscriminately. For example, Adams (1971) introduced his closed loop theory of motor learning and Schmidt (1975) developed an alternative approach with an explicit cognitive orientation, schema theory.

This era also brought together work being conducted by neural control and behaviour oriented scientists, often based outside both psychology and physical education. For example, electrophysiological recordings of animals engaged in complex motor activity facilitated an understanding of the organization of the motor system, with an emphasis on finding associations between motor behaviour and the neurological process. Much of the earlier work of the Russian physiologist Nikolai Bernstein was influential in directing thinking on these matters. Bernstein's work had been conducted in the 1920s but only made an impact in 1967 following its belated translation into English. Bernstein's argument was that movement control can only be understood by recognizing the totality of forces, both muscular and non-muscular, and establishing the manner in which they interact. Bernstein's approach, in conjunction with Gibsonian views of perception and action (Gibson, 1979), has had a profound effect on recent work conducted within motor behaviour by so-called ecological psychologists.

Motor Learning: Contemporary Issues

As we are all aware, learning, defined as a relatively permanent change in behaviour as a result of experience, has long been a concern of psychologists. Many early investigations were concerned with isolating certain components of the learning process and used complex motor skills as the experimental tasks. What is important to bear in mind is that the primary concern was the product or outcome of learning rather than the process of motor skill acquisition. However, through subsequent analysis of this work, it has been possible to glean a great deal of knowledge about motor behaviour. For example, in order to establish that learning has taken place it is necessary to chart changes in behaviour over time. For example, over the course of an eight week practice period, a basketball coach would expect to see an improvement in the performance of basketball players. If the coach were to graph the shooting scores of players s/he might expect to see a performance curve like the one presented in Figure 5.1.

Many of the early studies of performance curves established that those representing learning of motor skills exhibited periods where there was no apparent improvement in performance. Each of these periods was known as a plateau and it was thought that during this time the learner was consolidating knowledge already acquired. However, later research failed to replicate the earlier findings but it is interesting that most books on motor learning still refer to their existence. This is posssibly due to the wealth of anecdotal evidence. For example, when you first learn a totally new skill such as playing a video game, you appear to progress very rapidly before passing through a phase when you no longer improve, followed by another phase of rapid improvement.

An additional feature of the learning process of motor skills which was uncovered by this early research was the notion of reminiscence, a phenomenon frequently noted in sport and exercise. Try to recall a situation in which you were learning something new, for example a new aerobic dance routine or first riding a bicycle. You have practised long and hard, you are fatigued and your performance does not appear to reflect what you have learned. Two days later you attempt the same routine and you perform it perfectly. This is an example of reminiscence or improved performance following a period of no practice.

Figure 5.1: A Motor Performance Learning Curve

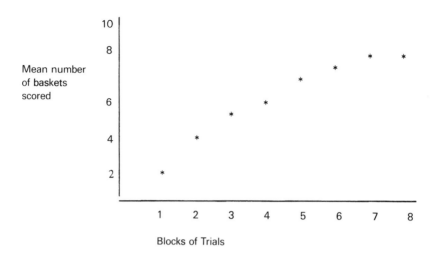

As the field of motor learning had such strong associations with 'learning psychology' as a whole it is not surprising that motor learning theories reflected current trends in psychology. Throughout the 1940s and 1950s the driving force was the stimulus–response (S–R) or behaviourist view of learning, and in particular Hull's (1943) learning theory. However, by the 1960s Hull's theory was found to be wanting as a general explanation of motor behaviour. A period of reassessment and often somewhat atheoretical empirical research followed during the 1960s, paving the way for the development of theories and models specific to motor learning in the 1970s. It was also during this time that contributions from other disciplines, including computer science, information technology and ergonomics established a wide base for the establishment of information processing models of human motor behaviour.

The approach which had the most profound influence amongst sport scientists was Adams's (1971) closed loop theory. In some ways as a reaction to Hullian ideas based on experiments conducted on animals, Adams outlined ways in which humans are set apart from the rest of the animal kingdom. First, immediacy of reinforcement is less critical for humans than other animals. With particular reference to sport, humans may continue to produce a response or performance without a teacher or coach reinforcing it. Second, we have the capacity for speech and often guide or mediate our motor responses through verbal instructions. Third, humans tend to use information to correct errors and vary their subsequent responses accordingly whereas animals tend to produce the same response continually until it is rewarded.

Adams's theory has two key elements, the perceptual trace which is essentially a reference standard acquired through practice, and the memory trace which is responsible for initiating movement. A key feature in the theory is the role played by feedback. According to Adams, the memory trace works by way of recalling the appropriate response from memory of previous correct responses. The memory trace simply selects and initiates the response but it does not control it. Feedback is provided both during and after movement production and over many practice attempts a perceptual trace is laid down. The perceptual trace is like a record of the movement which then operates as a reference of correctness in subsequent efforts. The learner compares feedback and knowledge of results of his or her action with this reference of correctness and any appropriate error adjustments can be made (this gives the theory its closed-loop character).

For sport psychology, Adams's theory was such a significant milestone as it was the first attempt at developing a theory of motor learning *per se*, rather than being a general learning theory which had been adapted to explain motor phenomena. As such, the theory represented a major shift in the whole motor behaviour domain and marks the point in time where the field matured into a recognizable subdiscipline within psychology. The theory also acted as a catalyst, generating a great deal of motor skills research. Issues such as the role of practice in establishing the perceptual trace, the influence of knowledge of results and the mechanisms of error detection and correction remain popular research topics to this day. Nevertheless criticisms have also been levelled against the theory, in particular in relation to novelty and storage problems and the nature of the research pursued.

The concern with novelty is associated with the observation by Bartlett (1932) that human motor action is never an exact replica of earlier performance. There are always slight variations in controlling aspects of the movement, such as the speed or force at which it is produced. Similarly, one of the attributes of skilled motor performance is that it is adaptable, so we recognize a skilful player as much for the way s/he adapts to unexpected circumstances as for his/her fluent movements. By suggesting that there is one reference of correctness for each action Adams's theory does not take this naturally accommodating variation into account. A second problem for the closed loop theory concerns storage or how the information is stored. It is assumed that separate memory traces and separate perceptual traces are developed for each and every movement. This implies an enormous burden on the central nervous system both for storage and retrieval purposes. A final criticism of Adams's theory centres around the nature of the research which is cited in support of the theory. Much of Adams's work and that of subsequent researchers was conducted on slow, linear positioning movements using only one limb segment whereas most sport related movement is very fast in nature and usually involves many body parts. It is probably unfair to criticize the theory itself on this account but this point is important in considering future directions to be followed by those hoping to advance our understanding in this field.

Schmidt's (1975) schema theory of motor learning goes some way towards addressing these problems. The approach moves even further away from traditional behaviourist concepts, turning instead towards cognitive psychology and the notion of the schema or set of complex cognitive relationships. Schmidt argued that every time movement is produced four items of information are stored: the initial conditions (for example starting position in a throw); certain aspects of a general motor programme for action (for example how much force was used); knowledge of the results of the action (did you hit the target); sensory consequences of the action (what the movement felt like). Abstract relationships are then made between these items of information and it is these relationships which make up the recall schema and the recognition schema. The recall schema is based on both knowledge of the goal of the task (initial conditions) and knowledge of results of previous attempts and is responsible for generating a motor programme for the action which is appropriate for novel circumstances. The recognition schema is based on the relationship found between the actual sensory feedback experienced during movement and the consequences of movement. The recognition schema is thought to guide movement production by comparing expected sensory consequences with the actual consequences.

A key distinction between this approach and that proposed by Adams is that the individual actions are not stored; rather, we make reference to abstract relationships or general rules about movement production. In this way it is predicted that learners will be more able to cope with novel situations where they are required to adapt already existing movements rather than necessarily devising new patterns of movement. As regards applied sport psychology, the most significant implications relate to the suggested usefulness of varied practices and routines, as opposed to specific practice for one movement or performance. Schmidt and a number of other researchers have conducted studies in which one group of learners practise a motor task in a variety of conditions and the other group is required to practise the specific task. When both groups are then asked to produce a response in a third and different situation (the transfer task) the group with varied practice produce the best performance. This finding is stronger for children than for adults and the implications for the design of teaching programmes of, for example, ball skills are thus immediately obvious.

No discussion of motor learning would be complete without reference to the influence of feedback and knowledge of results. Information available during and after movement can take several forms. The term feedback is used to delimit the information received by the performer as a result of the movement produced. For example when a tennis player serves the ball s/he receives information about how the movement felt, looked and sounded, as well as information about the result of the movement (for example, did it land in court). Information received as a direct result of producing a movement is referred to as intrinsic feedback. Examples of this are hearing the basketball hit the ring rather than dropping silently into the basket; sensing the off-balance position you were in before shooting; seeing the ball rebound away from the basket. A distinction is made between this type of information and that known as extrinsic feedback which refers to any additional information not inherent in the movement itself but which augments intrinsic feedback. There are a number of dimensions of extrinsic feedback but sport scientists have focused almost exclusively on one category, known as knowledge of results or KR, and this has predominated the research interests over the past few decades. There are many examples of KR in sport, both in practice and competition. For example, a coach might shout split times to swimmers as they train over a number of lengths, or in competition a gymnast receives a visible score from a judge after completion of a routine.

A great deal of research has been undertaken over the years on KR with the general agreement that it is one of the most important variables which influences learning effectiveness. In fact Bartlett (1948: 36) put this in context when he said, 'The common belief that "practice makes perfect" is not true. It is practice *the results of which are known* that makes perfect.' In trying to understand more about this learning process, many motor behaviourists have followed the lead provided by Edward L. Thorndike (1874–1949). He argued that learning ordinarily took place without conscious awareness, and is greatly influenced by the rewards associated with behaviour. His ideas are encapsulated in the simple law of effect which states that when a response is rewarded there is an increased likelihood of its occurring again.

One of Thorndike's most often cited experiments on motor learning was carried out in 1927. In it he compared the effect of practice alone against practice with KR on the performance of a motor task. Subjects were required to draw three, four, five or six inch lines while blindfolded. Subjects who received feedback telling them 'right' or 'wrong' improved by 55 per cent whereas subjects who did not receive KR showed no improvement (but remarkable stamina!) after drawing 5,400 consecutive lines. These findings have been the impetus for continuing research into the role of KR in motor learning until the present day, and numerous good reviews of this empirical research abound (e.g. Adams, 1987). In general, researchers have been interested in establishing how much KR (and how often) is optimal for skill learning in sport. Similarly, issues regarding delay in provision of KR or withdrawal of KR have received some attention. Most of this work followed closely, and in fact grew directly from, the enormous amount of work being conducted by the early learning theorists.

In the area of motor behaviour in recent years we can discern a shift away from the lead given by the verbal learning theorists and towards addressing the kinds of problems encountered by movement experts from a variety of disciplines. In particular, the notion of knowledge of performance has become popular in order to differentiate between information given about the actual movement pattern produced and information given regarding the end result or movement outcome. Typically, in laboratory experiments learners are shown kinematic information which is information about the mechanics of the movement itself, without reference to the forces involved. Several recent studies show that learners receiving kinematic information perform better than learners who only receive outcome knowledge. Obviously, coaches and teachers of motor skills do not usually have access to highly technical equipment with which to measure and present kinematic information. However, most schools and clubs now have video cameras and monitors but unfortunately these are not often used to their full potential. Reviews of studies utilizing videotaping as a means of providing knowledge of performance suggest that more will be learned by directing the performer's attention to specific aspects of the performance or even segments of the movement sequence, rather than simply reviewing the tape.

Despite these recent studies appearing to have more practical relevance, there is still the criticism that motor behaviour research uses tasks which are not representative of true-to-life motor skills. For example, much of the work concerning kinematic information feedback is laboratory based and uses single limb movements requiring very little coordination and control. These are necessary conditions in order to control for intervening variables but typically arguments arise as to the practical utility of findings based on these kinds of studies. However, this topic is currently experiencing a resurgence of interest and many more investigators are attempting to use applied research in an effort to uncover principles of KR which will have immediate practical relevance to teachers and learners. An example of this is the work being conducted at the Free University in Holland looking at the role of kinematic information feedback in learning the complex motor skills involved in tennis and skiing (Vereijken *et al.*, 1992).

A related area of contemporary study which received initial interest amongst developmental (for example Rosenthal and Zimmerman, 1978) and cognitive psychologists (for example Bandura, 1977) is that known as observational learning. Observational learning is rooted firmly in a social learning tradition and is concerned with learning by observing and imitating another person, the model. In sport, the 'watch me, do it this way' approach to teaching and learning has always been popular, if for no other reason than it saves the teacher or coach a long list of detailed verbal instructions which may not be understood by the learner. Despite this, it was not until the 1970s that physical educationists actually took an active research interest in the phenomenon. According to Bandura, the learner (observer) develops a cognitive representation of the modelled action which then acts as a blueprint to guide subsequent learner imitation of the modelled movement. Almost all of the work conducted on observational learning of motor skills throughout the 1970s used Bandura's social learning theory as the conceptual framework, thus making heavy demands on cognitive explanations of learning and performance (for a review see McCullagh, 1993). However, despite the many studies conducted and variables investigated no firm conclusions regarding observational learning could be drawn and the results of investigations, taken together, can at best be described as equivocal.

More recent attempts to explore the nature of observational learning have highlighted some key methodological and theoretical difficulties with the earlier work. In particular, investigators are now much more keenly aware of the limitations imposed by focusing only on single degree of freedom movements (i.e. simple movements). More convincing effects are now being found for complex or multi-degree of freedom movements which also have greater ecological validity (see Whiting *et al.*, 1987). A central issue which concerns a number of contemporary investigators is the nature of the supposed cognitive representation (Carroll and Bandura, 1987). As yet, it is not known precisely what visual information is picked up by the observer of the model, let alone how such information is translated into subsequent action. A number of studies now appear to support the contention that the relative movement of body segments and the trunk convey much meaningful information to an observer of human action (see Scully and Newell, 1985). These issues have also been combined with previous suggestions regarding the role of kinematic information emanating from the feedback literature. A number of recent studies have compared the effects of modelling with and without KR and KP (knowledge of performance). There seems to be some indication that the provision of information about the form or technique to be produced, whether by cueing attention to relevant aspects of the display or providing feedback in the form of KP, may enhance learning of multi-degree of freedom movements. It seems likely that the resurgence of interest in this area will continue to come together with recent work looking at feedback. This is encouraging as both areas of research, while traditional in their routes, have attempted to take on board some of the criticisms levelled against motor learning research as a whole. We now see an increase in the number of applied issues being considered worthy of study, as well as an increase in the use of more ecologically valid tasks, a trend which can only be for the best.

Motor Control: Contemporary Issues

Theories of motor control developed alongside those of motor learning during the mid-1960s and it was during this period that researchers became interested in how isolated movements were actually controlled, irrespective of the extent of learning. Again the link with mainstream psychology was strong where the rapid growth in technology during and after World War II led to the development of theories of human behaviour based on computer analogies. Welford's (1968) information processing model became popular within sport science at this time and has maintained its popularity over the years (see Chapter 3). According to this approach, the brain functions in a similar way to a computer with input, translation and output facilities. The input stage is concerned mainly with the detection of available sensory information (for example, does a player see a white tennis ball against a black background?). The central stage of the model is concerned with perceiving and making sense of the information, making an appropriate decision and planning the necessary action (for example the player identifies certain characteristics of the ball coming towards him/her, including direction, speed and spin, decides how to return the shot and then issues the appropriate muscle commands). An integral part of this process is the idea of a motor program to explain the planning and control of movements. This stage of the model is thought to be limited in terms of the amount of information it can handle, brought home to us by those occasions when we are unable to perform two tasks simultaneously. For this reason Welford speculated that the central mechanism may be a single channel mechanism, and hence we are limited in terms of the amount of information it is possible for us to process at any one time. The output stage of the model is concerned with actual movement production; once a decision has been made the appropriate instructions are issued to the body and limbs and action results. (A thorough discussion and explanation of the information processing model is provided in Chapter 3.)

The concept of the motor program, as outlined above, has been central to motor control for some considerable time. The idea was first proposed by Lashley (1917) when he discovered that a patient with a gunshot wound to the back experienced total anaesthesia of the lower limbs but could still accurately move his leg when deprived of visual feedback. This suggested that the movement was organized centrally. Hence the information was still being fed to the limbs via the intact efferent nerve pathways (brain to periphery), with little need for sensory feedback from the severed afferent nerve pathways (periphery to brain). By 1951 Lashley was arguing that a central motor program explanation could account for the planning and controlling of very fast, ballistic movements where there is insufficient time for feedback to be used by the performer. However, it was Keele (1968: 387) who offered the now classic definition of a motor program as 'a set of muscle commands that are structured before a movement sequence begins, and that allows the entire sequence to be carried out uninfluenced by peripheral feedback'. Evidence for the existence of motor programs has mainly been provided by three sources of investigation. First, there are differentiation studies involving non-human species (where it is shown that movement planning and production is still possible when the afferent pathway to the spinal cord is severed and no feedback is available). Second, there is research investigating the relationship between movement complexity and reaction time (RT) (more complex movements have longer RTs because more time is required to plan the response). Finally there are those studies which record the muscle activity patterns of human performers producing rapid actions. In these latter studies, when the performer is mechanically prevented from completing the action a similar EMG trace emerges, suggesting that even though the limb does not move there is a similar movement organization process.

Originally strict interpretations of the motor program have since been modified to incorporate less rigid formulations, and current programming notions include more abstract and generalized concepts such as the schema notion which is thought to account for not only the use of feedback during movement execution but also storage and novelty problems associated with motor programs. This more economical view of motor programming suggests that rather than recalling a detailed response specification for each and every action performed, instead an abstract programming rule is applied, a rule which has developed on the basis of numerous repetitions of similar actions within general classes of movements. For example, an overhand throw may have similar specifications to other types of throwing action in terms of speed, force, and sequencing requirements. It has been suggested that these programming rules form a 'grammar of action' which functions at the interface between thought and action (Mulder, 1991). Much of the research on behavioural aspects of motor control over the past decade has concentrated on establishing the structure of such generalized motor programs, i.e. exactly what is specified in advance by the program? It is generally agreed that two processes are involved in the programming of movement, planning the action and specifying parameters. Planning an action is believed to include rules for action regarding the orderly sequence of events, including the relative timing and the relative forces which are to be specified. Parameter specification refers to the addition of context-dependent and task-dependent information, including the overall duration of the movement, the overall force of the contractions and the specific muscles to be used (see Schmidt, 1988). In this view, the acquisition of motor control is proposed as being synonymous with the acquisition of programming rules, rather than in terms of muscle-specific motor programs.

An alternative view of motor control has been proposed by a group of individuals critical of traditional motor control concepts and has been called the ecological or dynamical perspective. This position relies heavily on the earlier writings of the Russian physiologist Nikolai Bernstein (Whiting, 1984) regarding what he terms the degrees of freedom problem. This concerns the problem of coordinating all our limbs, joints and muscles, each capable of moving independently, into a single controlled action. According to Bernstein (1967) any account of motor control must take into consideration both the muscular and non-muscular forces and the manner in which they interact rather than only focusing on the muscular forces as is true of traditional accounts. The ecological psychologists argue that previous accounts of motor control assume a hierarchical control system where there is assumed to be an executive at a higher level and the executive issues command to lower levels which then carry out the actions. However, the problem with this type of system is that it assumes 'too much organization, neural computation, and direct organization by the brain and spinal cord mechanisms, so that every movement must have an explicit representation stored in the central nervous system' (Schmidt, 1991). Also, there is no way to account for how the hierarchy itself is formed or how the independent units come under the control of the executive.

The ecological perspective focuses on the impact of naturally occurring physical laws emerging from interacting elements, such as the person and his/her environment. According to Turvey (1977), the various muscles and joints operating together as a single unit form coordinative structures. For example, a coordinative structure for kicking might involve muscle groups in the leg, ankle and foot but it is important to note that muscle groups working together need not be anatomically related. Rather than thinking in terms of an executive issuing commands to muscles, Turvey suggests that these coordinative structures are constrained to act as units given the requirements of the task and the context in which it is taking place. Constraints generally take the form of being either task, environmental or organismic. For example, in rugby, players are constrained by task and environmental requirements to advance the ball by kicking or passing by hand. Individuals may vary the way in which they kick or pass but again such variations are within the constraints of the particular circumstances. Not all combinations of muscle actions are as valid as each other, some methods will be more appropriate than others depending on the circumstances.

This dynamic perspective is gaining popularity in the motor behaviour literature and an increasing number of journal articles have adopted this perspective. In addition the recently established International Society for Ecological Psychology publishes the journal *Ecological Psychology* which regularly features a variety of articles dealing with the issues relating to motor skills as they occur within the constraints of an animal-environment synergy (as opposed to dealing with issues arising from a consideration of animals or environments in isolation from each other). However, as is true with so many modern process models, because of their complexity and the range of sources from which they are derived, the temptation remains to turn to simpler models to explain human motor behaviour. This is likely to be a fruitless quest. Furthermore, traditionalists criticize the theory because it fails to deal adequately with cognition and the role of an executive. According to Turvey and colleagues, the theory is still slowly evolving and will inevitably deal with cognitive issues in due course and once a firm grasp on the perception–action synergy has been duly established.

Undoubtedly, the way forward will be characterized by greater development of both theory and empirical research within the ecological perspective and a continuing healthy scientific debate with traditionalists (see Meijer and Roth, 1988). This, in turn, will open the way for a greater synthesis of motor learning, motor control and indeed, motor development research. In fact, a number of recent studies have already adopted an integrated approach in order to find empirical support for Bernstein's views on skill acquisition, empirical support which has been conspicuous by its absence over the past 20 years. Karl Newell and his colleagues from the University of Illinois and the Free University in Holland have embarked on a series of investigations into Bernstein's 'degrees of freedom problem' with general support being found across a variety of complex motor actions. A significant theoretical contribution to emerge from this work has been the suggestion that formerly held 'principles of motor development' may in fact reflect on local constraints evident in the organism–environment interaction rather than on universal principles (Newell and van Emmerik, 1990). A further worthwhile challenge for motor behaviour theorists and physical educationists/sport scientists alike is to build on this work with a view to developing practical programmes and guidelines with the athlete and coach very much in mind. It is toward issues relating to the learning environment that we now turn, as this has traditionally formed one of the main avenues of applied research in the motor behaviour area.

The Learning Environment

A widely held view of skill acquisition is that there are qualitative changes in the way a task is performed. One of the most common descriptions of how skills are acquired was that put forward by Fitts and Posner (1967). In the first or cognitive stage, when a learner is trying to come to grips with understanding the new task, learning is characterized by the high degree of verbal and cognitive input. The learner appears to rely heavily on words (or demonstrations) in order to take on board all of the necessary information to perform the task. The second or associative stage occurs when the learner focuses on trying to produce effective motor actions. This is the stage in which new patterns of coordination emerge as the learner practises and tries to refine a skill. It has been demonstrated that during this phase performance often improves rapidly, with the consistency of performance increasing with practice and the amount of verbal activity becoming less important to the learner. It is also during this phase that learners start to learn how to interpret the context in which the skill is taking place, develop anticipation and monitor their own feedback in order to detect errors. This phase can often be lengthy, especially if the learner is experiencing difficulty. The final or autonomous stage is characterized by the ability of the learner to produce the skill almost automatically without taking a lot of attention. During this phase the performer often loses the ability to provide a verbal description of the action as cognitive control is minimized in case it interferes with performance. Learning can continue over a very long period of time, and often gains in automaticity will continue with continued practice of skills. A selection of important conditions for the practice of motor skills is now considered.

Massed and Distributed Practice

Obviously, practice is an essential element in acquiring any motor skill and something with which most individuals involved in sport and exercise are familiar. However, something that many individuals may not be aware of is that distribution of practice conditions may have varying effects on how much is learned or how well a skill is learned. Distribution of practice refers to the spacing of practice either in an individual session or the spacing between different practice sessions. For example, a coach could advise a young gymnast to spend one hour of a two hour practice session trying to improve a handspring vault, whereas another coach might favour having gymnasts practise the vault during three 15-minute blocks interspersed with other practice activities. Similarly, one coach may favour one two-hour session per day whereas another may prefer to use two one-hour blocks.

A number of studies were conducted during the 1940s and 1950s attempting to address the effects of massed as compared to distributed practice within individual practice sessions. The majority of these studies addressed organization within one session and showed that distributed practice is more beneficial than massed practice. These studies have not been without criticism, the most telling concern being the distinction which is offered between learning and performance. Later investigators have pointed out that massed practice may result in a lower level of performance at the end of an experimental session but reminiscence may be equally high for both massed and distributed practice groups when next performing the task.

The majority of work on distribution of practice was initially driven by the predictions of Hull's (1943) theory of learning, but as the theory declined in popularity so less research became available on this topic. Despite this a study frequently cited for its practical utility was that conducted by Baddeley and Longman (1978). These investigators were required to train postal workers on a task similar in many respects to typing. It was initially decided that 60 hours of practice would be required for workers to become proficient but the question concerned how this amount of time should be scheduled. Four practice conditions were devised, namely one or two-hour sessions conducted once or twice a day. Results favoured the one hour practice session offered once per day.

Individuals in this group learned the typing task in the least number of hours and nine months after the study they were still the most proficient workers. This study clearly suggests that motor skills are best learned during shorter amounts of practice time per session. However, even with this 'real life' skill arguments could be made as to how representative a typing task is of the kinds of motor skills involved in sport and exercise. Furthermore, in considering the results of this study practitioners need to take into consideration the fact that the one hour per day scheduling would have to be spread across almost four months in order to complete 60 hours of training, whereas the two hour, twice per day scheduling would be completed within three weeks. Clearly, the relative merits of massed or distributed practice need to be considered in light of the individual circumstances surrounding the skills being learned, the total amount of time available and the amount of time available per session. There is no doubt that research of this nature provides preliminary guidelines to practitioners but when set against the vast number of related variables it is also apparent that much more is required by way of applied and pedagogically related research.

Whole and Part Methods

Another issue which is of considerable importance to teachers and coaches alike concerns the best method of practising the skills being learned. Should skills be presented and practised in their entirety (the whole method) or should they be broken down into smaller component parts (the part method), or indeed should some combination of these approaches be used (whole-part or part-whole)? These were the kinds of questions prompted by the Royal Air Force during the 1940s, at a time when pilot training was so important. The general conclusion reached was that whole methods of training were superior, and even today pilots train using flight simulators which replicate the whole flying environment.

Most people who have been involved in sport are familiar with instances when they had to break a skill down in order to grasp precisely what was required of them. Similarly, many school children are all too familiar with the days and weeks spent on skills practices and short routines rather than just playing the game. So should whole or part methods be the mainstay of teaching practice? Naylor and Briggs (1963) argued cogently that the deciding factor has to be the nature of the task which is being learned. Generally speaking, the whole method should be used whenever possible; if the learner is capable of reproducing the desired action then it is better to practise as a whole than in parts. Nevertheless, there are occasions in sport and exercise when the desired action is so complex and demanding that it must be broken down in order for the learner to grasp what is required of them. Examples of this might be a complicated gymnastics or dance routine in which each sequence is made up of separate movements. However, gymnastics and dance routines also have another important element, that is the timing of the actions. So although practice of isolated elements of the sequence may assist in initially learning the correct movement patterns, it should be replaced with whole practice routines as soon as possible.

Blocked and Random Practice

A common problem facing teachers and coaches of motor skills is how to teach several essential skills within a given practice session. Intuitively, the teacher is faced with two choices. S/he can require the learner to spend a specified number of practice trials on one task, refining and correcting it, before progressing on to spend a similar amount of practice time on the next task (blocked practice). Alternatively, the learner could be required to rotate around the various tasks, never practising the same skill on two consecutive trials (random practice). This issue of blocked vs random practice has generated a good deal of research interest since the late 1970s. It was Shea and Morgan (1979) who first revealed that our intuition may be wrong, during a laboratory investigation into the learning of three types of rapid, sequential arm movements. Subjects practising under random conditions tended to perform worse than subjects practising under blocked conditions during the acquisition trials. However, when all subjects were given a retention test to evaluate learning 10 days after the experiment, it was the random practice group which consistently proved itself more effective than the blocked practice group. These findings suggest that more learning takes place when random practice conditions are used, even though actual performance at the time of acquisition may not be as good as when practising under blocked conditions. Similar results have been found for 'real world' motor skills, such as three different badminton serves (Goode and Magill, 1986).

These surprising empirical findings which ran counter to conventional wisdom generated considerable debate regarding the effectiveness of random practice. The reconstruction hypothesis suggests that random practice works because it forces the learner to generate the solution to a given movement (coordination) problem each and every time s/he meets it. Thus performance across a group of practice trials appears slower and more difficult because the learner is regenerating the solution each time (because s/he has forgotten the solution from one occasion to the next). This process of regenerating the solution to the problem has been called retrieval practice and is thought to facilitate learning by giving the learner practice in dredging up essential information from long term memory. An alternative explanation of random effects, known as the elaboration hypothesis, is offered by Shea and Zimny (1983). They argue that practising tasks randomly makes each task unique, therefore creating meaningfulness and distinctiveness in the learner's mind. Post-experimental interviews with subjects corroborated these suggestions and also established that blocked practice subjects tended not to think about the task but rather were inclined to 'run off' the motor performance automatically. Findings such as this clearly suggest that teachers and coaches should give random practice greater consideration than is currently evident from the common suggestion that a learner engage in an activity and practise it 'over and over again until they get it right'.

Physical and Mental Practice

The belief that mental rehearsal will enhance performance has become commonplace among most coaches today, a belief no doubt reinforced by the increase in popular sport psychology self-help manuals. Imagery, visualization and mental rehearsal are dealt with more thoroughly in Chapter 3, in relation to general intervention strategies. However, the efficacy of mental practice or mental rehearsal in relation to motor learning is also given due consideration here, in the context of motor learning. Mental practice refers to a situation in which the learner thinks about or imagines performing the task rather than physically practising it. Developmental and educational psychologists would be familiar with the literature that deals with such practice but more normally in the context of verbal learning or the acquisition of mathematical or computational skills. A variety of theories have been proposed to account for mental practice effects; the most popular of these are presented in Chapter 3.

Feltz and Landers (1983) reviewed over 60 studies that related to the effects of mental training on motor skills and concluded that performance can be improved by mental practice. However, and as would be expected, mental practice was better than no practice but physical practice was found to be better than mental practice. It has also been suggested that the type of task being practised will affect the usefulness of mental practice. Tasks with a large cognitive component seem to benefit more from mental practice than tasks requiring large amounts of strength. This benefit would affect sports such as gymnastics, ice skating or dance where the performer has to remember long sequences of movement, or indeed any team sport where the performer is attempting to learn a new game play or strategy. It appears that learning the sequence of actions is facilitated by mental practice but that learning the actions themselves benefits more from physical practice.

Given these findings it would be unwise to suggest that teachers and coaches use mental practice to replace physical practice! However, it is wise to encourage the use of mental practice, particularly in the early stage of learning when the learner is establishing the correct sequence of action. By using breaks in physical practice efficiently the time taken to learn new skills may be shortened. There is less scientific evidence for the use of mental practice at the élite performer's level but there are a great many anecdotal reports of the use of imagery by top class athletes (see Hemery, 1991). Obviously this is an area which has huge scope for development in terms of primary evaluative research and indeed it is surprising that more experimental evidence is not available, given the current popularity of techniques based on mental practice in applied sport psychology.

Retention

Increasingly, cognitive psychologists have come to regard memory not as distinct and distant from learning but as essentially 'different sides of the same behavioural coin' (Adams, 1976: 223). Thus, memory is a working process, constantly changing and being updated as new information is acquired. The term 'retention' is commonly used in the sports science literature to refer to the persistence of performance over a period of no practice. Similarly, the term 'forgetting' refers to the failure to maintain performance and this can come about for a number of reasons which we will come to shortly.

A distinction was made in the early psychological literature between short term retention (several seconds up to a few minutes) and long term retention (hours, days, weeks). A similar distinction was accepted by motor behaviourists with most interest being expressed in understanding short term retention. The reason for this was that various studies conducted over the first half of this century found very high long term retention for motor skills. Indeed, the finding was so consistent that research enthusiasm waned and attention then turned to short term retention and the process by which forgetting occurred.

Two main theories of forgetting currently dominate the literature, trace decay theory and interference theory. Trace decay theory is based on the law of disuse and suggests that the reason forgetting occurs is because, over time and without practice, the 'memory trace' decays. The theory relies on time as a key factor in the decay process. Interference theory, on the other hand, recognizes that individuals are not always totally passive between first learning something and then attempting to respond. Interference theory suggests that forgetting may occur because of the influence of other activities. Retroactive interference (RI) is thought to occur when a performer is asked to produce a different skill between learning something new and being asked to perform it. Proactive interference (PI) is thought to occur when a previously learned skill interferes with the retention of a newly learned skill. There is considerable evidence for both RI and PI effects in terms of verbal skills but the motor behaviour literature has concentrated almost exclusively on retroactive interference with very little evidence available on the role of proactive interference in motor forgetting.

Transfer of Learning

An issue closely related to that of retention is the transfer of learning, a process fundamental to so much of teaching and coaching. That is, rather than assuming learners start with a clean slate when learning new skills, teachers often assume that transfer will occur from previously learned skills. For example, most boys will have played soccer at some stage and therefore teachers may sometimes assume that the skills of kicking and heading may transfer to new situations. Such practice procedures actually support very early psychological thinking regarding learning in the shape of Thorndike's identical elements theory (Thorndike and Woodworth, 1901). More modern approaches explain transfer in terms of the degree of similarity between the tasks being learned (Osgood, 1949), and speculate as to two types of transfer which are seen as being akin to proactive and retroactive interference. Positive transfer (retroactive) is thought to occur when the task being learned is assisted by the learner's previous experience in tasks with similar elements, for example someone who has played soccer is likely to grasp the tactical requirements of field hockey fairly quickly. Negative transfer (proactive) is thought to occur when a previously learned skill interferes with learning a new skill, for example tennis players sometimes find it difficult to bend their arm when playing strokes in squash. Despite numerous practical examples of negative transfer in the sports domains, it has been very difficult to establish this phenomenon in the research setting. Typically, any initial negative influences are masked by the effects of positive transfer, such as racket to ball coordination or strategy development.

The popularity of Schmidt's (1975) schema theory has led to renewed interest in the issue of transfer of learning. This is due to the fact that schema theory advocates varying practice conditions so that learners learn more than simply the execution requirements of the task. In fact, it is assumed that what is learned is a set of relationships between particular conditions or sets of circumstances. Learners are exposed to practice conditions involving a range of requirements regarding distance, location and speed, with the underlying assumption that when they are next faced with novel circumstances in a game situation that transfer will occur. However, support for the variability of practice hypothesis remains equivocal although it has generated a significant amount of research in recent years (for a review see van Rosum, 1987). Recent publications emphasizing the practical applications of motor learning research (for example Schmidt, 1991) point out that although teaching for transfer may be an intuitive desire of many teachers and coaches, the research evidence in its favour is not overly supportive. First, research suggests that very little transfer occurs between motor skills, even when they appear to be very similar. Therefore to spend time teaching one skill simply so that it will transfer to another is possibly not cost effective. That time would be better spent on the particular skill of interest and if transfer from previously learned skills should occur automatically then so much the better. A second point to emerge from the literature is the obvious point that if transfer does occur then the extent of transfer will depend on the similarity of either the skills or the contexts. It is not always clear what is the basis of similarity but it has been proposed that similarity could refer to aspects of the physical action or perceptual characteristics, or indeed more global aspects such as game strategy, tactics, competition or cooperation demands. The onus is on the teacher or coach to highlight such similarities (or differences) to previously learned skills. A final point suggested by the research relates to fundamental abilities such as speed, balance, flexibility, speed of response and visual acuity. There is no point in wasting time and energy devising exercises to practise general abilities in the hope that transfer will occur; the time would be better spent on practice of the motor skill to which the abilities apply in the context of the sport.

In summary, these results demonstrate just how uncertain we still are as to the nature of transfer. Much of current teaching and coaching practice appears to be still based on intuition, common sense and what has worked for others. It would be encouraging to see this area of research receiving renewed interest, perhaps in light of more recent theoretical drives to emphasize the reciprocal relationships of the organism–environment and perception–action systems.

The Way Forward

In terms of the history and evolution of the subject, it is true to say that the development and refinement of theories of motor behaviour still remain the number one priority. As expected, the present period is characterized, quite naturally, by considerable soul searching and critical introspection. However, at least we can say that the right sort of questions are being asked; contributions from a number of specialisms are being taken on board and the future looks promising if far from plain sailing. The advances which have been made over recent years have established a platform but as the chief players themselves acknowledge, the development of theories designed specifically for the motor domain remains unfinished business. For example, although both Adams's and Schmidt's theories of motor learning provide more adequate explanation of motor learning than previous verbal learning theories, neither can yet explain two pervasive phenomena:

learning through observation of a model and learning through mental practice. In both these instances the performer is passive (either while watching a model or visualizing the appropriate action) and therefore there is no way for a perceptual trace to be laid down, or for an existing motor program to be strengthened. The learner effectively learns without responding. To explain this effect, Newell and Barclay (1982), drawing on cognitive psychology, suggest that different levels of schemata may exist in a hierarchical system ranging from the general and mainly abstract, down to the detailed and mainly motor. Such a system would account for mental practice and observational learning by inferring that they make their mark at the symbolic level of learning. An additional challenge is to continue to amass the kind of research evidence currently emerging for Bernstein's principles of skill acquisition. By doing this, greater support will be found not only in terms of skill acquisition but perhaps a way forward for a reintegration of various areas of motor behaviour will also become more clear.

Existing motor learning theories are also often criticized because of their inability to respond or account for the considerable body of knowledge accumulating on short term memory, long term memory and transfer of learning. Recent work has begun to take on board this criticism and research is currently being conducted on contextual interference. Interestingly, these recent suggestions regarding theoretical approaches to motor learning are prime examples of an interdisciplinary research orientation, and are surely to be commended. Within psychology itself, a spirit of healthy eclecticism abounds, such that, on the one hand, the suggested developments and extension of schema theory are based in cognitive psychology and, on the other hand, the notion of contextual interference and stimulus generalization is derived from behaviourism. It appears that the field has moved through various stages, originally based firmly in general psychology, through unique developments within motor domain and now these contributions are being refined with reference to contemporary cognitive psychology.

Similarly, motor control theories, once considered as being separate from motor learning, have now been accepted as intricately related. Major proponents of the information processing model, as used to explain skilled motor performance, also include the investigation of changes in performance associated with learning under certain conditions in their research programmes. Thus, by the 1970s it was difficult to distinguish between the two domains. Critics of the area are now calling for ever more comprehensive theories of movement coordination and control, and recent attempts by motor behaviourists to elaborate upon the work of Turvey and colleagues hints at a possible way forward.

It has to be ironic that one current major criticism of the motor skills literature is that it is too hide-bound by theoretical debate when other areas of sport psychology suffer chronically from a lack of theory! Historically, it can be seen that the area developed out of mainstream psychology and tended to align itself with basic theory-driven research rather than with applied concerns. Most research in motor learning and control has been conducted in highly controlled laboratory conditions using simple, single degree of freedom movements. An obvious criticism of this approach is that such experiments tell us little about real world situations. In the past, the key researchers in the field were quick to defend the pursuit of basic research which tried to find principles applicable to many aspects of skilled performance, rather than espousing applied research which attempted to find instant solutions to isolated problems at the expense of theoretical rigour. At a recent symposium (see Singer, 1990) concerned with future directions in the field, various eminent researchers proposed some necessary changes in research orientation. It was agreed that motor learning needs to become more applied, in the sense that researchers need to base their problems on real life situations. Similarly, it was suggested that motor control should now concern itself with improving task performance rather than simply examining the control process. However, it should be pointed out that applied research can still be theory driven and it is this type of research which is advocated, rather than applied research which seeks to answer isolated problems of practitioners. Answering isolated problems, while important for maintaining support for practitioners, will not ultimately assist in developing theory. Motor learning and control as a field of study has long suffered under the illusion that the only 'good' research was basic research and this in turn served to dampen enthusiasm for any applied research which was looked upon as inferior. Now, 20 years later, it is being recognized that while the field has made some advances in being recognized as a unique domain within psychology it has not been altogether successful in disseminating the knowledge which has been amassed to the practitioners who actually need to use it: teachers, coaches and athletes. A number of reasons have been proffered for this, including such notions as first, the theory is so removed from application that practitioners are not interested or find it too difficult to interpret; second, that student teachers and coaches are not made aware of the application of theory to practice in the limited time devoted to courses during training; and third, that an intermediary is necessary between those conducting research on the one hand, and those involved in teacher and coach education on the other. At present such people are as scarce as the proverbial hen's teeth.

References

ADAMS, J. A. (1971) 'A closed-loop theory of motor learning', *Journal of Motor Behavior*, 3, pp. 111–50.

ADAMS, J. A. (1976) *Learning and Memory: An Introduction*, Homewood, IL: Dorsey.

ADAMS, J. A. (1987) 'Historical review and appraisal of research on the learning, retention, and transfer of human motor skills', *Psychological Bulletin*, 101, pp. 41–74.

BADDELEY, A. D. and LONGMAN, D. J. A. (1978) 'The influence of length and frequency of training session on the rate of learning to type', *Ergonomics*, 21, pp. 627–35.

BANDURA, A. (1977) *Social Learning Theory*, Englewood Cliffs, NJ: Prentice Hall.

BARTLETT, F. C. (1932) *Remembering: A Study in Experimental and Social Psychology*, Cambridge: Cambridge University Press.

BARTLETT, F. C. (1948) 'The measurement of human skill', *Occupational Psychology*, 22, pp. 31–8.

BERNSTEIN, N. (1967) *The Co-ordination and Regulation of Movements*, Oxford: Pergamon Press.

BRYAN, W. L. and HARTER, N. (1899) 'Studies in the physiology and psychology of telegraphic language', *Psychological Review*, 4, pp. 27–53.

BUNGE, M. (1990) 'What kind of discipline is psychology: Autonomous or dependent, humanistic or scientific, biological or sociological?', *New Ideas in Psychology*, 2, pp. 121–37.

CARROLL, W. R. and BANDURA, A. (1987) 'Translating cognition into action: The role of visual guidance in observational learning', *Journal of Motor Behavior*, 19, pp. 385–98.

FELTZ, D. L. and LANDERS, D. M. (1983) 'The effects of mental practice on motor skill learning and performance: A meta-analysis', *Journal of Sport Psychology*, 5, pp. 25–57.

FITTS, P. and POSNER, M. I. (1967) *Human Performance*, Belmont, CA: Brooks-Cole.

FRITSCH, G. and HITZIG, E. (1870) 'Uber die elektrische Errerbarkeit des Grosshirns', *Archiv Anatomie Physiologie*, 37, pp. 300–22.

GIBSON, J. J. (1979) *The Ecological Approach to Visual Perception*, Boston, MA: Houghton-Mifflin.

GOODE, S. and MAGILL, R. A. (1986) 'The contextual interference effects in learning three badminton serves', *Research Quarterly for Exercise and Sport*, 57, pp. 308–14.

HEMERY, D. (1991) *Sporting Excellence: What Makes a Champion?* London: Harper Collins.

HOLDING, D. H. (1989) 'Final survey', in HOLDING, D. H. (Ed.) *Human Skills*, Chichester: John Wiley and Sons, pp. 282–92.

HULL, C. L. (1943) *Principles of Behavior*, New York: Appleton-Century-Crofts.

KEELE, S. W. (1968) 'Movement control in skilled motor performance', *Psychological Bulletin*, 70, pp. 387–402.

LASHLEY, K. S. (1917) 'The accuracy of movement in the absence of excitation from the moving organ', *American Journal of Physiology*, 43, pp. 169–94.

LASHLEY, K. S. (1951) 'The problem of serial order in behavior', in JEFFRIES, L. A. (Ed.) *Cerebral Mechanisms in Behavior*, New York: Wiley.

McCULLAGH, P. (1993) 'Modelling: Learning, developmental and social psychological considerations', in SINGER, R. N., MURPHEY, M. and TENNANT, L. K. (Eds) *Handbook of Research on Sport Psychology*, New York: Macmillan, pp. 106–27.

MEIJER, O. G. and ROTH, K. (Eds) (1988) *Complex Movement Behavior: 'The' Motor-Action Controversy*, Amsterdam: North-Holland.

MERTON, P. A. (1953) 'Speculations on the servo control of movement', in WOLSTENHOLME, G. E. W. (Ed.) *The Spinal Cord*, London: Churchill.

MULDER, T. (1991) 'A process-oriented model of human motor behavior: Toward a theory-based rehabilitation approach', *Physical Therapy*, 71, pp. 157–64.

NAYLOR, J. C. and BRIGGS, G. E. (1963) *Long-Term Retention of Learned Skills: A Review of the Literature*, ASD Technical Report 61-390, Washington, DC: US Department of Commerce.

NEWELL, K. M. and BARCLAY, C. R. (1982) 'Developing knowledge about action', in KELSO, J. A. S. and CLARK, J. E. (Eds) *The Development of Movement Control and Coordination*, New York: John Wiley, pp. 175–212.

NEWELL, K. M. and VAN EMMERIK, R. E. A. (1990) 'Are Gesell's developmental principles general principles for the acquisition of coordination?', in CLARKE, J. E. and HUMPHREY, J. H. (Eds) *Advances in Motor Development*, New York: AMS Press, pp. 13–36.

OSGOOD, C. E. (1949) 'The similarity paradox in human learning: A resolution', *Psychological Review*, 56, pp. 132–43.

ROSENTHAL, T. L. and ZIMMERMAN, B. J. (1978) *Social Learning and Cognition*, New York: Academic Press.

SCHMIDT, R. A. (1975) 'A schema theory of discrete motor learning', *Psychological Review*, 82, pp. 225–60.

SCHMIDT, R. A. (1988) *Motor Control and Learning. A Behavioral Emphasis*, 2nd edn, Champaign, IL: Human Kinetics.

SCHMIDT, R. A. (1991) *Motor Learning and Performance: From Principles to Practice*, Champaign, IL: Human Kinetics.

SCULLY, D. M. and NEWELL, K. M. (1985) 'Observational learning and the acquisition of motor skills: Toward a visual perception perspective', *Journal of Human Movement Studies*, 12, pp. 169–87.

SHEA, J. B. and MORGAN, R. L. (1979) 'Contextual interference effects on the acquisition, retention, and transfer of a motor skill', *Journal of Experimental Psychology: Human Learning and Memory*, 5, pp. 179–87.

SHEA, J. B. and ZIMNY, S. T. (1983) 'Context effects in memory and learning movement information', in MAGILL, R. A. (Ed.) *Memory and Control of Action*, Amsterdam: North-Holland, pp. 345–66.

SINGER, R. N. (1990) 'Motor learning research: Meaningful for physical educators or a waste of time?', *Quest*, 42, pp. 114–25.

THORNDIKE, E. L. and WOODWORTH, R. S. (1901) 'The influence of improvement in one mental function upon the efficiency of other functions', *Psychological Review*, 8, pp. 247–61.

TURVEY, M. T. (1977) 'Preliminaries to a theory of action with reference to vision,' in SHAW, R. and BRANSFORD, J. (Eds) *Perceiving, Acting and Knowing: Toward an Ecological Psychology*, Hillsdale, NJ: Erlbaum, pp. 211–65.

VAN ROSUM, J. H. A. (1987) *Motor Development and Practice: The Variability of Practice Hypothesis in Perspective*, Amsterdam: Free University Press.

VEREIJKEN, B., VAN EMMERIK, R. E. A., WHITING, H. T. A. and NEWELL, K. M. (1992) 'Free(z)ing degrees of freedom in skill acquisition', *Journal of Motor Behaviour*, 24, pp. 133–42.

WELFORD, A. T. (1968) *Fundamentals of Skill*, London: Methuen.

WHITING, H. T. A. (Ed.) (1984) *Human Motor Actions: Bernstein Reassessed*, Amsterdam: North-Holland.

WHITING, H. T. A., BIJLARD, M. J. and DEN BRINKER, B. P. L. M. (1987) 'The influence of a dynamic model on the acquisition of a complex cyclical action', *Quarterly Journal of Experimental Psychology*, 39A, pp. 43–59.

WOODWORTH, R. S. (1899) 'The accuracy of voluntary movement', *Psychological Review*, 3, (Supplement 2).

Further Reading

ADAMS, J. A. (1987) 'Historical review and appraisal of research on the learning, retention, and transfer of human motor skills', *Psychological Bulletin*, 101, pp. 41–74.

CHAMBERLIN, C. and LEE, T. D. (1993) 'Arranging practice conditions and designing instruction' in SINGER, R. N., MURPHEY, M. and TENNANT, L. K. (Eds) *Handbook of Research on Sport Psychology*, New York: Macmillan, pp. 213–41.

GLENCROSS, D. (1993) 'Human skill: Ideas, concepts and models' in SINGER, R. N., MURPHEY, M. and TENNANT, L. K. (Eds) *Handbook of Research on Sport Psychology*, New York: Macmillan, pp. 242–56.

GLENCROSS, D. J., WHITING, H. T. A. and ABERNETHY, B. (in press) 'Motor control, motor learning and the acquisition of skill: Historical trends and future directions', *International Journal of Sport Psychology*.

HOLDING, D. H. (1989) *Human Skills*, Chichester: John Wiley and Sons.

KELSO, J. A. S. (1982) *Human Motor Behavior: An Introduction*, Hillsdale, NJ: Erlbaum.

MAGILL, R. A. (1989) *Motor Learning: Concepts and Applications*, 3rd edn, Dubuque, IA: Brown.

SCHMIDT, R. A. (1991) *Motor Learning and Performance: From Principles to Practice*, Champaign, IL: Human Kinetics.

Chapter 6

Sport in Context

(Social Psychology)

Introduction

Sport and social psychology have been on friendly terms for a long time. In fact the earliest ties stem from Triplett's now famous work with American cyclists in 1898, and throughout this century the relationship between the two subdisciplines has endured and prospered. Almost by definition social psychology, as the study of social behaviour and experience, is uniquely placed to be able to comprehend what is taking place during sporting occasions of almost all types. With very few exceptions (such as at one extreme, the single-handed round-the-world sailor, at the other extreme the Super Nintendo fanatic!), sport involves social interaction, and accordingly, many of the concerns of social psychologists in general have continued to interest sport psychologists. For example, very basic questions include how is our performance influenced by those around us, how do we explain the success and failure of ourselves and others, and what makes a good team or a good team member? It is these three questions which form the mainstays of this chapter.

Sport psychologists have run alongside social psychologists in trying to answer these and other questions. Sometimes they have been a little behind, sometimes in front, and sometimes both could be accused of wearing blinkers and thus being blinded to the other's presence. Bearing this in mind, the chapter will give a flavour of the sorts of social psychological questions which concern sport, and the answers which have been forthcoming. Within the confines of this single chapter it is not possible to sample the full range of work in this area. Fortunately, most sport psychology texts tend to focus a good deal of their attention on social psychological issues, and any one of a number of recent texts offer extensive reviews to which you could usefully turn for more information. Rather than simply summarizing this material, what we hope this chapter may demonstrate is the nature of the special relationship which exists between sport psychology and social psychology, and how this has influenced the current state of our knowledge.

Individual Differences in Sporting Contexts

Social Facilitation

The sport psychology literature dealing with the effects of others (whether as fellow competitors or spectators) on individual performance is considerable and stretches back at least as far as Triplett's fishing line experiment (Triplett, 1898). Triplett's work was later taken up by a great many social psychologists, and his experiment has since become enshrined within social psychology as a classic example of social facilitation research. There followed literally hundreds of human and animal studies of social facilitation, both in the field and the laboratory, and across this research the results have been generally consistent. In a nutshell, it is generally true that the presence of others leads to enhanced performance on certain tasks, and specifically tasks which call for well learnt, dominant responses. If you can do something well, the presence of others will improve performance. On the other hand, if you are incompetent, learning a skill or attempting something for the first time, then you may perform worse in company than alone. Social facilitation represents one of the most popular research paradigms in experimental social psychology, and continues to exercise the minds of many, both inside and outside sport (Geen, 1989).

One example taken from sport itself was a delightful field experiment involving men shooting pool in an American pool hall (Michaels *et al.*, 1982). Initially a sample of players were secretly rated as being of above or below average ability, on the basis of the percentage of their shots which were successful. Subsequently, groups of four stooges came and stood by the tables, as if just casually watching the game. In the presence of these spectators, above average players increased their shot accuracy from 71 to 80 per cent; the below-average players slipped from 36 to 25 per cent. To use sporting parlance, the good got going, the bad went off.

Although social facilitation has enjoyed a high profile in sport psychology textbooks and despite examples such as this field experiment, it is interesting that the number of cited studies which actually involve real-life sports is relatively small. Instead the research which is routinely referenced, or carried out by sport psychologists themselves, tends to be common to social psychology as a whole, with particular emphasis on motor learning and/or motor performance and normally involving isolated tasks in laboratory settings. The results of these experiments were often very predictable and the effect was shown to be robust. At the same time there was and is an understandable cry of 'so what?' because the crucial link to applied settings was rarely made successfully. The research could tell us something about how particular motor skills (e.g. balancing on a stabilometer) were influenced by specific variables (e.g. skill level, size of audience) but little about social facilitation involving the complex packages of skills which combine to produce sporting performance. Probably as a direct result of this problem, research interest declined throughout the 1980s. In the words of Diane Gill (1986:177),

> Perhaps the main reason sport psychologists have abandoned social facili-
> tation research is the failure to demonstrate any notable effects in real life

sporting settings. Although many social facilitation experiments were conducted in the 1960s and 1970s, the experimental variables were often
trivial . . . and the results of the few field investigations were disappointing.

How was it possible to deal with this impasse? Well, above all else there was a
need to look again at the theoretical underpinnings of the research, and to develop
more sophisticated and cognitively based models as to how others have an influence on
our behaviour (Landers, 1980). This has been a slow process and even by the 1990s
hard evidence of change is thin on the ground but at the same time there are
encouraging signs of better things to come. Traditionally, Zajonc's drive theory of social
facilitation (Zajonc, 1965) has been very prominent and is still routinely cited, albeit
with an increasing awareness of the limitations of this approach (Wankel, 1984). In
many ways the endurance of Zajonc's work is to be expected given sport psychology's
longstanding preoccupation with the effects of arousal on performance. Indeed, arousal
models such as those derived from the inverted-U hypothesis (see Chapter 4) have
been applied to the interpretation of social facilitation effects. (As an aside it is
interesting to note that the PhD dissertation of Rainer Martens (1969), who later
became so prominent in competitive anxiety research, dealt with motor skills and
audience effects.)

Despite the simple appeal of Zajonc's argument that the mere presence of others
increases arousal and hence causes social facilitation, his primary thesis did not remain
unchallenged for long (Cottrell, 1968). Since the 1970s, support was gradually eroded in
the light of accumulating empirical evidence that it is not merely presence itself but the
type of presence which is significant. More specifically, social facilitation effects increase
in proportion to the extent that we feel we are being evaluated by those around us,
whether these are spectators or fellow competitors. Even accomplished performers may
crack when playing in front of a crowd, home or away, which they know has high
expectations (Baumeister and Steinhilber, 1984). It is now accepted that evaluation
apprehension is the key to social facilitation, although the larger 'why' questions still
remain more elusive. At the present time, a number of different explanations are in
competition (Harkins and Szymanski, 1987). Evaluation apprehension has been variously linked to terms such as heightened self-awareness, self-consciousness, self-
presentational concern, self-monitoring or self-attention. Precisely how each of these
concepts relates, or is distinguishable from the others, is not clear. To some authors, social
facilitation still relates to drive and our ability to monitor others, to others it relates to
attentional overload, to others attentional shift, and to others attentional conflict
(Harkins and Szymanski, 1987: 171). At this point, rather than becoming drawn into a
rather futile discussion of subtle differences in the use of terminology, it is probably best
to conclude that social facilitation research now recognizes the psychological impact of
different sorts of audiences and coactors, and this recognition has helped us begin to
understand, for example, how home and away crowds can have differential and complex
effects on performance (Benjafield *et al.*, 1989).

It has taken some time but finally theory has begun to catch up with empirical
research, and perhaps as a consequence, this material now sits more comfortably
alongside a general discussion of social influence processes as a whole. This discussion
encompasses terms such as conformity, compliance and obedience, terms which at one
time were neatly and conveniently compartmentalized but which are increasingly seen in
a more holistic and integrative framework of analysis. These changes also reflect upon a
long and tortuous self-examination of the nature of social psychological enquiry, ending

with a recognition that a reductionist and an individualistic approach to understanding social phenomena had been getting us nowhere fast for a long time.

Social Loafing

The lowering of artificial barriers between social phenomena is also revealed in recent research relating social facilitation to social loafing. Social loafing is a term with a history nearly as long as social facilitation. In 1913, a French agricultural engineer called Max Ringelmann discovered that on average, one man pulling on a rope alone was likely to exert over twice as much pull (an average of 63 kilograms) as when his efforts were combined as part of a team of eight (31 kilograms). Even when later ingenious experimental designs were able to measure individual effort directly, uncontaminated by the effects of coordination losses (for example, Ingham *et al.*, 1974), a substantial residual effect was still found which must reflect upon a personal, motivational deficit. This deficit, the Ringelmann effect or social loafing, is defined as the reduction of individual effort when working as part of a group or team (Latané *et al.*, 1979), and quite naturally has been and still is the subject of close attention by sport psychologists (Hardy, 1990).

A substantial literature, again chiefly based on laboratory tasks, demonstrates that many factors will impact upon the extent of social loafing (Hardy and Crace, 1991). These factors include the size of the group, the identifiability of individual effort, the strength of group identity, the nature and attractiveness of the task, the degree of trust between group members, the interdependence of group members, the extent of involvement with the group, group cohesiveness, intergroup comparisons and personal responsibility. Obviously the extent of overlap between a great many of these factors is considerable and this web of interaction reflects in the theoretical explanations which have been offered (Widmeyer *et al.*, 1992). Indeed almost as many explanations have been advanced to explain why people should social loaf as how they do it. Theories and models have focused on one or more of the factors mentioned above. Some concentrate on the psychological, and perhaps subconscious, consequences of placing people in situations where they know their efforts are not easy to identify and where they are not being personally evaluated. Following from Latané's early work in this area, social impact theory, coupled with the notion of diffusion of responsibility, still enjoys considerable popularity. The principal argument here is that, even allowing for large variations in personal commitment to the task, in a group we feel able to share responsibility with other group members and this may well lead to a diminution of effort. Other commentators, who perhaps have been more influenced by social exchange models of social behaviour, emphasize the strategies which people will use to 'get by' in groups. It is assumed that we are motivated to exert the minimum effort for the maximum reward, otherwise referred to as free riding or, more politely, the allocation strategy (Widmeyer *et al.*, 1992). Yet others place greater emphasis on group cohesiveness, arguing that the more closely we identify with the group, the less likely we are to loaf (Hogg, 1992).

From amongst all these competing theories there may be a natural tendency to try to find a winner, the theory which best fits the facts. This enterprise is unlikely to be rewarding as this competitive model of science, grounded in the physical sciences, is clearly inappropriate in the case of social psychology. Following on directly from a re-evaluation of the nature of social psychological enquiry, in all probability we will have to adopt a less cut and dried view of the social world. However difficult it may be for those with a background in the physical, human and natural sciences, we must learn to accept that various theories are able to complement each other in providing a comprehensive account of the different ways in which people are influenced by those around them. Whether this is labelled as social facilitation, social loafing or just plain social influence is of relatively small importance. In this spirit of analysis, over recent years authors such as Harkins and Szymanski (1987) and Mullen and Baumeister (1987) have discussed social loafing and social facilitation not in splendid isolation but side by side, as two faces of the same coin. To Harkins and Szymanski, the emphasis is on the effects of evaluation by either self or others; Mullen and Baumeister focus on self-attention theory and our self-awareness in a variety of social contexts. What is entirely laudable in both cases is not only their willingness to transcend the traditional boundaries between social psychological 'themes' but also the fact that both openly acknowledge that their contributions do not stand alone but must be considered alongside alternative and complementary theoretical perspectives. This spirit of deconstructionism may sit uneasily with many but at least it offers a more productive way forward. Perhaps in the longer term, through an acceptance of complexity and complementarity, this may open the door to the development of multifaceted theories, models and frameworks which are genuinely capable of interpreting everyday sporting situations.

Playing at Home

Standing as a counter-example to the general shortage of literature which is of direct relevance to real-life sporting events, there is one practical issue which has attracted considerable interest, namely the effects of home advantage on team performance. Intuitively we would probably believe that playing at home brings an immediate advantage, and an interesting archival literature is available dealing with the playing records of teams drawn from a variety of sports over the years. For example, Schwartz and Barsky (1977) collated and catalogued the results of literally thousands of professional games. They found home advantage in the major American sports of baseball (53 per cent home wins), ice hockey (64 per cent), American football (60 per cent) and basketball (64 per cent). Likewise Edwards (1979) found in a variety of sports, including both college (59 per cent home wins) and professional American football (54 per cent home wins), and professional baseball (56 per cent home wins) that home advantage held, and was most noticeable for those teams which were already on a tide of success.

As expected, this effect does appear to be dependent on a number of factors (Courneya and Carron, 1991) including the types of behaviour associated with a particular sport. For example, Glamser (1990) found professional English soccer players from a particular club were more likely to be either booked or sent off the further from home they played. Similarly, Varca (1980) found that American professional basketball players displayed 'functionally aggressive behaviour' at home, whereas away players were more likely to exhibit 'dysfunctionally aggressive behaviour', that is they accumulated more recorded fouls. (Whether referees were more likely to call foul against away players was not investigated but must surely be a significant factor here.)

In addition, the nature and size of the crowd, as well as the design of the venue itself also play their part. Certain stadia are renowned for their intimidating atmosphere, and the home advantage which is assumed to accompany this atmosphere. One example from rugby union was Cardiff Arms Park (before it was renamed the National Stadium), a ground which visiting teams traditionally regarded as affording the Welsh a 10-point advantage before a ball was touched. Other sporting venues, usually involving not team but individual sports, are regarded as 'user friendly' for all competitors. One example from track athletics is Bislett in Norway which élite athletes routinely include in their end of season itinerary as it has a reputation as a record breaking track. This particular stadium is regarded as being 'tight', with tight bends and spectators virtually down to track side. How these design features, or the running surface itself, specifically facilitate athletic performance (or indeed how social facilitation influences runners in both sprints and middle distance races) has yet to be considered systematically but in some respects the records and Bislett's reputation possibly speak for themselves.

In terms of the nature of the crowd, predictably research shows that verbally aggressive crowds have been shown to have a more powerful inhibitory effect on away teams (Greer, 1983). When we also consider the previous literature on evaluation effects, then obviously the expertise as well as the intimacy of the crowd, both home and away, will each play their part in determining performance. Moving beyond the home advantage hypothesis and with these thoughts in mind, recent authors have begun to describe a less simple relationship between success and venue. Baumeister and Steinhilber (1984) considered the history of baseball and basketball results and found that home advantage disappeared in the latter stages of major competitions. Benjafield *et al.* (1989) took this work further and found an even more complex relationship. They relied upon similar data to those used by Baumeister and Steinhilber, including World Series baseball games between 1924 and 1982, NBA (basketball) playoffs between 1967 and 1982, and NHL (ice hockey) Stanley Cup games between 1968 and 1988. Overall they found home advantage did appear to be in evidence in deciding games, but the exception was when the team was defending a title. That is, recurrent champions were performing in front of fans whose expectations were high, self-attention was therefore raised, and there was more chance of a team cracking under the pressure. In the light of this finding, it would be interesting to speculate as to whether the passionate, knowledgeable and increasingly evaluative Welsh crowd in Cardiff has helped or hindered the Welsh rugby team during the leaner years of the late 1980s and 1990s.

Team Dynamics

For the sport psychologist with an interest in team dynamics, there have long been rich pickings lying waiting within social psychology. Small group research has been a mainstay of experimental social psychology for decades, bringing together traditions which have long roots embedded in both sociological and psychological social psychology. To give an example of the breadth of this literature, the reference list included with Forsyth's (1990) comprehensive introductory text on group processes extends to over 1800 citations, many of which are primary source articles based on empirical research with small groups. Not surprisingly, a considerable number of themes have been explored over the years, including most prominently the work on group decision making, communication networks, social influence, group structures, conflict, cooperation and competition, group dynamics, role differentiation and leadership. A sport team is one clear cut example of a small, discrete group, and sport psychologists have not been slow to recognize the value of small group research for understanding team processes. They have also not been reticent in selectively borrowing and using this material when appropriate or expedient (Carron, 1988). This has been an active process of filtering however, or at least active in the sense that only certain lines of enquiry have been pursued. Unfortunately the quality control which has operated in terms of sifting though the good and the not-so-good in these selected fields has not always been of the highest order. For this reason perhaps as much as any other, there is some dissatisfaction with the current state of the science (Widmeyer *et al.* 1992: 176), with criticism levelled against the atheoretical nature of much group research, the reliance on univariate statistical procedures which do not permit an appreciation of interacting variables, together with the under representation of longitudinal research in the literature and the focus on team sports to the exclusion of all other sports' groups (for example classes, committees and boards).

Widmeyer, Brawley and Carron name three areas which they regard as the most significant for sport practitioners. These are group size, group composition and group cohesion. Apart from a few recent articles by these authors themselves (see Widmeyer *et al.*, 1992), there is virtually no sport psychology literature dealing specifically with group size or group composition. If sport psychologists are committed to exploring these issues in more detail, they should take warning from the methodological nightmares which confronted social psychologists who endeavoured to consider size and heterogeneity effects in small groups, and quickly realized that the combinations and permutations of members of even groups of five made the feasibility of empirical research extremely difficult.

As regards group cohesion, then here sport psychology has made a very valuable research contribution, and particularly in terms of the effects of cohesiveness and team maturity on performance. Interestingly, it is only recently that this contribution has been recognized within social psychology (Hogg, 1992), one of several occasions where mainstream psychology has in the past ignored the potential which sport psychology may have for advancing the common stock of psychological knowledge. In comparison with other branches of sport psychology, the number of active 'group' researchers is relatively small in sport psychology, although their work does enjoy a high profile. For example, almost all sport psychology texts from the mid-1980s contain chapters devoted to group processes. In addition, a book solely devoted to group dynamics in sport appeared in 1988 (Carron, 1988), and in 1990, the prestigious *International Journal of Sport Psychology* devoted an entire issue to 'The Group in Sport and Physical Activity' (Volume 21, Number 4), again edited by the Canadian sport psychologist Albert Carron. This issue included articles on group composition, group size, social loafing, leadership, group cohesion and collective efficacy. These articles reveal precisely where the primary focus of interest lies in sport psychology, although once more they also highlight the paucity of research in certain areas and the underdevelopment of theoretical frameworks. To avoid simply reiterating findings obtained from general social psychology, this chapter deals only with those topics where a substantial body of sport related research exists, namely group cohesion and social loafing (see above), with the leadership research covered more extensively in Chapter 7.

Team Cohesion and Team Spirit

Research dealing with team cohesion (alternatively called cohesiveness), or indeed group atmosphere in general, is fascinating for many reasons. Not least this work stands as an example of the quirky relationship between scientific knowledge and common sense. Social psychological research has repeatedly found that what makes an effective group is far removed from what 'common sense' tells us should be the case, but amazingly the message repeatedly fails to make its mark on popular consciousness. We appear to be strongly conditioned to respect group decisions, to assume that two heads will be better than one, and that within sport, the team which drinks together will be the team which plays and wins together. By way of support for this argument, over recent years a large and lucrative industry has developed to provide 'team building' courses for business managers. Often these courses use outdoor adventure training to foster team spirit, with very little regard to the true mechanics of group development or the actual relationship between group atmosphere and performance. Instead they are underpinned by what common sense tells us is the truth, that tight management teams are good management teams.

Sport has not been immune from this influence. A commonly held belief amongst coaches and players alike is that a tight, cohesive sports team will be a successful team. Indeed psychologists have added fuel to this fire by stressing the need for coaches to emphasize team goals rather than individual aspirations (for example, Zander, 1975). As a consequence of these and similar influences, many practising sport psychologists still believe that their primary task remains to engender good team spirit. In reality the answer is not so simple, and there is a good deal of research which has begun to help us unravel the complexities of the relationship between team cohesion and performance. This research reveals a number of significant points. First, that many factors interact to determine group cohesion. Second, that cohesion does not always predict team success but more often success may predict cohesion. Third, that the concept of cohesion is multifaceted, and finally, that measurement of cohesion itself then presents major difficulties. Each of these issues will now be explored in turn.

In terms of the determination of group or team cohesion, numerous factors have been identified as playing a part (Carron, 1988; Mudrack, 1989), including group size, propinquity (i.e. physical proximity) between members, the costs incurred in joining the group, leadership styles, competition, success and similarity. The final factor, similarity, has been the focus of a great deal of interest, with some authors arguing that similarity encourages cohesiveness (Eitzen, 1975) while others maintain that it may inhibit healthy group development (Janis, 1982) while others ignore the issue entirely. In a recent meta-analysis incorporating over 200 studies, Anthony *et al.* (1992) found that there was a tendency for groups which were made up of similar members to be more cohesive, although this was more true of laboratory than real groups, and the effect was also dependent on group size. Overall the strength of the relationship was described as 'significant but weak', thereby indicating that the issue has yet to be satisfactorily resolved.

Within sport psychology, Carron (1982) has been most influential in developing our understanding of how team cohesion develops (the antecedents of cohesion), what it is (defining cohesion), and how it subsequently influences group and individual performance (the consequences of cohesion). In terms of antecedents, Carron distinguishes between four sets of determinants, namely situational (for example size, organizational orientation), personal (for example gender, similarity, personality), leadership (for example coach and captaincy styles of management) and team (for example ability, achievement orientation, experience, stability and maturity).

As regards dimensions of cohesion itself, Carron makes the important distinction between task cohesion (or group integration) which refers to how well the group or team operates as a working unit, and social cohesion (or individual attraction) which refers to how well members like each other and the extent of team identity. Finally, regarding consequences, Carron distinguishes between group outcomes (team performance, group stability) and individual outcomes (satisfaction, individual performance). Despite the usefulness of this general framework, very few parts of the model have actually been tested empirically. In reality by far the greatest attention has been devoted to the relationship between cohesion and performance. The nature of this relationship is problematic to say the least but where an association has been found it has tended to hinge solely upon task cohesion, and social cohesion does not appear to enter into the equation. In later work, Carron and his co-workers (Widmeyer *et al.*, 1992) establish yet finer distinctions between terms and specifically how cohesion is perceived by team members. Four categories of perceptions are described, with the two major categories (group integration; individual attractions to the group) each subdivided into task and social domains. 'Group integration' is defined as members' perceptions of the group as a totality, while 'individual attractions to the group', as the name suggests, represents each members' personal attractions to the group. To date this formulation has been most significant not in generating primary research but in helping to develop a multidimensional measure of group cohesion, the Group Environment Questionnaire or GEQ (Widmeyer *et al.*, 1985).

It would be fair to say that despite the high level of interest in measurement and in theoretical debate, with few exceptions (for example, Spink, 1990; Williams and Widmeyer, 1991) primary sport-related research is sparse and yet discussion continues to return to the relationship between sporting success and cohesiveness (Carron, 1988). The conclusions which have been reached from sport research have been equivocal to say the least. On the one hand, studies of team sports, including basketball, American football, soccer, volleyball and baseball, at various times have shown that the success of teams can depend more on cohesion than skill level of individual members (see Gill, 1986: 226). However other research has shown the contrary, and that conflict and rivalry within a team can be a spur to success, or can drive individual team members to great things. One example of this was the West German rowing eight in the 1960s, who were on the point of breaking up because of internal disputes and yet went on to win the Olympic gold in 1968 (Lenk, 1969). A further example would be the Carrera team's victory in road cycling's Giro d'Italia in 1987. The Carrera team had decided that the Italian Roberto Visentini was to be their principal rider, given the race was based in Italy. The in-form Irish team member, Stephen Roche, was decidedly unhappy with this decision but then confounded the pundits by winning the trophy for Carrera despite being unpopular within a highly fractured team, and despite the verbal and indeed physical interventions from a partisan Italian crowd. The recent history of Formula One racing also contains countless examples of team conflicts which have not reflected in team failures, except where those conflicts directly influenced how team members 'came together' (quite literally in the case of Ayrton Senna and Alain Prost) in incidents during a race.

The literature continues to struggle with the relationship between cohesion and performance, albeit with growing awareness of the subtleties of debate. Above all else, the direction of causality remains questionable — does cohesion engender success or does success engender cohesion? Very recently group cohesion has been the subject of a timely meta-analysis, an analysis which included sports teams alongside other small group research (Mullen and Cooper, 1992) and included reference to over 200 studies in total. This analysis concluded that a cohesion–effectiveness relationship does exist, and that it is often at its strongest amongst sport teams. Indeed the difference between sports teams and other non-sport real-life groups were so noticeable that the authors caution attempts at generalizing from one set of studies to the other. They also confirmed that the effect derives most significantly from task commitment or cohesion, and not from social or interpersonal cohesion, a further example of the need to confront complexity. A final conclusion derived from a select sample of longitudinal studies, and one which is very important in the context of this discussion is that 'the stronger direction of effect seems to be from performance to cohesiveness, and not from cohesiveness to performance'. This is not to argue that cohesion cannot influence performance but that the performance to cohesion link is the more definite, a conclusion endorsed by other sport psychologists and social psychologists.

Looking at this literature as a whole, three factors emerge as vital in any discussion of cohesion. First, the type of sport or the type of task obviously mediates any effects. The more that the sport requires that team members must rely on each other and are interdependent (*interactive sports*) then the more significant cohesion is likely to be (Carron, 1988). In other sports where athletes may represent the same team but individual performance does not depend on team work (*coacting sports*) then the research shows team cohesion is less important in determining outcome. With an awareness of how important sporting context is likely to be, over recent years attempts have been made to classify sports according to where they fall along some notional continuum between being predominantly a coacting sport, or being an interacting sport (Cratty, 1983). The implicit assumption is that these two constructs, coaction or interaction, occupy opposite extremes along a continuum and hence are inversely related — high on coacting (that is low-means interdependent tasks) automatically implies low on interacting (that is high-means interdependent tasks). The authors suggest that this implicit model needs to be subjected to closer scrutiny, for these two dimensions may not be related at all but indeed may be independent. Therefore some sports may be both highly interactive and coactive (for example rowing, tug-of-war), whereas some may be highly interactive but involve less identifiable coaction (for example volleyball). Others may be low on both dimensions (for example fell running, chess) and yet others may be coactive but not interactive (for example archery, bowls). Certainly the more that players are interdependent on each other, and ultimately the team's performance is a reflection on the synergy or coordinated action of the team, then the more salient cohesion will be, and in order to be able to genuinely apply research to sport itself then this issue of how to categorize sports must remain high on sport psychology's agenda.

In reviewing this material, a second point always to bear in mind from social psychology is the downside or the negative effects of high team cohesion. Group research of various kinds, from traditional conformity experiments through to the varied literature dealing with group decision making (Forsyth, 1990), reveals that the tighter or more cohesive the group, the less likely it is that people will be motivated to express their individuality. In team sports, one consequence may be that players may all perform to the same standard and thus minimize intragroup competition. On the one hand, this may encourage high levels of cooperation amongst players. On the other, this self-determined norm may not always be of the highest standard. This work also suggests that the more pressure a team is under, for example following a string of defeats, the more team members will be inclined to turn inwards and rate their behaviour in comparison with their teammates (Festinger, 1954).

The final point concerns how to proceed given a recognition that cohesion is multifaceted, and that earlier research consistently neglected to appreciate that fact (Mudrack, 1989). In the light of more sophisticated descriptions of the concept itself, measures of cohesion in turn are now far more sophisticated. Sport psychologists have undoubtedly been at the cutting edge in terms of developing measures of team cohesion. The four most significant measures are described briefly below, although it must be pointed out that the psychometric properties of some of these scales, together with the theoretical bases are still somewhat contentious (Hogg, 1992) and they should be used with due caution.

Team Cohesiveness Measures

Sports Cohesiveness Questionnaire (SCQ). Seven-item scale developed by Martens *et al.* (1972) from earlier eight-item scale, traditionally the most popular measure and still routinely used to measure interpersonal attraction, personal power, value of membership, sense of belonging, enjoyment, teamwork and closeness.

Team Cohesion Questionnaire (TCQ). A 13-item scale used to consider seven domains (team performance satisfaction, self-performance satisfaction, value of membership, leadership, task cohesion, desire for recognition and affiliation cohesion) (Gruber and Gray, 1982).

Multidimensional Sport Cohesion Instrument (MSCI). A 22-item, 11-point response scale, yielding four scores (attraction to the group, sense of purpose, quality of teamwork, valued roles) (Yukelson *et al.*, 1984).

Group Environment Questionnaire (GEQ). An 18-item Likert scale, yielding four scores (group integration — task, group integration — social, individual attractions to the group — task, individual attractions to the group — social) (Widmeyer *et al.*, 1985).

In a call to arms, or more correctly a call for more research, Widmeyer *et al.* (1992) argue that far more sport based research is needed and that this research must have strong roots in theory, adopt a longitudinal perspective, use multivariate analyses and look at a wide range of groups in sport and not simply competitive teams. Whether such a research strategy will come close to unravelling the intricacies of the relationship between team dynamics, including cohesion, and actual performance remains to be seen, but once more, a due recognition of complexity is a step along the way.

Membership Continuity and Team Development

A closely related literature concerns the maturity of teams, and the influence of group development on team performance. Within social psychology, stage models of group development now enjoy widespread acceptance, with the early work of Tuckman (Tuckman and Jensen, 1977) still very much to the fore as a framework within which various group processes are identified. Tuckman described group development in terms of four basic stages. The group initially gets together and works through the somewhat formal orientation stage (forming). Next, there may well be heightened tension associated with role differentiation and competition for status and influence (storming), before norms, rules and standards of behaviour begin to stabilize (norming). Finally, the group will have matured to a stage where it is able to work together as a unit (performing). Clearly this all takes time, and when personnel change any group or team has to work through the process afresh, and performance will invariably suffer in this period of readjustment.

Despite the obvious relevance of such formulations for team sports, and the significance of group development in general for understanding performance in sports involving a high degree of interdependence, there has been a real scarcity of sport-related research since the 1970s dealing with group development and performance. During that decade a number of significant archival studies set the scene by identifying the relationship between team maturity and success. Research using data derived from sports such as soccer, baseball, basketball and gymnastics demonstrated that turnover rates and performance were negatively related, and also showed large differences between sports in terms of the time taken to reach maturity and then the period for which good teams stayed at the top. For example, Loy *et al.* (1978) cite a breakdown of results of American football teams in the National Football League between 1955 and 1959, by length of member tenure within the team. Those with mature teams (2.25 years or more average playing experience per player) had a winning record some 17 percentage points higher than those with young teams (less than 2.25 years). The effective half-life of successful teams is likely to depend on many factors including the age of players, the type of sport and various facets of group dynamics including cohesiveness and role differentiation. However, these issues remain largely unexplored and there must be tremendous scope, from both a practical and a theoretical viewpoint, to develop longitudinal research programmes in this area.

Social Cognition

Over recent years, social psychology on both sides of the Atlantic has come to regard social cognition as being at the heart of any analysis or interpretation of social behaviour and experience. Within social psychology, the early work of Bartlett on memory and Heider on naive psychology was crucial in setting the scene for the more recent flurry of activity. The term social cognition loosely embraces a wide range of material including that dealing with attribution processes, personal construct theory, social representations, stereotyping and social categorization, schema and self-schema, and knowledge structures, indeed all ways in which we internally represent and construe our social world (Fiske and Taylor, 1991). Sport psychology has long had an interest in one particular aspect of social cognition, causal attribution, and this continues to occupy a position of prominence within the discipline. At the same time, those with an interest in participation and exercise motivation are finding that the models which guide their research rely more and more heavily on social cognitive frameworks. These include Bandura's self-efficacy theory, Harter's work on perceived competence, and Ajzen and

Fishbein's theory of reasoned action (see McAuley, 1992). Indeed Edward McAuley sees Bandura's work as complementing attribution theories in providing an understanding of how our self-perceptions relate to causal attributions, although within sport psychology such integrative work remains very much in its infancy.

Sport psychology as a whole is increasingly coming to recognize the important mediating role which social cognition plays in framing sporting experiences, and it is noteworthy that during the early 1990s a growing number of research enterprises are introducing concepts derived directly from social cognition (for example Kendziereski, 1990). However, this does not represent genuinely pioneering work for one branch of social cognition occupies a well established niche in sport psychology, that being causal attribution.

Causal Attribution in Sport

Theories of causal attribution deal with how we interpret and understand our world, and have been well tried in a range of sports contexts for a great many years. Some of the most fundamental questions which are of interest to sport concern the attributions associated with success and failure, embedded in a wider discussion of achievement motivation. Interest really began in earnest in the early 1970s, following from the work of Bernard Weiner, and it is this work which continues to dominate discussion to the present day. Weiner's primary concern was not with sporting but academic success and failure. Fortuitously, with so many sport psychologists coming from a background not in psychology but in education, this work transferred painlessly and quickly to sport. Working from Fritz Heider's original formulations (Heider, 1958), in the first place Weiner placed the four major attribution elements, namely ability, effort, task difficulty and luck, into one of four cells of a two-by-two matrix, as shown in Figure 6.1 (derived from Weiner, 1972).

The two dimensions which were originally used to differentiate between these attributional factors were stability and locus of control, and ordinarily each was simply dichotomized to yield a two-by-two matrix. So, for example, effort was classified as an unstable, internal factor. More recently, and in the face of mounting criticism levelled against classification and misclassification problems, the two-by-two matrix has been elaborated upon to include other factors such as practice and fitness (unstable, internal) and environmental conditions (unstable, external). Subsequently the entire approach has been revised substantially by Weiner himself, who has now added a third dimension, namely controllability. This revision necessitated renaming locus of control as locus of causality to avoid confusion, although the construct remained essentially the same. The new dimension, controllability, refers to the extent to which the behaviour is either seen to be within the control of the individual, or reflects on outside factors (for example, the opposition), while causality refers to the extent to which the individual believes that he or she has control over internal factors in the first place. The distinction between these two dimensions is obviously quite subtle and continues to cause considerable difficulties (Biddle, 1988).

These difficulties aside, the two-by-two matrix has now been extended to a two-by-two-by-two matrix (see Biddle, 1993), usually represented as a three-dimensional cube

Figure 6.1: Weiner's Attribution Model

Locus of Control

	Internal	External
Stable	ABILITY	TASK DIFFICULTY
Unstable	EFFORT	LUCK

Stability

Source: Derived from Weiner (1986)

with controllability (split into controllable and uncontrollable), locus of causality (still represented as internal and external) and stability (stable and unstable) along the three axes of a cube (albeit with a tacit acceptance that it is impossible to fill all eight possible cells given the overlap between controllability and causality).

Despite unresolved methodological and theoretical problems with this model, Weiner's basic ideas continue to hold considerable appeal to sport psychologists, operating from both a practical and a research perspective. Pragmatically, through interview or more formal assessment procedures an applied sport psychologist would be able to determine if his/her client is favouring particular attributional styles and could then use intervention strategies so as to let the individual derive greater psychological satisfaction for success (perhaps by describing success and achievements with reference to stable, internal and controllable factors). Failures can also be redefined in ways which may be less psychologically damaging or which will at least present optimistic ways forward (for example, through training and coaching recommendations). A major methodological problem here is that it is the sport psychologist who must translate and then assign the athlete's attributions to one of the cells of the matrix, largely irrespective of whether or not the person has such convenient pigeonholes in their own mind. To try to go some way towards addressing this problem, Russell (1982) developed the Causal Dimension Scale (CDS) whereby athletes are asked to describe their own reasons why they believe events occurred and then he or she rates this reason or cause in terms of Weiner's three attribution dimensions, controllability, causality and stability. Again, an implicit assumption here is that we always attribute events to causes, and yet research indicates that this may not invariably be true.

Scanning the sport psychology literature on causal attribution even the casual reader is likely to be surprised by the amount of work which has taken place in sport. Given the scope of this literature there is neither the time nor the space to present anything other than a very brief sketch of the most significant research findings. For more detailed information, you are recommended to turn to Stuart Biddle's comprehensive recent review (Biddle, 1993). A number of general conclusions emerge from this and other recent review articles. First, probably the single most popular topic to be empirically investigated continues to be related to what is known as the self-serving attributional bias hypothesis. This hypothesis suggests that we are inclined to attribute success to internal causes, and to blame failure on external factors. From a meta-analysis of 22 sport related studies, Mullen and Riordan (1988) found evidence to suggest that successful performance was more likely to be attributed to stable, internal factors (such as ability), especially in sports involving larger teams and where the attributions related to team performance. At the same time there was little evidence to suggest that failure was attributed to external factors (task difficulty or luck). The only gross conclusion which it is possible to reach from this work is that we tend not to be entirely logical in how we attribute success and failure but that we may often subconsciously make internal attributions and thus reward ourselves for success; this is especially true of younger athletes who are thus better able to protect their egos from the psychological consequences of failure (Whitley and Frieze, 1985).

To those sport psychologists with an interest in psychometrics, the next logical research step had to be the development of scales or measures of athletes' attributional styles. One recent example is the Sport Attributional Style Scale (SASS) which asks athletes to generate causes for eight positive and eight negative events, and then to rate each in terms of five attribution dimensions (internality, stability, globality, controllability and intentionality) (Hanrahan *et al.*, 1989). To date, apart from these same authors' initial tests of internal consistency, construct validity and test–retest reliability, the scale remains untested and has generated little published research. We would predict that this is unlikely to remain the case for long, given that the existing attribution literature once more reflects sport psychology's preoccupation with individual differences. This interest has extended in a variety of ways, for example looking at attributional differences in terms of culture, age, gender and type of involvement, and the relationship with other personality dimensions including self-esteem and learned helplessness (Biddle, 1993). It could be presumed that the considerable attention afforded to actor–observer differences (where actors tend to attribute their own behaviour to external causes while observers tend to attribute others' behaviour to internal factors) in attribution research within social psychology as a whole would reflect in similar interest within sport psychology. However, with very few exceptions (for example, Grove *et al.*, 1991) this rich research seam has remained unexploited.

One area which has attracted somewhat more attention from sport psychologists is that dealing with the relationship between causal attribution and emotion or affective state. In his review, Biddle cites nine articles derived from sport psychology, and concludes that emotional processing (perhaps another expression for job satisfaction) involves the outcome (success, failure and individual performance), intuitive appraisal (immediate evaluation of performance), reflective appraisal (later evaluation of performance) and attribution dimensions (whether the result is attributed to internal or external factors). The relationship is far from straightforward but intuitive appraisal and attributions appear to play the major roles such that 'a major predictor of sport emotion is the intuitive appraisal (performance satisfaction) but with attributions accounting for significant additional variance' (Biddle, 1993: 452).

Undoubtedly attribution research will continue to enjoy a prominent position within sport psychology, and the cross fertilization of ideas between sport research and other fields, most especially education, will ensure that model development continues apace. However, there is a need to proceed with some caution in the light of very general and possibly insurmountable criticism of attribution research from within social psychology as a whole. Here, attribution theories are increasingly labelled and castigated for, amongst other things, presenting far too individualistic and nomothetic (i.e. searching for generalities in behaviour) a view of social cognition. Their inability to accommodate huge individual differences have led many authors to conclude that in the past attribution theories have been afforded too high a profile and now they should be embedded more deeply within a general social cognitive framework, as simply one facet of human information processing. The impact of this debate on sport psychology has yet to be truly felt but it will be interesting to watch the coming years.

This point should never detract from the growing significance of social cognition as a perspective within sport psychology, whether in relation to gender schema, stereotypes in sport, participation motivation or whatever. Here as elsewhere, the evergrowing appreciation of our complexity and sophistication as infomation processors ensures that social cognitive research is here to stay.

Spectators

The majority of this chapter, and indeed the book as a whole, considers psychology in sport with the emphasis firmly on those who actually participate in the sport itself. This is a reflection on sport psychology's priorities. However, we should never ignore the fact that millions of people have an involvement with sport which is extremely intense and time consuming and yet they may never have kicked a ball, run on an athletics track or seen the inside of a snooker hall. The majority of those who would identify themselves as sport psychologists have rarely turned their attention either to the behaviour of spectators or how spectators perceive their sport. In contrast, sport sociologists have a long history of spectator research, albeit with a particular emphasis on fan violence (Young, 1991). For some reason this literature rarely receives attention in standard sport psychology texts. This could be because the methodologies which have been used have tended not to be experimental but have usually been a combination of the historical, observational and qualitative. An exception to this rule is found within European sport psychology, where fan violence in particular is accorded due attention (see 'Aggression and Violence in Sport' later in this chapter). European ideas have not always travelled well across the Atlantic, hence it was encouraging to note a recent article by Murrell and Dietz (1992) of the University of Pittsburgh which dealt with the relationship between fan support and group identity. The authors used Tajfel's Social Identity Theory (SIT) (Tajfel, 1981) to explain the way in which a common group identity amongst university students predicted fan support for university teams.

In terms of spectator research as a whole, Iso-Ahola and Hatfield's book is exceptional amongst general sport psychology texts in having a chapter devoted exclusively to the effects of athletics on spectators (Iso-Ahola and Hatfield, 1985, Chapter 14). Under two headings, 'Socialization into the role of sport consumer' and 'Attributional determinants of spectator sports attendance', the literature dealing with why people attend sports events and what they derive from their experience is reviewed. Briefly, the conclusions which the authors draw are first, that growing up in a sports culture (including the influence of peers, family, school and community) make it more likely that in turn individuals will become 'sports consumers'. Second, that spectators are drawn most powerfully towards contests between equal but successful teams. Third, that watching violent sport may decrease inhibitions against violence. Fourth, that fans personalize victory and 'bask in reflected glory', and finally, that external attribution biases psychologically insulate spectators from the pain of defeat, and internal biases make winning that much sweeter. The limited work available on actor–observer differences has already been dealt with; as to the other conclusions which are reached, while they may be valid they are hardly inspirational and it is perhaps little wonder that research in these areas is sparse.

This research apart, it has tended to be the case that spectator research has been reactive rather than proactive, often generated in response to social problems or even major disasters rather than accumulating slowly and progressively over time. Examples include the work associated with the 1986 Popplewell Inquiry into Crowd Safety and Control at Sports Grounds in the UK (see Canter *et al.*, 1989). This inquiry was set up following the tragic events in early 1985 including the West Stand fire at Bradford City Football Club and the Heysel stadium disaster in Brussels which led to 39 fatalities. In their book *Football in Its Place*, Canter *et al.* (1989) turn to 'environmental psychology' in order to explore a great many themes which they regard as relevant to the Popplewell Inquiry. These include stadium design, spectators' attitudes and experiences, soccer club cultures, crowd and emergency behaviour and violence in sport. While the book contains interesting factual information, from a theoretical or even a psychological point of view it does not attempt to offer a genuine framework for understanding. Instead it sets out positive conclusions in terms of the social and physical environment within which sport takes place; it is primarily a piece of *post hoc* action research. It has been the task of other authors, often outside the discipline of psychology, to tie these themes together into a coherent theoretical framework (see 'Aggression and Violence in Sport' later in this chapter).

Although these are very early days, work on social cognition is beginning to make some impact on spectator research. For example, Wann and Branscombe (1990) primed subjects by having them work on sentence construction tasks which were associated with either violent (boxing) or non-violent (golf) sports. When subjects subsequently watched an unrelated man's behaviour, those primed with the violent sport cues were more likely to construe his behaviour as aggressive. In a somewhat related vein, Long (1991) has recently provided an interesting discussion on the social perceptions of people in sport. Using some of the parlance of social cognition, he begins to outline a number of stereotypes or social images which he believes we carry with us when we watch sport. The stereotypes which he identifies, but does not even begin to substantiate, nevertheless appear to ring true.

The Dumb Jock

'The dumb jock could play many sports, but he [*sic*] is most likely to be linked with sports that require the greatest physical strength, size and aggressiveness.

American football, boxing, wrestling, weight lifting and ice hockey are well suited for the dumb jock but he may also be frequently found in basketball and baseball. He is rarely seen playing competitive golf, swimming, or at the tennis court because these sports are seen as employing less size and strength as major contributors to success.' (Long, 1991: 229)

The Flawed Hero

'There are numerous examples, fictional examples, and some well-known real life stories of the athlete who excels in his sport but falls short in some other area that is not necessarily intelligence. The flaw is often one related to the character of the individual. Perhaps he [*sic*] drinks, gambles, gets into bar fights, or has unfortunate personal relationships with the wrong sort of opposite sex. Some have referred to Mike Tyson, Pete Rose, Jim Thorpe, Babe Ruth, Steve Garvey, Billie Jean King and Billie Martin as examples of having one or more of the flaws.' (Long, 1991: 231-2).

The Superstar

'It is not enough to see the superstar as a truly superior athlete. To justify the superstar's success he [*sic*] must also be seen as having other outstanding qualities such as high moral character and a great personality. He should be a model for children and adults in every way. The true superstar may also be a super family man, community leader, and all round super person. If the male superstar is not married, he must then be a super bachelor like Joe Nameth at his peak.' (Long, 1991: 232)

Clearly there are considerable cultural variations in these stereotypes, and this study represents very much an early attempt but a valuable one nevertheless. For example, do the British have a cultural predisposition to want to flaw (or floor) their superstars? Anecdotal information would suggest this is the case, and surely such stereotypes could be examined in a more systematic way. This is yet another area where the potential for further research is considerable.

The Psychology of Officialdom

Spectators have been generally ignored but even they have received more attention than those people who make sport possible, that is the referees, judges, umpires, linesmen and sundry officials who form an integral and essential part of all sporting occasions. If it had not been for the role played by a Soviet linesman in allowing England's goal to stand in the 1966 World Cup Final then soccer history would have been different. If it had not been for the controversial actions of two officials at the start of the ill fated 1993 Grand National horse race, bets worth in excess of £75,000,000 would not have been declared void and the Chancellory of the Exchequer would have been £6,000,000 richer. With very few exceptions the 'men in the middle' remain very much on the sidelines of sport psychology. One such exception involved a survey of fans' attitudes to umpires prior to two major league baseball games in the US (Rainey *et al.*, 1990). Suffice it to say, ratings of umpires' performance were consistently low.

While this result is predictable, it is still interesting that the psychology of sports officialdom as a whole remains under researched. Perhaps the authority and power which their role assumes has served psychologically to distance officials from mere mortals who are able to feel precompetition anxiety, who are influenced by audience effects, whose decision making and risk taking strategies are open to scrutiny, and whose humanity makes or breaks so many sporting occasions. There is clearly a topic here for discussion by historians of science and sport sociologists; for sport psychologists there remains a large gap in our understanding of the sporting experience.

In terms of available literature, virtually no references to sports officials appear in standard sport psychology texts, nor in sport science abstracts. In 1990, Weinberg and Richardson co-authored a text entitled *Psychology of Officiating*. This represented a laudable attempt to partially fill the void and does present good advice to sports officials. This is clearly its primary function, to help officials cope with their job, but it is disappointing that the authors were able to draw on so few primary research sources in compiling this text. We live in hope that the second edition will not encounter such a problem, although the omens do not look good.

Violence and Aggression in Sport

The literature on violence and aggression conveniently divides in two. First, there is participants' aggression itself; second, there is spectator violence and including the effect of game behaviour on fans. With regard to the former, it may be assumed that this topic would yield a rich seam of interesting and worthwhile psychological insight. Unfortunately this is not always the case. Certainly there is a literature available on aggression and violence in sport but in the main this work tends to disappoint. According to Diane Gill (1986: 206), 'Many people have written about and discussed aggression in sport, but few have conducted systematic research on aggression in sport and exercise settings.' Why this is the case is a more difficult question to answer but two issues in particular present considerable obstacles to progress. In the first case, progress of any sort is bound to be difficult when there is confusion as to what is being studied in the first place. That is, how can we define aggression? This is not a problem peculiar to sport. Across psychology as a whole, the concept of aggression has never stood close scrutiny. According to the sport psychologists Bakker *et al.* (1990: 81–82), 'It is almost impossible to arrive at a decisive definition of aggression. The concept can be viewed as a personality trait, a learned habit or as a biological process. Intention or, on the contrary, consequences can be emphasised. Aggression can be expressed in socially acceptable or unacceptable forms.'

Having acknowledged the huge problems surrounding the question of how to define, most psychological definitions then normally proceed to incorporate both intention (motivation to harm, whether physically, mentally or emotionally) and outcome (behaviour rather than emotion or cognition). Sport psychologists can then find themselves impaled on the horns of a tricky dilemma for *the intention to hurt someone who is motivated to avoid such treatment* could actually be used to define competitive sport itself where athletes are normally motivated to win and therefore hurt the other person, the loser. Ergo, competitive sport is aggression!

This may seem a petty argument to pursue much further but behind this mischief there lurks a serious problem. That is, having recognized the impossibility of defining aggression adequately, we must then ask the question as to whether the concept is psychologically valid and whether aggression is genuinely distinguishable from other forms of social behaviour. This is not the occasion to delve further into these murky waters; instead we will simply acknowledge that the problem will never go away and then we will retreat to see how sport psychology has traditionally dealt with this elusive term, aggression.

As a way of avoiding this sort of academic conundrum, sport psychologists have tended to be selective, concentrating their attention on a restricted range of behaviours and specifically those which deliberately and illegally cause physical injury to another person. The justification for this stance is provided by the convenient distinction which the psychobiologist Moyer (1976) originally made between two forms of 'aggression', instrumental or rule governed aggression, and reactive or angry/hostile aggression. It is the latter, reactive aggression, which normally forms the focus of attention. Sport psychologists, along with sports writers in general, appear to find it difficult to avoid prefacing their work with ever more gory tales of blood and guts as evidence of the prevalence of violence in sport, and the albeit disputed claim (Young, 1991: 578) that 'sports related violence on and off the field is spiralling alarmingly.'

Where aggression appears in general sport psychology texts, authors also seem compelled to follow standard psychology texts in presenting various theories of aggression (usually psychoanalytic, ethological, drive [frustration–aggression hypothesis] and social learning) before quickly moving to a review of empirical work and thereby leaving most theoretical debate far behind. However, as most researchers appear loosely to adopt either the frustration–aggression hypothesis or a social learning perspective, it is inevitable that psychoanalysis, with its emphasis on instinctive drives, is presented as a counterpoint. Writing in the psychoanalytic tradition, Dervin (1991) argues that sport represents merely a cultivation or refinement of the aggressive instinct. In the first place, sports of all kinds represent a socially acceptable medium for displaying our basic destructive instincts. Freud would almost certainly have endorsed the Duke of Wellington's alleged comment that 'the battle of Waterloo was won on the playing fields of Eton'. Furthermore, psychoanalysts would go on to argue that without such playing fields there may well continue to be a great many more Waterloos.

This brings us to the second and most substantive psychoanalytic assumption, that without sport our aggressive tendencies would find vent in some other potentially more dangerous and life threatening pursuit, such as war. The evidence to support this idea of catharsis is difficult to find, either with reference to spectators or participants. Instead, sport psychology has considered either individual differences in reactive and instrumental aggression (the most popular measure of both being a shortened, 28-item version of the Bredemeier Athletic Aggression Inventory or BAAGI-S; Wall and Gruber, 1986), or how we are socialized to be aggressive in sport, and the specific factors which influence displays of predominantly reactive aggression. A great many variables have been shown to be associated with an increase in reactive aggression amongst competitors. These include whether a team or competitor is losing, playing away from home, the distance from home, the type of sport, current values and norms in that particular sport, and the importance of the game to the individual (Bakker *et al.*, 1990). It is noteworthy that the overwhelming majority of this research focuses on contact sports which already have some association with violence. High on this list are ice hockey and soccer, and the most common dependent variable which is measured, either through observation or archival research, is the number of fouls or rule infringements, which in turn must be influenced by the referee's interpretation of the laws.

Regarding fan violence and aggression, as previously mentioned sport sociologists have long had an interest in this field, as have European sport/social psychologists (Bakker *et al.*, 1990). Sport sociologists, and especially European writers such as Dunning (*et al.*, 1988), would argue that hooliganism and fan violence have a long and ignoble history certainly in Europe and particularly in Britain. At the same time, Kevin Young would also argue that North America has not been immune from what is euphemistically and incorrectly known as 'the British disease', but that North America's sports crowd disorders have been downplayed, primarily for political and economic reasons. One related example is a recent study by White (1989) which considered the incidence of murders in US cities which had American football teams through to the National Football League playoff games. He found that in those cities where the team lost a playoff, there was a subsequent increase in reported homicides in the following six days, however the crime rate remained unchanged if the team was successful.

Fan violence represents a classic example of a research area which is ripe for multidisciplinary research, and indeed it is very gratifying to see recent attempts at developing psychosocial models which draw on both sociological and psychological traditions and methodologies. Simons and Taylor (1992) have developed such a causal model, incorporating potentiating or general predisposing factors (socio-economic conditions, politics and geography, media influences and community norms), critical factors (social and personal identification, group solidarity, de-individuation, dehumanization of the opposition, leadership), on-field contributing factors (type of sport, modelling, score configuration and competitive events) and off-field contributing factors (alcohol, crowd density, frustration and role modelling). This model seems to provide an extremely useful framework for understanding fan violence at a great many levels of analysis, and sits easily with developments across social psychology as a whole.

The Way Forward

There has been a sea change in the relationship between sport and social psychology over the last few years. Sport psychology no longer unceremoniously borrows convenient ideas from social psychology in order to provide simple answers to complex social phenomena. Now the mood is shifting and, in common with social psychology as a whole, sport psychology is beginning to become more critical and self-reflective in recognition of the complexity of the social world. Sport psychologists are now willing to recognize the need to develop research methodologies and theoretical frameworks which can cope with a higher level of sophistication. Whether this recognition will act as a spur to future generations of sport psychologists, or as a discouragement, only time will tell.

Inevitably, it has only been possible to scratch the surface here but we hope that it is now obvious not only how much relevant research already exists in key areas but also the scope for development in others. Many sport psychologists pepper their work with pleas for more theory, and undoubtedly in certain areas the lack of adequate frameworks for understanding have certainly hindered progress. The varied work on social influence is a case in point. At the same time, this plea should not be a naïve cry for some ready-made theoretical panacea awaiting to cure all ills. This approach fails to recognize the role of theory in social psychology, and the fundamental nature of social psychological enquiry. In the past, many panaceas have been tried but far too often they have proved merely to be snake oils which flatter to deceive. To search for sovereign, grandiose theories with which to tie all loose ends together is to follow a false trail to enlightenment. This search goes against the grain of modern social psychology where multiple perspectives and the judicious employment of mini-theories and the development of multifaceted process models appears to be the order of the day. It is vital that sport psychologists make sure that they take on board not only the successes but also the failures which have led social psychology to this endpoint. The failures, blind alleys and false dawns can be just as revealing of where to go in the future as where not to go. There is no doubt that the gap between social psychology and sport psychology is narrower at present than for some considerable time, and the future certainly looks rosy if challenging. To paraphrase that hackneyed Chinese curse, we live in interesting times. To some this will be a source of inspiration, to others this new dawn may be difficult to accept. We side with the former.

References

ANTHONY, T., COPPER, C., DOVIDIO, J.F., DRISKELL, J. E., MULLEN, B. and SALAS, E. (1992) 'The effect of group member similarity on cohesiveness: Do birds of a feather really flock together?' unpublished manuscript, Department of Psychology, Syracuse University, New York.

BAKKER, F. C., WHITING, H. T. A. and VAN DER BRUG, H. (1990) *Sport Psychology: Concepts and Applications*, Chichester: John Wiley and Sons.

BANDURA, A. (1990) 'Perceived self-efficacy in the exercise of personal agency', *Journal of Applied Social Psychology*, 2, 2, pp. 128–63.

BAUMEISTER, R. F. and STEINHILBER, A. (1984) 'Paradoxical effects of supportive audiences on performance under pressure: The home field disadvantage in sport championships', *Journal of Personality and Social Psychology*, 47, pp. 85–93.

BENJAFIELD, J., LIDDELL, W. W. and BENJAFIELD, I. (1989) 'Is there a homefield advantage in professional sports championships?' *Social Behavior and Personality: An International Journal*, 17, 1, pp. 45–50.

BIDDLE, S. (1988) 'Methodological issues in the researching of attribution-emotion links in sport', *International Journal of Sport Psychology*, 19, pp. 264–80.

BIDDLE, S. (1993) 'Attribution research and sport psychology', in SINGER, R. N., MURPHEY, M. and TENNANT, L. K. (Eds) *Handbook of Research on Sport Psychology*, New York: Macmillan, pp. 437–64.

CANTER, D., COMBER, M. and UZZELL, D. L. (1989) *Football in Its Place: An Environmental Psychology of Football Grounds*, London: Routledge.

CARRON, A. V. (1982) 'Cohesiveness in sport groups: Interpretations and considerations', *Journal of Sport Psychology*, 4, pp. 123–8.

CARRON, A. V. (1988) *Group Dynamics in Sport*, London, Ontario: Spodym.

COTTRELL, N.B. (1968) 'Performance in the presence of other human beings: Mere presence, audience and affiliation effects', in SIMMEL, E. C., HOPPE, R. A. and MILTON, G. A. (Eds) *Social Facilitation and Imitative Behavior*, Boston: Allyn and Bacon.

COURNEYA, K. S. and CARRON, A. V. (1991) 'Effects of travel and length of home stand/road trip on the home advantage', *Journal of Sport and Exercise Psychology*, 13, 1, pp. 42–49.

CRATTY, B. J. (1983) *Psychology in Contemporary Sport: Guidelines for Coaches and Athletes*, Englewood Cliffs, NJ: Prentice-Hall.

DERVIN, D. (1991) 'Sports, athletes and games in a psychoanalytic perspective', in DIAMANT, L. (Ed.) *Mind-Body Maturity: Psychological Approaches to Sports, Exercise and Fitness*, New York: Hemisphere, pp. 163–80.

DUNNING, E., MURPHY, P. and WILLIAMS, J. (1988) *The Roots of Football Hooliganism: An Historical and Sociological Study*, London: Routledge and Kegan Paul.

EDWARDS, J. (1979) 'The home field advantage', in GOLDSTEIN, J. H. (Ed.) *Sports, Games and Play: Social and Psychological Viewpoints*, Hillsdale, NJ: Lawrence Erlbaum, pp. 409–38.

EITZEN, D. S. (1975) 'Group structure and group performance', in LANDERS, D. M., HARRIS, D. V. and CHRISTINA R. W. (Eds) *Psychology of Sport and Motor Behavior*, University Park, PA: Pennsylvania State University Press.

FESTINGER, L. (1954) 'A theory of social comparison processes', *Human Relations*, 7, pp. 117–40.

FISKE, S. T. and TAYLOR, S. E. (1991) *Social Cognition*, New York: McGraw-Hill.

FORSYTH, D. R. (1990) *Group Dynamics*, 2nd edn, Monterey, CA: Brooks/Cole.

GEEN, R. G. (1989) 'Alternative conceptions of social facilitation', in PAULUS, P. B. (Ed.) *Psychology of Group Influence*, 2nd edn, Hillsdale, NJ: Lawrence Erlbaum Associates, pp. 15–51.

GILL, D. L. (1986) *Psychological Dynamics of Sport*, Champaign, IL: Human Kinetics.

GLAMSER, F. D. (1990) 'Contest location, player misconduct and race: A case from English soccer', *Journal of Sport Behavior*, 13, 1, pp. 41–49.

GREER, D. L. (1983) 'Spectator booing and the home advantage: A study of social influence in the basketball arena', *Social Psychology Quarterly*, 46, pp. 252–61.

GROVE, J. R., HANRAHAN, S. J. and MCINMAN, A. (1991) 'Success/failure bias in attributions across involvement categories in sport', *Personality and Social Psychology Bulletin*, 17, pp. 93–97.

GRUBER, J. J. and GRAY, G. R. (1982) 'Responses to forces influencing cohesion as a function of player status and level of male varsity basketball competition', *Research Quarterly for Exercise and Sport*, 53, pp. 27–36.

HANRAHAN, S. J., GROVE, J. R. and HATTIE, J. A. (1989) 'Development of a questionnaire measure of sport related attributional style', *International Journal of Sport Psychology*, 20, pp. 114–34.

HARDY, C. J. (1990) 'Social loafing: Motivational losses in collective performance', *International Journal of Sport Psychology*, 21, 4, pp. 305–27.

HARDY, C. J. and CRACE, R. K. (1991) 'The effects of task structure and teammate competence on social loafing', *Journal of Sport and Exercise Psychology*, 13, pp. 372–81.

HARKINS, S. G. and SZYMANSKI, K. (1987) 'Social loafing and social facilitation: New wine in old bottles', in HENDRICK, C. (Ed.) *Group Processes and Intergroup Relations*, Newbury Park, CA: Sage, pp. 167–88.

HEIDER, F. (1958) *The Psychology of Interpersonal Relationships*, New York: John Wiley and Sons.

HOGG, M. (1992) *The Social Psychology of Group Cohesiveness: From Attraction to Social Identity*, Hemel Hempstead: Harvester Wheatsheaf.

INGHAM, A., LEVINGER, G., GRAVES, J. and PECKHAM, V. (1974) 'The Ringelmann effect: Studies of group size and group performance', *Journal of Experimental Social Psychology*, 10, pp. 371–84.

ISO-AHOLA, A. and HATFIELD, B. (1985) *Psychology of Sports: A Social Psychological Approach*, Dubuque, IA: Wm C. Brown.

JANIS, I. (1982) *Victims of Groupthink*, 2nd edn, Boston: Houghton-Mifflin.

KENDZIERSKI, D. (1990) 'Exercise self-schemata: Cognitive and behavioral correlates', *Health Psychology*, 9, pp. 69–82.

LANDERS, D. M. (1980) 'The arousal/performance relationship revisited', *Research Quarterly for Exercise and Sport*, 51, pp. 77–90.

LATANÉ, B., WILLIAMS, K. and HARKINS, S. (1979) 'Many hands make light work: The causes and consequences of social loafing', *Journal of Personality and Social Psychology*, 37, pp. 822–33.

LENK, H. (1969) 'Top performance despite internal conflict', in LOY, J. W. and KENYON, G. S. (Eds) *Sport, Culture and Society* New York: Macmillan.

LONG, G. T. (1991) 'Social perceptions of sports figures: Dumb jocks, flawed heroes and superstars', in DIAMANT, L. (Ed.) *Psychology of Sports, Exercise and Fitness: Social and Personal Issues*, New York: Hemisphere, pp. 227–36.

LOY, J. W., MCPHERSON, B. D. and KENYON, G. (1978) *Sport and Social Systems: A Guide to the Analysis, Problems and Literature*, Reading, MA: Addison-Wesley.

MARTENS, R. D. (1969) 'Effect of an audience on learning and performance of a complex motor skill', *Journal of Personality and Social Psychology*, 12, pp. 252–60.

MARTENS, R., LANDERS, D. and LOY, J. (1972) *Sports Cohesiveness Questionnaire*, Washington DC: AAHPERD Publications.

MCAULEY, E. (1992) 'Self-referent thought in sport and physical activity', in HORN, T. S. (Ed.) *Advances in Sport Psychology*, Champaign, IL: Human Kinetics, pp. 101–18.

MICHAELS, J. W., BLOMMEL, J. M., BROCATO, R. M., LINKOUS, R.A. and ROWE, J. S. (1982) 'Social facilitation and inhibition in a natural setting', *Replications in Social Psychology*, 2, pp. 21–24.

MOYER, K. E. (1976) *The Psychobiology of Aggression*, New York: Harper and Row.

MUDRACK, P. E. (1989) 'Defining group cohesiveness: A legacy of confusion?' *Small Group Behavior*, 20, pp. 37–49.

MULLEN, B. and BAUMEISTER, R. F. (1987) 'Group effects on self-attention and performance: Social loafing, social facilitation and social impairment', in HENDRICK, C. (Ed.) *Group Processes and Intergroup Relations*, Newbury Park, CA: Sage, pp. 189–206.

MULLEN, B. and RIORDAN, C. A. (1988) 'Self-serving attibutions for performance in naturalistic settings: A meta-analytic review', *Journal of Applied Social Psychology*, 18, 1, pp. 3–22.

MULLEN, B. and COOPER, C. (1992) 'The relationship between group cohesiveness and performance: An integration', unpublished manuscript, Department of Psychology, Syracuse University, New York.

MURRELL, A. J. and DIETZ, B. (1992) 'Fan support of sport teams: The effect of a common group identity', *Journal of Sport and Exercise Psychology*, 14, pp. 28–39.

RAINEY, D., SCHWEICKERT, G., GRANITO, V. and PULLELLA, J. (1990) 'Fans' evaluation of major league baseball umpires' performances and perceptions of appropriate behavior toward umpires', *Journal of Sport Behavior*, 13, 2, pp. 55–72.

RUSSELL, D. (1982) 'The Causal Dimension Scale: A measure of how individuals perceive causes', *Journal of Personality and Social Psychology*, 42, pp. 1137–45.

SCHWARTZ, B. and BARSKY, S. F. (1977) 'The home advantage', *Social Forces*, 55, pp. 641–61.

SIMONS, Y. and TAYLOR, J. (1992) 'A psychosocial model of fan violence in sports', *International Journal of Sport Psychology*, 23, pp. 207–26.

SPINK, K. S. (1990) 'Group cohesion and collective efficacy of volleyball teams', *Journal of Sport and Exercise Psychology*, 12, 3, pp. 301–11.

TAJFEL, H. (1981) *Human Groups and Social Categories: Studies in Social Psychology*, Cambridge: Cambridge University Press.

TRIPLETT, N. (1898) 'The dynamogenic factors in pacemaking and competition', *American Journal of Psychology*, 9, pp. 505–23.

TUCKMAN, B.W. and JENSEN, M. A. (1977) 'Stages of small group development revisited', *Group and Organizational Studies*, 2, pp. 419–27.

VARCA, P. E. (1980) 'An analysis of home and away game performance of male college basketball teams', *Journal of Sport Psychology*, 2, pp. 245–57.

WALL, B. R. and GRUBER, J. J. (1986) 'Relevancy of athletic aggression inventory for use in women's intercollegiate basketball: A pilot investigation', *International Journal of Sport Psychology*, 17, pp. 23–33.

WANKEL, L. M. (1984) 'Audience effects in sport', in SILVA, J. M. and WEINBERG, R. S. (Eds) *Psychological Foundations of Sport*, Champaign, IL: Human Kinetics, pp. 293–314.

WANN, D. L. and BRANSCOMBE, N. R. (1990) 'Person perception when aggressive or nonaggressive sports are primed', *Aggressive Behavior*, 16, 1, pp. 27–32.

WEINBERG, R. S. and RICHARDSON, P. A. (1990) *Psychology of Officiating*, Champaign, IL: Human Kinetics.

WEINER, B. (1972) *Theories of Motivation: From Mechanism to Cognition*, Chicago: Rand-McNally.

WEINER, B. (1986) *An Attributional Theory of Motivation and Emotion*, New York: Springer-Verlag.

WHITE, G. F. (1989) 'Media and violence: The case of professional football championship games', *Aggressive Behavior*, 15, pp. 423–33.

WHITLEY, B. E. and FRIEZE, I. H. (1985) 'Children's causal attributions for success and failure in achievement settings: A meta-analysis', *Journal of Educational Psychology*, 77, pp. 608–16.

WIDMEYER, W. N., BRAWLEY, L. R. and CARRON, A. V. (1985) *The Measurement of Cohesion in Sport Teams: The Group Environment Questionnaire*, London, Ontario: Sports Dynamics.

WIDMEYER, W. N., BRAWLEY, L. R. and CARRON, A. V. (1992) 'Group dynamics in sport', in HORN, T. S. (Ed.) *Advances in Sport Psychology*, Champaign, IL: Human Kinetics, pp. 163–80.

WILLIAMS, J. M. and WIDMEYER, W. N. (1991) 'The cohesion-performance outcome relationship in a coacting sport', *Journal of Sport and Exercise Psychology*, 13, 4, pp. 364–71.

YOUNG, K. (1991) 'Sport and collective violence', *Exercise and Sport Sciences Review*, 19, pp. 539–86.

YUKELSON, D., WEINBERG, R. and JACKSON, A. (1984) 'A multidimensional group cohesion instrument for intercollegiate basketball teams', *Journal of Sport Psychology*, 6, 1, pp. 103–17.

ZAJONC, R. B. (1965) 'Social facilitation', *Science*, 149, pp. 269–74.

ZANDER, A. (1975) 'Motivation and performance in sports groups', in LANDERS, D. M., HARRIS, D. V. and CHRISTINA, R. W. (Eds) *Psychology of Sport and Motor Behavior*, University Park, PA: Pennsylvania State University Press.

Further Reading

BAKKER, F. C., WHITING, H. T. A. and VAN DER BRUG, H. (1990) *Sport Psychology: Concepts and Applications*, Chichester: John Wiley and Sons.

BIDDLE, S. (1993) 'Attribution research and sport psychology', in SINGER, R. N., MURPHEY, M. and TENNANT, L. K. (Eds) *Handbook of Research on Sport Psychology*, New York: Macmillan, pp. 437–64.

CARRON, A. V. (1988) *Group Dynamics in Sport*, London, Ontario: Spodym.

COX, R. H. (1990) *Sport Psychology: Concepts and Applications*, 2nd edn, Dubuque, IA: Wm C. Brown.

GILL, D. L. (1986) *Psychological Dynamics of Sport*, Champaign, IL: Human Kinetics.

HORN, T. S. (Ed.) (1992) *Advances in Sport Psychology*, Champaign, IL: Human Kinetics.

ISO-AHOLA, A. and HATFIELD, B. (1985) *Psychology of Sports: A Social Psychological Approach*, Dubuque, IA: Wm C. Brown.

SINGER, R. N., MURPHEY, M. and TENNANT, L. K. (1993) *Handbook of Research on Sport Psychology*, New York: Macmillan.

Chapter 7

Making Sport Work

(Occupational Psychology)

Introduction

Of all the branches of psychology which have yet to reveal their full worth to the world of sport, occupational psychology must surely head the list. Looking across the gamut of potentially relevant material the casual reader is struck not by the way in which occupational psychology has been picked clean but instead by the exciting opportunities which remain to be discovered. Two exceptions to this rule do stand out however, these being the areas of leadership/effective management and goal-setting. While a plentiful sport psychology literature exists dealing with both, neither is without its problems, and these will be discussed later. Alongside this material, we have also identified areas which we consider are ripe for further research. Possibilities which spring to mind and which have long interested occupational psychologists include work on personnel selection and recruitment, and on work motivation and job satisfaction. Both have immediate relevance to so many sport settings, and we would suggest, eagerly await closer attention. To structure this material, the chapter is divided into four primary sections. The first reviews the management of sport, encompassing work on leadership and coaching styles. The second deals with goal-setting in sport, while the third and fourth sections, dealing with selection and work motivation respectively, look more towards the future and suggest possibilities for further work. The first topic to be addressed is leadership and management in sport. You could easily imagine that this issue will also be covered in Chapter 8 under teacher effectiveness, but in actual fact the two literatures remain very much distinct, one focusing on teaching and delivery techniques in physical education, the other with how to manage and motivate athletes. Whether this is an artificial divide is up to you to decide when you have had the opportunity to read both chapters; we are certainly of the opinion that the distance separating the two at present cannot be healthy.

Managing Sport

The Psychology of Coaching

Without doubt one of the primary consumers of sport psychology has been, and presumably always will be, sports coaches. Many applied sport psychologists have come to acknowledge that the most effective way to get their message across is not by working directly with athletes but instead by working as part of a support team, with the coach or manager acknowledged as the leader of the pack. After all, the sport psychologist may come and go but it is the coach or manager who, day in and day out, maintains the most contact with an athlete and whose influence remains paramount. Accordingly, if the coach can learn how to convey messages which have a sound foundation in psychological knowledge, and thus can act as the agent or mouthpiece for sport psychology, then the messages are likely to have that much more impact. Within the United Kingdom, this principle is institutionalized through the work of the National Coaching Foundation (NCF). Coaches working for national sporting organizations must progress through a series of levels in order to be eligible to work with particular squads or individuals, and these NCF courses include several dealing with aspects of sport psychology.

There is usually no shortage of takers for sport psychology courses and perhaps in some way as a response to market demand in general, over recent years the sport psychology literature evidences increasing interest in the psychology of coaching as a specific topic. To meet this demand, a number of practical sport psychology guides for coaches are now available (for example see Martens, 1989). On occasion these take standard sport psychology knowledge and present it in a 'user friendly' way for those with no previous experience of the subject. Unfortunately, far too often these guides present practical advice relating to basic teaching principles but only offer fleeting or casual reference to basic psychology. This is regrettable but certainly understandable given that the research base could best be described as fragile.

A glance at the reference list to this chapter will show just how vital a mere handful of researchers have been, with Packianathan Chelladurai in particular having had a hand in almost all research initiatives in this field over the last 15 years. Despite the best and considerable endeavours of Chelladurai and his co-workers, there is a limit to what any small group can achieve and consequently primary sport related research on leadership in sport is somewhat sparse. An added problem may be that without the normal checks and balances which arise from healthy rivalries and differences of opinion across a broadly based research community, then life may be altogether too comfortable and as a result growth may actually be stunted. Whether this is true in this particular field is a matter for pure speculation. Certainly a number of very important topics have been opened up for sport, and inspiring theories have been specifically adopted for use in sport. Unfortunately the pace at which these ideas are then tested, developed and finally fully operationalized can be disappointing to say the least.

Against this backcloth, most sport psychology texts are left with a dilemma. They recognize the significance of this area for sport but at the same time they have a fairly select literature on which to draw (see Horn, 1992; Chelladurai, 1993). For obvious and very practical reasons, the most important question which has driven this research has been, which leadership or coaching styles are likely to be most effective in sport? To try to answer this question, the typical response has been to begin with a standard overview of leadership research in psychology. This type of presentation would be familiar to most introductory social psychology students, relying heavily on theories and models from mainstream social and occupational psychology but then using these to interpret leadership in sport. Coverage typically moves from a description of the inadequacy of the trait approach (see Chapter 2), to the work on leadership functions and behaviours. This work began in earnest in the 1950s, led by work at Ohio State University, and saw the identification of the two principal leadership functions which still guide so many models to this day. These functions or behavioural styles have been given various labels over the years but looking beyond these labels, essentially each refers to a cluster of either task or socio-emotional concerns. The principal research instrument to emerge from the post-war years was the Leader Behaviour Description Questionnaire (LBDQ) which measured leaders' behaviour in relation to two independent constructs, initiating structure (the task dimension) and consideration (the socio-emotional dimension).

Measuring Leadership in Sport

Given sport psychology's longstanding concern with psychometrics, it will probably come as little surprise to learn that in the fullness of time sport psychologists used this work to help develop a number of sport-specific scales. These measures included two direct derivatives of the LBDQ, the Coach Behaviour Description Questionnaire or CBDQ (Danielson *et al.*, 1975) and the Leadership Scale for Sports or LSS (Chelladurai and Saleh, 1980). The CBDQ is a 20-item scale which includes eight categories, dealing with competitive training, initiation, interpersonal team operations, social behaviour, representation behaviour, organized communication, recognition and general excitement. The CBDQ has not generated a great deal of research since the 1970s, but the same cannot be said of the LSS. The LSS is a 40-item scale, made up of five subscales, namely training and instruction, autocratic behaviour, democratic behaviour, social support and positive feedback. The LSS continues to attract considerable attention (for example, Chelladurai *et al.*, 1988), albeit with two primary reservations remaining to be resolved. The first concerns the over-reliance on university students as subjects in LSS research, and the second relates to whether or not the LSS subscales genuinely capture the most salient dimensions of coaching behaviour.

The LSS can be administered in one of two forms. The first considers the way in which the athlete perceives his or her coach ('My coach . . .'), the second deals not with athletes' experience of the coach but with preferred behaviour ('I prefer my coach to . . .'). Differences between scores derived from both question types (known as the discrepancy score) have been used to quantify the mismatch between experience and preference, and beyond this to relate discrepancy to satisfaction (for example, Schliesman, 1987). On several occasions, levels of satisfaction with the coach have been found to correlate negatively with discrepancy scores, and particularly those derived from two subscales ('positive feedback', and 'training and instruction'). Other research has used the 'preferred' LSS version ('I prefer my coach to . . .') to compare coaching preferences in various sports along numerous dimensions, for example between males and females, Americans and non-Americans, the young and the old, and élite and non-élite athletes (see Horn, 1992: 186–9). Typically (and very much in line with other leadership research), men have a greater preference for autocratic styles whereas women prefer democracy, age and maturity of an athlete do not have a clear effect on preference, and preference is influenced both by the nationality of the athlete and the specific sport in question. These and other findings are normally set in the context of Chelladurai's Multidimensional Model of Leadership (Chelladurai, 1993), a model which will be outlined later.

A further scale, the Coaching Behaviour Assessment System or CBAS (Smith *et al.*, 1977) was also developed in the 1970s to quantify directly the behaviour of coaches and to categorize that behaviour under 12 headings. This scale has continued to generate interest along a number of research fronts (for example Horn, 1984), and Smoll and Smith (1989) have now incorporated it as part of a sport-specific, interactional model of leadership behaviour known as the mediational model. This model considers the relationship between the coach, the player and the situation in determining coaching behaviour, players' perception and recall, and players' evaluative recall. The same authors have used the CBAS to look at the interaction between children's self-esteem and their responsiveness to different coaching styles. They found that those children with low self-esteem most needed coaches who valued their contribution and provided positive feedback for successful work (Smith and Smoll, 1990) .

Another behavioural measure, the Arizona State University Observation Instrument or ASUOI, has also been developed to assess coaches' verbal and non-verbal behaviour, this time using 13 categories (Lacy and Goldston, 1990). Unfortunately, to date research using this scale is limited.

Contingency Models of Leadership

Moving on from measures of leadership behaviours, sport psychology textbooks have traditionally rounded off their coverage of leadership research with extensive descriptions of recent contingency models. From the wide range of available contingency models on offer, the common conclusion to emerge is that, in sport as elsewhere, there is simply no magic formula for predicting who will be a successful leader. In addition, no single leadership, management or coaching style will ever be successful across a range of situations. Instead, the only general advice which can be offered is that to be as effective as possible then sports coaches, managers or indeed captains must develop the ability to assess changing situations, and then employ a management style which is appropriate to the needs of their followers and the demands of the situation.

Fiedler's Contingency Theory

Of the most significant theories to guide discussion, Fred Fiedler's still enjoys a degree of popularity, despite the accumulated criticisms which it has attracted from within occupational psychology (Bryman, 1986). As briefly as possible, the theory argues that different individuals will be more or less effective as leaders in different situations. Individuals are categorized by their score on the Least Preferred Co-worker scale (or LPC), a scale which measures what they think of the person they least liked working with. Situations are categorized in relation to three factors (task structure, leader-member relations and position power of the leader), factors which are thought to influence the degree of control which the leader is likely to have in a given situation. Of all the criticisms levelled against Fiedler's work perhaps the most fundamental is that which attacks his contention that our LPC score is permanent, almost akin to a personality trait. According to Fiedler, we are either low, moderate or high LPC people, and hence when operating as leaders we are best advised to change situations to suit our predispositions rather than vainly trying to change or adapt our preferred leadership style. This sentiment is enshrined in his Leader-Match programme for managers (Fiedler and Chemers, 1984). Fiedler himself did work with certain sports, including basketball, in the development of his original theory (Fiedler, 1967), although subsequent research in the sport domain has been both very limited and equivocal in terms of offering support for the approach. It is almost as though commentators feel duty bound to pay lip service to the model but then move quickly on to more productive fields.

Three alternative contingency approaches have had a far more significant impact in sport psychology. These are Vroom and Yetton's normative theory, Hersey and Blanchard's situational leadership theory, and House's path-goal theory. Each theory concentrates on a particular aspect of the leadership function, the first with decision-making, the second with social responsiveness to followers' maturity, and the third with motivating subordinates. To this extent the three do not directly compete but instead with a little imagination they can complement each other, and especially as each places great emphasis on how effective leadership involves adapting to changing situations. They are also eminently practical theories, developed with the needs of managers, albeit business managers, very much to the fore.

Vroom and Yetton's Normative Theory

Vroom and Yetton argue that one of the primary leadership functions is decision-making. When making decisions, the theory postulates that a leader or manager must weigh up two considerations. These are the quality of the decision and the acceptance of the decision by those who must implement it. On some occasions it is vital that the decision itself is of high quality irrespective of its acceptance by the group, at other times acceptance is of paramount concern, and on other occasions both may be equally important. Depending on which is true then one or more leadership style is likely to be most effective. The way in which these ideas are traditionally presented is in the form of a decision tree, where questions are asked sequentially from left to right until a terminal mode is reached; this determines which style to adopt. In a rare but highly commendable step, Chelladurai took this original decision tree and rather than testing it out in sport, he straightaway modified the basic model for use with sports coaches (see Figure 7.1).

Decisions made at each point in the tree lead sequentially on to further decisions (from left to right), before a terminal node signifying a leadership style is finally reached. The seven key questions or dimensions to be asked in this process are: time pressure (quick decision?), decision quality required (quality required?), the source and quality of information (good info?), the complexity of the problem (complex problem?), the need for the group or team to be behind the decision (acceptance critical?), the manager/coach's power base (strong power base?) and the extent of group integration (integrated team?). The model assumes that for each of these dimensions, the coach can choose whether or not that issue is important or even relevant. Depending on these choices then eventually the coach will reach one of three decision making styles which is deemed the most appropriate given that set of circumstances, these styles being either autocratic, delegative or participative. Autocratic implies that the decision is reached by the coach

Figure 7.1: *Chelladurai's Normative Model of Decision Making Styles in Coaching*

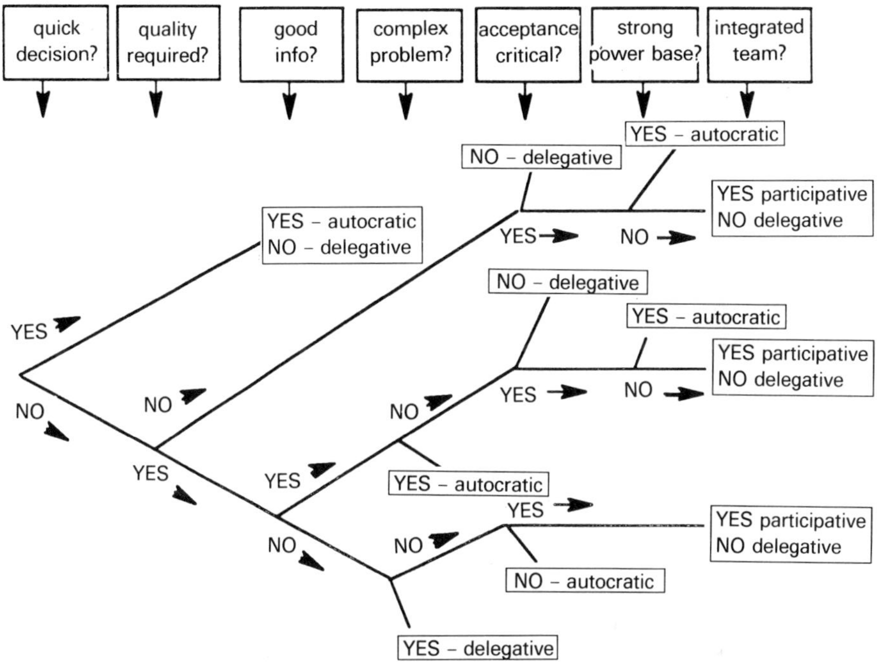

Source: Adapted from Chelladurai and Haggerty, 1978: 6-9. Used with kind permission of authors.

with little consultation; delegative assumes that the coach delegates responsibility to others; and a participative style is one where the team or group as a whole makes the decision.

Although Vroom and Yetton normally refer to a range of decision strategies, the underlying principles remain very similar in both models. Research based on Vroom and Yetton's original model was very slow to appear in occupational psychology but a scattering of recent articles have generally been supportive, while at the same time arguing that the model needs to accommodate discrepancies between leaders' and subordinates' perceptions of what makes an effective manager and in particular a greater preference for participative styles amongst subordinates (Field and House, 1990). In sport psychology, there is if anything a more substantial research base, clustered around Chelladurai's Normative Model for Decision Styles in Coaching. Since the original publication of the model, Chelladurai and others (for example, Gordon, 1988; Chelladurai *et al.*, 1989) have once more demonstrated sport psychology's preoccupation with matters psychometric by refining and fine tuning a coaching decision style questionnaire based on the variables which constitute the decision tree. The questionnaire includes various sporting situations where choices must be made and problems must be solved. The solutions offered to these problems then reflect in particular decision styles. This questionnaire is designed to be completed either by coaches themselves or by athletes as they perceive (or prefer) their coaches would respond to hypothetical situations, but as yet research is still at a developmental stage.

Hersey and Blanchard's Situational Leadership Theory

The second contingency theory to make a substantial impact in sport is Hersey and Blanchard's Situational Leadership Theory, formerly known as the life cycle theory and originally derived from the Ohio State Leadership Studies (Hersey and Blanchard, 1982). This approach focuses on the characteristics of followers and most especially their level of maturity. In essence, when subordinates are inexperienced then the leader must be directive (task oriented). As they become more experienced then the leader must show greater concern for emotional support (socio-emotionally oriented) and when they are fully mature then the leader must learn how to back off on all counts, giving space to develop further by being neither directive nor over concerned about offering social support. Although virtually no research has been carried out to test this theory, it remains extremely popular and at an intuitive level, does seems eminently sensible. The overriding message which the original theory conveys is that coaches must remain responsive to the changing needs of their athletes, and this message continues to strike some sort of a chord with applied sport psychologists.

While Chelladurai and Carron (1983) support this central thesis, they go on to argue that this industrial model must be tailored to sport. In contrast with paid workers, they suggest that young, immature athletes need considerable social support early in their careers but this need decreases as time goes by. In contrast, early in a sporting career too much emphasis on skills training may be a turn off. The time for this technical advice is in mid-career, before once more backing off as the mature athlete learns to become self-sufficient. In a field test of this model with basketball players, Case (1987) found general support for these suggestions. However, an additional finding was that those who went on to élite level then looked for even greater social support from their coaches, presumably at a time when the pressures of competition were that much more fierce.

House's Path-Goal Theory

A final contingency model to enjoy prominence in the sport psychology literature is that formulated and gradually extended by House, known as the Path-Goal Theory. This theory has close ties originally with the Ohio State Leadership Studies, and more recently with expectancy-value theories of work motivation (see the section on 'Motivating Athletes'). The theory deals with how leaders can influence motivation and perceptions of work by using one of a number of leadership styles (directive, supportive, achievement-oriented or participative). The style is chosen which best reflects environmental demands (for example, the tasks, the organizational structure and interpersonal relationships at work), and followers' characteristics (for example, their ability, locus of control and authoritarianism). The leader is expected to maximize effort by showing how rewards can be reached, by clearing obstacles in the path and by providing positive feedback for work well done. As with the previous theory, relatively little work has been carried out in sporting contexts (Vos Strache, 1979) but it is nevertheless recognized as potentially valuable, and is likely to be 'one to watch' as expectancy-value theories become more significant across sport psychology as a whole.

Chelladurai's Multidimensional Model of Leadership

These three theories have each been embraced by sport psychology, and their efficacy has been duly acknowledged. At the same time (and in contrast to other areas in sport psychology), there has been a refreshing reluctance simply to borrow such theories wholesale. Instead, from the late 1970s onwards Chelladurai and his colleagues have sought to develop sport-specific theories and models of leadership which are able to accommodate ideas and concepts from a great many sources and especially the world of paid work. This sentiment is firmly behind Chelladurai's Multidimensional Model of Leadership, a model which considers the process whereby coaches actually coach (see Figure 7.2).

The effectiveness of the leader is determined by two principal outcomes, how well athletes perform and how satisfied they are with the process. The three interacting aspects of the leader's behaviour which can produce these outcomes are first, the behaviour which is required of a leader in these circumstances, second, the actual behaviour displayed by the leader, and third the behaviour which is preferred by the athletes themselves. In turn, each of these are influenced by other factors or antecedents. According to Chelladurai, the behaviour required of the coach in any situation will depend on the sport itself, the goals of the organization and indeed the whole environment within which the sport exists. His or her actual behaviour as leader will depend on ability, knowledge and interpersonal skills, while his or her preferred behaviour reflects both characteristics of the members and the situation.

This model remains untested in its entirety but it should be regarded as a good start towards integrating a number of themes which crop up in the literature. In line with other process models in psychology, it is likely that as time passes, the model will become increasingly complex. For example, the number of further interconnections between components could be almost limitless. Each of the antecedents is likely to influence each of the leader behaviours to a greater or lesser degree. In turn, the consequences or outcomes will subsequently have a dynamic effect on the characteristics of both the leader and the members (and also the situation?) which will then influence the leader behaviour. In this manner the model could become fundamentally more dynamic, dealing with change and development over time. However, despite these reservations the strength of

Figure 7.2: *Chelladurai's Multidimensional Model of Leadership*

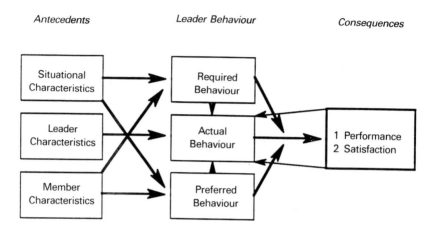

Source: Derived from Chelladurai, 1993: 648. Used with permission of the author.

the model remains its ability to bring together interacting behavioural and cognitive variables within a common framework, and to prescribe certain factors which coaches must take into account in order to maximize their chances of success. It is it be hoped that the basic model acts as a spur for further work.

Social Exchange and the Leadership Process

At the risk of prolonging this discussion yet further, the theories which have been employed within sport psychology have undoubtedly been valuable but that is not to say that there are not other approaches which could also make useful contributions. For example, the recent literature on vertical dyad linkage focuses attention on the one-to-one interpersonal relationship between leader and follower, while a separate literature has begun to question our preoccupation with always having to be led and instead talks of neutralizers and substitutes for leadership (see Bryman, 1986). In this vein, there is one final social psychological approach which rarely features in the sport literature but which could comfortably be included and which could help further our understanding of leadership in sport. This is the somewhat disparate body of leadership research originally derived from social exchange theory (Hollander, 1985). The fundamental postulate is that followers will only continue to invest in a leader and allow that person to influence them so long as the personally valued rewards which they gain exceed the costs which they incur. Therefore leadership in sport as elsewhere is represented as a basic exchange process, where influence is bought, but at a price. Adopting this perspective, one important task for the coach or manager is to identify what each athlete regards as rewards and costs in this exchange, essentially to understand their followers. Following from both House's and Hersey and Blanchard's work, Lee (1991) has argued that followers can be categorized along two dimensions, whether they are active or passive, and whether they show independent and critical thinking, or generally don't think. People low on both are described as 'sheep', the 'yes people' are those who are active but unthinking, 'alienated followers' (or 'blockers') are those who are critical thinkers but are passive in the team or group, and 'effective followers' are those who are high on both dimensions. A final category, 'survivors', encompasses those who fall somewhere in the middle. Recognition of these tendencies, alongside what the athlete values from their involvement in the sport, can go a long way towards helping coaches deal effectively with athletes, young and old.

A further idea derived from social exchange is that of idiosyncrasy credit (Hollander, 1985). According to Hollander, one of the most dangerous strategies which a coach or manager can adopt is that of a new broom sweeping clean. It is much more sensible to spend time evaluating the structure of the group, determining its needs, norms and routines, and over time accumulating what are known as idiosyncrasy credits in the eyes of the followers for a competent if predictable job well done. Eventually, when sufficient credits have accumulated then the leader will be given freedom to press his/her individual stamp on the team or organization. Anecdotally, it is possible to think of occasions where potentially very good managers or coaches have failed to make an impact on a particular team, individual or organization not because of a lack of technical expertise but because they tried to initiate a new regime before the time was ripe, or failed to respond to the needs of the situation. Brian Clough's brief reign as manager of the English soccer club Leeds United, following in the wake of Don Revie's successful stewardship, may well be a case in point here. Under Don Revie, Leeds had become a mature, well established and highly integrated team, a team which had learnt to respect Revie's own style of management. It is more than likely that Clough's idiosyncratic and sometimes eccentric approach to the game would have come as something of a culture shock to the players. Rather than being a breath of fresh air, he was more likely to be seen as the cold wind of change, or even just puffs of hot air! Taken as a whole, Brian Clough's entire career in football management, including his early working relationship with Peter Taylor at Derby County, through to his final demise at Nottingham Forest, would surely provide a fascinating case study for students of leadership and management.

Leadership and Playing Position

Looking briefly at other leadership domains, there is a fascinating if somewhat isolated pocket of research which deals with playing position and leadership roles. For some unknown reason, this relies exclusively on findings from one sport, baseball (see Cox, 1990: 404–6). This work has shown that infielders and catchers are more likely to be captains and in turn are more likely to go on to become managers and coaches themselves. The more central the position, not only in terms of the play but also in terms of visibility and observability, the greater the leadership opportunities. Unfortunately the existing research is unable to establish cause and effect but the potential for further research involving other sports has to be considerable.

Recent Research

Given the previous discussion of leadership theories and models, it is somewhat disappointing to find not a heady debate about fundamental leadership processes but instead merely a steady trickle of articles which deal with a variety of coaching issues, some of which are also covered in Chapter 8 under the guise of teaching sport. One example is a study by Hanson and Gould (1988) which considered the ability of coaches to recognize their athletes' anxiety state prior to competition. It was found that very few coaches were able to predict their athletes' anxiety levels, and suggest that there is a significant lesson here for coaches: to get to know their athletes better! More recently, Gould *et al.* (1990) considered the training needs of 130 élite coaches in the United States and found that perceived needs were still not being met. Although sport sciences are seen as one of three most important influences in the development of these élite coaches, they regarded that the most significant influence on their coaching styles came not from books, manuals or courses but from hands-on experience and international networking, that is watching other élite coaches in action.

One issue which has emerged recently and is likely to continue to generate interest is gender in coaching. Traditionally, leadership research across psychology as a whole has been androcentric, that is it has dealt first and foremost with men. As women have moved in increasing numbers into management so gender research has increased dramatically (Eagly and Johnson, 1990). Mirroring this trend, gender has only recently emerged as an issue in the sport psychology of coaching but already the signs are that this research will move in a similar direction, emphasizing the similarities in leadership behaviours of men and women but pointing to the structural obstacles and stereotypes which still serve to hold women back. In this vein, Hasbrook *et al.* (1990) have successfully started to debunk some of the myths and the stereotypes about women coaches. For example, women coaches were more likely to have physical education qualifications, or actually to teach physical education, and interestingly it was men who were more inclined to mention 'incompatibility with family life' as a possible reason for leaving coaching than women.

Overall, there still remains considerable ground to be explored in terms of coaching effectiveness. There is a real need for the messages coming from sport psychology to be translated into practical advice and indeed a variety of training packs now exist, often including their own handbooks, seminars, workshops and lectures. Some if not all of this material has initially been theory-driven although inevitably it has been popularized with frequent use of cartoons, presumably to appeal to coaches who are not considered to be academically oriented. As is true of textbooks dealing with topics such as motor skills, once more this is an occasion which continually cries out for close collaboration between those who work at the cutting edge in terms of research, and those who see delivery as their main priority.

Table 7.1: Locke's Four Principles of Goal Setting

Difficulty:	More difficult goals lead to a higher level of performance than easy goals.
Specificity:	Specific goals are more effective than general subjective goals (e.g. 'do your best') or no goals.
Acceptance:	To be effective goals must be accepted by the performer whether they are self-instigated or assigned by someone else.
Feedback:	Goals will not be effective in the absence of feedback.

Goal Setting

Alongside work on coaching styles, goal setting represents one of two primary areas where occupational psychologists have made a direct and considerable impact on the world of sport, in both a theoretical and a practical sense. While the use of goal setting within sport is widespread, the adoption of formal goal setting principles has not been without controversy and it is interesting that a recent review article actually refers to goal setting not as the blue-eyed boy of sport psychology but as its Jekyll and Hyde (Burton, 1992). Within psychology as a whole the idea of setting goals to guide or direct our behaviour has a well established history. However, the recent use of goal setting as a performance enhancement technique in sport can be traced directly back to Edwin Locke's goal setting theory. Underlying his theory is the notion that behaviour is regulated by values and goals, with a goal defined as a conscious intention or, more simply, what the person is setting out to accomplish. Goal setting research has been conducted in a wide variety of settings over the past 25 years but laboratory based work has tended to dominate the scene (see Locke and Latham, 1990). Regardless of the type of task or the subjects used, the overwhelming majority of studies (approximately 90 per cent) indicate that setting goals leads to improved performance on experimental tasks. According to Locke, goals affect performance by way of four mechanisms. First, goal setting focuses attention, second, it mobilizes effort in proportion to the demands of the task, third, goals enhance persistence, and finally goals have an indirect effect in that they encourage the individual to develop strategies for achieving their goals. Furthermore, Locke and his co-workers claim that a number of features relate to these performance effects, and these features have taken on the status of accepted principles in the goal setting literature. These four principles are shown in Table 7.1.

Goal setting has been embraced enthusiastically by consultants in the worlds of business and management and more latterly by sport psychologists (Burton, 1992; Weinberg, 1992) who often employ it as an integral part of psychological skills training programmes. Over the years, basic goal setting procedures have been made more readily accessible to coaches and athletes alike, and the principles have been frequently translated into popular parlance to encourage practical use. One example is the widespread use of the acronym SCAMP as a way of teaching athletes simple goal setting procedures.

S *Specific* Don't set vague goals, e.g. improve performance. Specify exactly how much you want to improve and how you can measure it. Predict the extent of your improvement and you will work hard to achieve it.

C *Challenging/Controllable* Set performance goals at a level slightly ahead of your current ability: this means that goals are within the realm of possibility but also provide challenge. Keep goals within personal control rather than depending on performance of others.

A *Attainable* Don't burden yourself with an impossible goal. All goals should relate to where you are now and you should aim to improve yourself step by step. Don't be afraid to reassess goals if they prove unrealistic.

M *Measurable/Multiple* Sense of achievement is greatest and motivation enhanced most when progress can actually be seen. Goals are best expressed in a form which can be measured objectively, e.g. seconds off time. Failing that, measure performance or characteristic on a subjective rating scale of 1 to 10, e.g. rate ability to cope under pressure on scale of 1 to 10. Also, multiple goals increase probability of achievement.

P *Personal* The goals you set (in conjunction with your coach) must relate to you as an individual. Decide what *you* want to achieve; don't borrow other people's goals. This will enhance your commitment to these objectives.

It is also relatively easy to come up with programmes to deal with a wide range of sports related skills. The following shows an example of a typical programme used by the authors when working with athletes (in this case Gaelic fooballers), beginning with a worked example and progressing to the development of a goal setting regime to deal with each player's particular problems.

Worked example: A goalkeeper wishes to improve his dead ball clearance accuracy. The biggest obstacle to achieving this is recognized as simple practice of the skill and he has decided that he is committed to increasing the accuracy of his clearances and will devote the time which is necessary to achieve this. At present he works out that he is able to hit a ball from 35 metres into a 10 metre circle three times out of 10 (his baseline). He then sets himself a realistic goal of hitting the target seven times out of 10 by the start of the season. How does he achieve this? He works out a training programme which involves going out to a field three times a week, marking a circle and hitting 30 shots each from 35 metres. He records his success rate on each occasion and charts improvement over time. In the light of this continual feedback he is able to check whether he is on line for achieving his goal and can adjust his practice over the weeks if necessary.

Instructions: Now think of one aspect of your own game performance which you would like to improve and informally start to see how you can put in place a programme to realize that goal.
1 Identify one aspect of performance which you wish to see improved.
2 What skills/qualities are needed to develop to bring about this improve-ment?
3 What routine/practice will help improve this skill/quality?
4 How can you measure or quantify this skill/quality?
5 What is the present level of attainment in terms of this skill/quality?

6 What level of performance would you like to achieve by a certain date?

7 Work out what targets you would like to meet by certain dates, what training routines you must put in place to reach these targets and how you will measure performance. Always remember that timetables can be adjusted to take into account changing circumstances, e.g. illness, injury, other commitments.

So far all may appear rosy; here is what appears to be a relatively simple psychological technique which allows athletes to maximize their potential through structured training and planning. Unfortunately, this optimistic presentation deliberately flatters to deceive for goal setting is a prime example where popularity is based on perceived practical utility but where application has proceeded while turning a blind eye to a number of serious theoretical and conceptual problems. One of the most fundamental of these is the way in which sporting applications differ from the industrial domains for which, and in which, goal setting was originally developed (see Hall and Byrne, 1988). Examples of differences are not hard to find. For instance, although competition between business organizations is the essence of capitalism, within industrial organizations competition may be confined to particular functions (for example, promotion) and may be positively discouraged amongst co-workers. In sport, and particularly individual sports, competition is considered to be an essential component, whether during training or competition. In addition, there are also obvious differences in terms of the reasons why individuals are actually involved in work or sport in the first place. Principally, the extrinsic rewards which accrue from work stand in contrast to the intrinsic motivators which have been identified as being so crucial to maintaining an interest in amateur sport (see Roberts, 1992). A further major distinction rests upon how goal setting is applied in sport and in work, and in particular the relative emphasis which is placed on either product or process. Performance enhancement in business is normally directly related to an end product, increased productivity. However, in sport, although there may be an implicit outcome goal (for example winning a major tournament), sport psychologists have repeatedly asserted that goal setting should focus on the process not the outcome (Martens, 1989; Bull, 1991). Hence goal setting in sport is typically associated with improving motivation and self-confidence through setting process goals rather than outcome goals (Gould, 1986; Hardy and Fazey, 1990). Despite this fundamental difference the two literatures are still regarded as interchangeable yet clearly they are not. This fact is highlighted further when each of Locke's four principles are examined.

In terms of goal difficulty, rather than challenging goals enhancing motivation some authors now suggest that setting unrealistically high and distant goals may actually be de-motivating and hence inhibit performance (Gould, 1986), while others maintain that challenging, long term goals must be subdivided into short term or intermediate goals (Martens, 1989). In advocating the use of subgoals in sport, it is interesting that Locke himself used an example taken from élite sport, that of John Naber, the 1976 Olympic 400 m backstroke gold medallist (Locke and Latham, 1985). Apparently John Naber spontaneously adopted a goal setting programme after failing to win the gold medal in the 1972 Olympics. He established that he would need to knock four seconds off his time over four years and he broke this down so minutely (literally) that he was able to calculate that this amounted to improving his time by four milliseconds for every hour of training. He was meticulous in his planning, and he was successful in winning his gold. Although this example is appealing in its apparent simplicity, it has recently been pointed out by Beggs (1991) that the practicalities of implementing such a highly structured training regime would be almost impossible for all but a very small minority of dedicated, élite athletes.

In terms of goal specificity, in contrast with evidence from industrial psychology, the sport psychology literature has failed to find any differences between subjects who were assigned specific, difficult goals and subjects who were simply told to do their best (Beggs, 1991). It has also been proposed that competition in sport may contaminate the goal difficulty/specificity to performance relationship. With this in mind, it is fascinating to note recent practical guidelines on swimming coaching emanating from a 'think-tank' seminar in Canada (Dennis, 1991). Here North American coaches were advocating a shift away from over-reliance on specific performance goals and towards greater concern with competitive goals, that is, to beat the person in the next lane. Swimmers' use of goal setting strategies may actually have become so ingrained that times or personal bests (PBs) have become the primary focus, and winning and competing, the essence of sport, have been forgotten.

Goal acceptance or commitment was the third of Locke's principles of goal setting, but yet again, when examining goal acceptance and commitment in sport, it has been found that subjects who were assigned tasks of varying degrees of difficulty, accepted their goals regardless of goal difficulty (Weinberg *et al.*, 1985). Finally, Locke's claim that goals will only be effective when feedback is provided has also found little support in the sports literature (Giannini *et al.*, 1988). Taken together these findings make it difficult to offer sports coaches firm guidelines as to whether or not to use goal setting. Indeed it could be argued that if coaches worked solely on augmenting intrinsic or extrinsic feedback then specific goal setting programmes would become virtually redundant, or at least for élite athletes. It seems reasonable to suggest that most high level performers are intrinsically motivated to improve performance and would therefore use feedback naturally and spontaneously to set personal goals. In addition, the literature suggests that overly ambitious goal setting may be positively dangerous for athletes who are already experiencing stress or low self-esteem (Jones *et al.*, 1990). Certainly, goal setting can promote intrinsic motivation when practice tasks have low intrinsic interest but it can actually de-motivate athletes when tasks inherently have high intrinsic interest or are complex in nature, as is so often true of actual competition.

Goal Setting: The Way Forward

As you can now appreciate, what began as a simple story involving one routine intervention strategy has evolved into a tale with a beginning but without a happy ending. The reasons why sport must handle goal setting with care are manifold. In the first place, the international world of sport presents a radically different context from that used by Locke to develop his original theory, namely American business. Sport psychologists need to ask themselves whether a theory based primarily on industry actually translates to different sporting contexts. Perhaps we are trying to make sport suit the theory but instead the theory should be modified and adapted to suit sport. Locke (1991) has advocated looking at goal setting in laboratory conditions, removed from the reality of sport. We would suggest that such laboratory research has to be complemented by many more applied field studies and experiments in order to consider issues such as the incidence of intuitive or spontaneous goal setting, and the effects of unrealistic goals, competition or feedback. Other topics include differences between élite performers and mere mortals, gender, age, task complexity and task variety within any one sport. Certainly at the present time the message appears to be that caution is the watch-word when employing goal setting as a psychological technique for practice and competition in sport.

At a more practical level, a number of concerns have been raised about current goal setting guidelines. Many of these assume a one-to-one coach to athlete ratio, and also make considerable assumptions as to the athlete's or coach's ability to analyse current performance and predict future performance. These assumptions should not be taken for granted, especially when dealing with young athletes or those who have enjoyed fewer educational opportunities. It may be the case that sport psychologists can eventually assist the development of good coaching practice not by laying down laws based on abstract theory but by first of all examining just what good coaches already do. In this way, once more the relationship between good theory and good practice will be cemented ever stronger.

Personnel Selection in Sport

As mentioned earlier, there are areas of occupational psychology which have aroused precious little interest in sport psychology but which nevertheless have the potential to be highly significant in years to come. One prime example concerns player selection and recruitment, traditionally a bone of contention in almost all sports and at all levels. As mentioned in Chapter 2, sport psychologists must remain extremely cautious about advocating the use of psychological measures for selection purposes but this certainly does not preclude the use of psychological principles for helping understand and improve the process of selection itself and most especially how we make decisions. Too often selectors make important choices on the basis of fragile and suspect judgements, judgements which are subsequently open to question and which are not easily translated into positive feedback to those players involved.

In the wake of ever increasing interest amongst occupational psychologists in the selection process and how best to select fairly (Kremer, 1991), it was inevitable that attention should fall on the role played by human judgement. There is not the time to delve deeply into the vast psychological literature on human judgement here. Suffice it to say that the processes by which we intuitively arrive at decisions, either individually or collectively, are far from mechanical and are also far from being perfect. Information from both the environment and our experience is used idiosyncratically to help us arrive at a decision. To save time and effort, we are not averse to using simplifying strategies or cognitive shortcuts to reach opinions quickly. While these strategies reduce the cost of processing information, they are prone to induce errors that could be avoided by more systematic but effortful procedures. Fortunately, such procedures are available to improve upon and systematize basic human decision making. The extent to which these models are in some way prototypes of natural processes, or are radical alternatives to how we normally process information, has yet to be determined, but this debate should not prevent us now proceeding to prescribe how the selection process in sport may be improved.

Selecting Fairly

It is widely recognized that the development and use of job related criteria forms an essential part of a fair personnel selection process (see Muchinsky, 1993, Chapters 3 and 5). To demonstrate how such a process could operate in sport, an example used by the authors when working with coaches from one particular sport is shown below. It is not our intention to become bogged down in theory here but suffice it to say, the process has a sound theoretical basis in the personnel selection literature. It enables all relevant information to be quantified and combined within the decision making process and simultaneously allows the relative importance and salience of each piece of information to be taken into account.

The process operates according to simple mathematical principles (loosely adapted from Multi Attribute Utility Theory), essentially combining all available information in such a way as to arrive at the optimum solution, in this example the selection of a player for a particular position in field hockey. Initially, the selectors must draw up a list of all relevant attributes for that particular position (the equivalent of a job analysis), noting qualities which are specific to that position itself but also those qualities which are needed to complement other positions on the pitch as well as other players' strengths and weaknesses in the team. For the sake of example, these attributes could possibly include the following:

>   Speed
>   Vision/distribution
>   Close ball skill
>   Passing accuracy
>   Strength
>   Tackling ability
>   Team member
>   Age
>   Fitness
>   Competitiveness
>   Durability

Selectors then assign each attribute a particular weight, depending on its importance for that position and for the team at that time. Possible candidates for that position are then rated in terms of each attribute (out of 10), and that rating is then multiplied by the weighting to produce a score which can then be compared with other candidates as shown in Table 7.2.

Player A, with a score of 40.3, is therefore 'given the nod' over Player B with 33.5. What is more the selectors can now go back to both players and give precise feedback as to why the decision was made, and hopefully what Player B can do to improve his/her

Table 7.2: Selecting a Hockey Player

		PLAYER A		PLAYER B	
	Weight (W)	Rating (R)	W × R	Rating (R)	W × R
Speed	0.7	4	2.8	6	4.2
Vision/distribution	0.6	7	4.2	6	3.6
Close ball work	0.4	5	2.0	3	1.2
Passing	0.3	8	2.4	7	2.1
Strength	0.8	9	7.2	2	1.6
Tackling	1.0	3	3.0	6	6.0
'Team member'	0.5	6	3.0	4	2.0
Age	0.2	8	1.6	4	0.8
Fitness	0.7	7	4.9	5	3.5
Competitiveness	0.8	8	6.4	8	6.4
Durability	0.3	6	1.8	7	2.1
TOTAL			**40.3**		**33.5**

chances in the future. In this way, team selection, either by individuals or committee, may more accurately reflect upon relevant skills of individual players, and if biases and prejudices still exist then at least they will have had to be quantified. To summarize, the steps in this process are listed below.

1   List all possible candidates for the position.
2   List all attributes salient to the position itself and its place in the team as a whole.
3   Assign numerical weights (from 0 to 1) to each attribute according to its significance.
4   Give each candidate a score on each attribute depending on past performance.
5   Multiply the score on each attribute by the assigned numerical weight.
6   Add together the total score for each candidate.
7   Select the candidate with the highest total score.

The procedure appears straightforward. However steps two and three, involving making choices and assigning weights, is far from easy, especially when it is part of a group or committee exercise. Selectors may also feel that this process lacks the 'human touch' but in reality it may be doing little more than formalizing the process which was already working at a very informal level. Selection research does not suggest that formulae should replace people altogether but it does suggest that formulae should be used by people to facilitate the task of combining a set of piecemeal judgements into an overall summary score to aid decision-making. That is all, and for most judgements that is but a small part of the total task. While such techniques may not be a cure for all selection ills, they do provide practical methods for arriving at complex decisions. They aid in the thorough examination of selection problems and in the bringing together of all relevant information systematically. As many athletes would agree, selectors are not always, or usually, good judges of their own ability as judges. Possibly this process could help them improve.

Motivating Athletes

As other chapters amply demonstrate, over recent years considerable attention has been paid to the development of theories and models dealing with participation motivation in sport (Scanlan *et al.*, 1993). This work deliberately focuses on young athletes and highlights the significance of intrinsic motivators in maximizing an individual's long term commitment to sport. At the same time, the dangers associated with either parents or coaches emphasizing extrinsic rewards are openly acknowledged. It is also true to say that much of the research on sport motivation both in the UK and North America has concentrated on school populations using as subjects high school students and primary or secondary school pupils. While this research may be very revealing of drop-out and participation amongst amateur sportspeople, the limitations of the analysis with regard to professionals should not be ignored. This distinction between professional and amateur careers is brought home by Whitehead (1987) when she writes:

> Results from fifty interviews with children who dropped out of sport are now
> being analysed. These show that some of the teenagers are concerned to use
> their time for whatever will be of greatest long-term benefit in their lives (e.g.
> a career), and they don't see sport in that light.

While in no way devaluing the importance of this work on amateur and voluntary sport, unwittingly this research may be ignoring a considerable and growing number of young people who may realistically regard their involvement in sport not as recreational activity but as the first stage in a professional career. For these individuals, alternative models of motivation may be appropriate, and it is at this point that occupational psychology may be able to help. When long term careers and professional sport enter the equation then it may be necessary to consider participation in the context of process models of work motivation. These models enjoy a prominent role within industrial and occupational psychology but with notable exceptions, until very recently, they have rarely been cited within sport psychology (see Eccles and Harold, 1991).

In brief, the history of research on work motivation has shown a gradual shift from traditional content models of work motivation which endeavoured to list or classify motivators (for example the work of Maslow, Alderfer and Herzberg), and towards an appreciation of the complexities of the process of motivation, exemplified by the various expectancy-value models which describe how personal and environmental variables play their part in determining the relationship between effort, performance, rewards and job satisfaction, and thus future motivation (see Greenberg and Baron, 1993).

The argument advanced by Porter and Lawler (1968) is that motivation (otherwise referred to as effort) is related to performance, to reward and to satisfaction in a definable way. Three principal components are taken to determine motivation, namely expectancy, instrumentality and valence. Our motivation or the effort we are prepared to expend will depend first, upon our belief that we are capable of influencing our performance through increasing effort (expectancy), second, our knowledge that an increase in performance will be reflected in an increase in rewards (instrumentality), and finally, the value which we place on the rewards (both internal and external) that we expect to receive (valence). Diagrammatically, the model is shown in Figure 7.3.

One important feature of this model is the emphasis which it places on feedback. Accordingly in the context of coaching the model has considerable practical utility for

Figure 7.3: An Expectancy-Value Model of Work Motivation

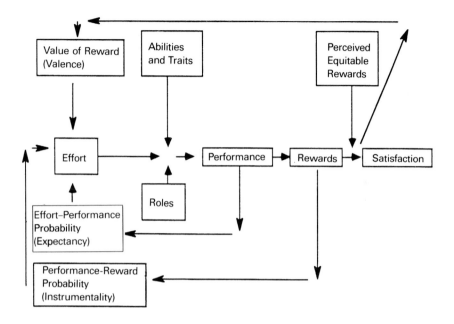

identifying and dealing with management problems effectively. In a research context, the model also has great heuristic value for considering the interaction between a number of cognitive and environmental factors in determining satisfaction and future effort. However, the complexity of the model also means that practically, it is difficult to develop a research project which is able to look at each component systematically, or to take into account all other possible intervening factors, for example, attributional style (see Chapter 6). Using a very rudimentary expectancy-value model to frame discussion, a preliminary study by Kremer and Robinson (1992) considered the attitudes and motivations of professional apprentice soccer players from Northern Ireland who had travelled to join English and Scottish clubs, often to return to Ireland after being rejected. Contrary to predictions based on intrinsic motivation models, these players did not return disenchanted and lost to the game, but almost invariably they slotted comfortably into life in the Irish League, often older and wiser as to their potential but still continuing to take a very active part in the game which they continued to enjoy. Clearly the reward structure which motivated these young professionals was very different from that which is described in relation to participation rates and drop-out amongst young, amateur athletes. Once more, occupational psychology may present genuine opportunities for understanding and there is a need to ensure that an awareness of the many faces of sport, both amateur and professional, voluntary and compulsory, are kept very much to the fore in any future discussion of sport motivation.

The Way Forward

This chapter has brought together a diversity of material, bound loosely together because of its association with research originating in occupational and industrial psychology. The range of material covered makes it difficult to draw sweeping conclusions. Instead, future directions have been suggested at various points throughout the chapter. Progress has proceeded at very different rates in each of the four areas covered. Sports related research dealing with leadership and goal setting is well developed, the work on selection and professionalism in sport is in its infancy. It is to be hoped that in the case of leadership and goal setting that the transfer process between occupational and sport psychology continues to open up opportunities for advancement of our knowledge, tempered always by an awareness of the special context which sport provides. In the case of the latter two topics, and other related possibilities, it is to be hoped that an increasing number of sport psychologists can be drawn towards working in this area. The payoffs for themselves, and for sport, could be considerable.

References

BEGGS, W. D. A. (1991) 'Goal setting in sport', in JONES, J. G. and HARDY, L. (Eds) *Stress and Performance in Sport*, London: Academic Press, pp. 135–70.

BRYMAN, A. (1986) *Leadership and Organizations*, London: Routledge and Kegan Paul.

BULL, S. J. (Ed.) (1991) *Sport Psychology: A Self-help Guide*, Wiltshire: The Crowood Press.

BURTON, D. (1992) 'The Jekyll/Hyde nature of goals: Reconceptualizing goal setting in sport', in HORN, T. S. (Ed.) *Advances in Sport Psychology*, Champaign, IL: Human Kinetics, pp. 267–97.

CASE, R. W. (1987) 'Leadership behavior in sport: A field test of the situational leadership theory', *International Journal of Sport Psychology*, 18, pp. 256–68.

CHELLADURAI, P. (1993) 'Leadership', in SINGER, R. N., MURPHEY, M. and TENNANT, L. K. (Eds) *Handbook of Research on Sport Psychology*, New York: Macmillan, pp. 647–71.

CHELLADURAI, P. and CARRON, A. (1983) 'Athletic maturity and preferred leadership', *Journal of Sport Psychology*, 5, pp. 371–80.

CHELLADURAI, P. and HAGGERTY, T. R. (1978) 'A normative model of decision-making styles in coaching', *Athletic Administration*, 13, 1, pp. 6–9.

CHELLADURAI, P., HAGGERTY, T. and BAXTER, P. (1989) 'Decision style choices of university basketball coaches and players', *Journal of Sport and Exercise Psychology*, 11, pp. 201–15.

CHELLADURAI, P., IMAMURA, H., YAMAGUCHI, Y., OINUMA, Y. and MIYAUCHI, T. (1988) 'Sport leadership in a cross-national setting: The case of Japanese and Canadian university athletes', *Journal of Sport and Exercise Psychology*, 10, pp. 374–89.

CHELLADURAI, P. and SALEH, S. D. (1980) 'Dimensions of leader behavior in sport: Development of a leadership scale', *Journal of Sport Psychology*, 2, pp. 34–35.

COX, R. H. (1990) *Sport Psychology: Concepts and Applications*, 2nd edn, Dubuque, IA: Wm C. Brown.

DANIELSON, R. R., ZELHART, P. F. and DRAKE, C. J. (1975) 'Multidimensional scaling and factor analysis of coaching behavior as perceived by high school hockey players', *Research Quarterly*, 46, pp. 323–34.

DENNIS, P. (1991) Personal correspondence from Swimming Coaching Development Officer for Northern Ireland.

EAGLY, A. H. and JOHNSON, B. T. (1990) 'Gender and leadership style: A meta-analysis', *Psychological Bulletin*, 108, pp. 233–56.

ECCLES, J. S. and HAROLD, R. D. (1991) 'Gender differences in sport involvement: Applying the Eccles expectancy-value model', *Journal of Applied Sport Psychology*, 3, pp. 7–35.

FIEDLER, F. E. (1967) *A Theory of Leadership Effectiveness*, New York: McGraw-Hill.

FIEDLER, F. E. and CHEMERS, M. M. (1984) *Improving Leadership Effectiveness: The Leader Match Concept*, 2nd edn, New York: John Wiley and Sons.

FIELD, R. H. G. and HOUSE, R. J. (1990) 'A test of the Vroom-Yetton model using manager and subordinate reports', *Journal of Applied Psychology*, 75, pp. 362–6.

GIANNINI, J. M., WEINBERG, R. S. and JACKSON, A. J. (1988) 'The effects of mastery, competitive and cooperative goals on the performance of simple and complex basketball skills', *Journal of Sport and Exercise Psychology*, 10, pp. 408–17.

GORDON, S. (1988) 'Decision styles and effectiveness in university soccer', *Canadian Journal of Sport Sciences*, 13, pp. 56–65.

GOULD, D. (1986) 'Goal setting for peak performance', in WILLIAMS, J. (Ed.) *Applied Sport Psychology*, Palo Alto, CA: Mayfield, pp. 143–58.

GOULD, D., GIANNINI, J., KRANE, V. and HODGE, K. (1990) 'Educational needs of élite US national team, Pan American, and Olympic coaches', *Journal of Teaching in Physical Education*, 9, pp. 332–44.

GREENBERG, J. and BARON, R. A. (1993) *Behaviour in Organizations*, 4th edn, Needham Heights, MA: Allyn and Bacon.

HALL, H. K. and BYRNE, T. J. (1988) 'Goal setting in sport: Clarifying recent anomalies', *Journal of Sport and Exercise Psychology*, 10, pp. 184–98.

HANSON, T. and GOULD, D. (1988) 'Factors affecting the ability of coaches to estimate their athletes' trait and state anxiety levels', *The Sport Psychologist*, 2, pp. 298–313.

HARDY, L. and FAZEY, J. A. (1990) *Mental Training*, Leeds: The National Coaching Foundation.

HASBROOK, C. A., HART, B.A., MATHES, S. A. and TRUE, S. (1990) 'Sex bias and validity of the believed differences between male and female interscholastic athletic coaches', *Research Quarterly for Exercise and Sport*, 61, 3, pp. 259–67.

HERSEY, P. and BLANCHARD, K. H. (1982) *Management of Organizational Behavior: Utilizing Human Resources*, 4th edn, Englewood Cliffs, NJ: Prentice-Hall.

HOLLANDER, E. P. (1985) 'Leadership and power', in LINDZEY, G. and ARONSON, E. (Eds) *The Handbook of Social Psychology*, Volume 2, 3rd edn, New York: Random House, pp. 485–537.

HORN, T. S. (1984) 'Expectancy effects in the interscholastic athletic setting: Methodological considerations', *Journal of Sport Psychology*, 6, pp. 60–76.

HORN, T. S. (1992) 'Leadership effectiveness in the sport domain', in HORN, T. S. (Ed.) *Advances in Sport Psychology*, Champaign, IL: Human Kinetics, pp. 181–99.

HOUSE, R. J. and MITCHELL, T. R. (1974) 'Path-goal theory of leadership', *Journal of Contemporary Business*, 3, pp. 81–97.

JONES, J. G., SWAIN, A. and CALE, A. (1990) 'Antecedents of multidimensional competitive state anxiety and self-confidence in élite intercollegiate middle distance runners', *The Sport Psychologist*, 4, pp. 107–18.

KREMER, J. (1991) *Recruiting and Selecting Fairly: A Summary Report*, Belfast: Fair Employment Agency.

KREMER, J. and ROBINSON, F. (1992) 'The boy didn't always done great: Apprentice footballers in Northern Ireland.' British Psychological Society (Northern Ireland Branch) Annual Conference, Virginia, County Cavan, Ireland.

LACY, A. C. and GOLDSTON, P. D. (1990) 'Behavior analysis of male and female coaches in high school girls' basketball', *Journal of Sport Behavior*, 13, 1, pp. 29–40.

LEE, C. (1991) 'Followership: The essence of leadership', *Training*, 28, pp. 27–35.

LOCKE, E. A. (1991) 'Problems with goal-setting research in sports — and their solution', *Journal of Sport and Exercise Psychology*, 8, pp. 311–16.

LOCKE, E.A. and LATHAM, G. P. (1985) 'The application of goal setting to sports', *Journal of Sport Psychology*, 7, pp. 205–22.

LOCKE, E. A. and LATHAM, G. P. (1990) *A Theory of Goal Setting and Task Performance*, Englewood Cliffs, NJ: Prentice Hall.

MARTENS, R. (1989) *Coaches Guide to Sport Psychology*, Champaign, IL: Human Kinetics.

MUCHINSKY, P. M. (1993) *Psychology Applied to Work*, 4th edn, Pacific Grove, CA: Brooks/Cole.

PORTER, L. W. and LAWLER, E. E. (1968) *Managerial Attitudes and Performance*, New York: Irwin Dorsey.

ROBERTS, G. C. (Ed.) (1992) *Motivation in Sport and Exercise*, Champaign, IL: Human Kinetics.

SCANLAN, T. K., CARPENTER, P. J., SCHMIDT, G. W., SIMONS, J. P. and KEELER, B. (1993) 'An introduction to the sport commitment model', *Journal of Sport and Exercise Psychology*, 15, pp. 1–15.

SCHLIESMAN, E. (1987) 'Relationship between the congruence of preferred and actual leader behavior and subordinate satisfaction with leadership', *Journal of Sport Behavior*, 10, pp. 157–66.

SMITH, R. and SMOLL, F. L. (1990) 'Self-esteem and children's reactions to youth sport coaching behaviors: A field study of self-enhancement processes', *Developmental Psychology*, 26, 6, pp. 987–93.

SMITH, R. E., SMOLL, F. L. and HUNT, E. (1977) 'A system for the behavioral assessment of athletic coaches', *Research Quarterly*, 48, pp. 401–7.

SMOLL, F. L. and SMITH, R. E. (1989) 'Leadership behaviors in sport: A theoretical model and research paradigm', *Journal of Applied Social Psychology*, 19, 18, pp. 1522–51.

VOS STRACHE, C. (1979) 'Players' perceptions of leadership qualities for coaches', *Research Quarterly*, 50, pp. 679–86.

VROOM, V. H. and YETTON, P. W. (1973) *Leadership and Decision Making*, Pittsburgh: University of Pittsburgh Press.

WEINBERG, R. S. (1992) 'Goal setting and motor performance: A review and critique', in ROBERTS, C. G. (Ed.) *Motivation in Sport and Exercise*, Champaign, IL: Human Kinetics, pp. 177–98.

WEINBERG, R. S., BRUYA, L. D. and JACKSON, A. J. (1985) 'The effects of goal proximity and specificity on endurance performance', *Journal of Sport Psychology*, 1, pp. 296–305.

WHITEHEAD, J. (1987) 'Why children take part', *The ISCiS Journal*, 1, (i), pp. 23–31.

WILLIAMS, J. (1986) *Applied Sport Psychology: Personal Growth to Peak Performance*, Palo Alto, CA: Mayfield.

Further Reading

BEGGS, W. D. A. (1991) 'Goal setting in sport', in JONES, J. G. and HARDY, L. (Eds) *Stress and Performance in Sport*, London: Academic Press, pp. 135–70.

BURTON, D. (1992) 'The Jekyll/Hyde nature of goals: Reconceptualizing goal setting in sport', in HORN, T. S. (Ed.) *Advances in Sport Psychology*, Champaign, IL: Human Kinetics, pp. 267–97

CHELLADURAI, P. (1993) 'Leadership', in SINGER, R. N., MURPHEY, M. and TENNANT, L. K. (Eds) *Handbook of Research on Sport Psychology*, New York: Macmillan.

ECCLES, J. S. and HAROLD, R. D. (1991) 'Gender differences in sport involvement: Applying the Eccles expectancy-value model', *Journal of Applied Sport Psychology*, 3, pp. 7–35.

HORN, T. S. (1992) 'Leadership effectiveness in the sport domain', in HORN, T. S. (Ed.) *Advances in Sport Psychology*, Champaign, IL: Human Kinetics, pp. 181–99.

MARTENS, R. (1989) *Coaches Guide to Sport Psychology*, Champaign, IL: Human Kinetics.

ROBERTS, G. C. (Ed.) (1992) *Motivation in Sport and Exercise*, Champaign, IL: Human Kinetics.

SCANLAN, T. K., CARPENTER, P. J., SCHMIDT, G. W., SIMONS, J. P. and KEELER, B. (1993) 'An introduction to the sport commitment model', *Journal of Sport and Exercise Psychology*, 15, pp. 1–15.

WILLIAMS, J. (1986) *Applied Sport Psychology: Personal Growth to Peak Performance*, Palo Alto, CA: Mayfield.

Chapter 8

Growing through Sport

(Developmental Psychology)

Introduction

Traditionally, developmental psychology has been selective in the way it views our lives from cradle to grave. High on its priority list have been topics such as early childhood experience and learning, motivation, perception, intelligence, language and concept development, personality and socialization. From the point of view of sport, one topic is very notable by its absence from this list, motor development. That is not to say that the acquisition of motor skills has been ignored but too often physical accomplishments have been used as no more than developmental milestones, marking out what were seen as more psychologically significant developments in terms of cognitive, perceptual or social skills. Indeed it is only in the last few years that motor development has gained recognition as a valued and separate area within the subdiscipline, with a growing literature devoted solely to the topic (see Gabbard, 1992).

As well as focusing on selected topics, developmental psychology has also tended to concentrate its attention on certain stages of life, most notably childhood and adolescence. Again only recently has development throughout life, and including middle and old age, come under the research spotlight. This shift in emphasis promises to be highly significant for sport psychology, particularly given an ageing population which includes a growing number who have cast aside the walking frame and instead have donned a swimming costume or leotard! Attendance figures for adult sport and exercise classes bear testimony to this trend. For sport and exercise psychologists, as for the general population, there has been a need to change our perception of old age as principally a sedentary period of life and to begin to recognize the value of sport and exercise throughout life (Ostrow and Dzewaltowski, 1986). Without doubt, the 1990s represents a most exciting time for those sport scientists with an interest in motor development. On the one hand they must continue to maintain and consolidate a foothold within developmental psychology; on the other they must grapple with the new priorities which have emerged across the field as a whole. Whether they are successful on one or both fronts remains to be seen.

Motor Development

Motor development is concerned with describing and explaining changes in movement behaviour from infancy to adulthood. To achieve this goal, many of the theories and research methods which had been derived from general developmental psychology were borrowed wholesale, but in turn, subsequent motor development research was singularly unsuccessful in influencing or being recognized in mainstream developmental psychology. As a result, although many of the early developmental scales and measures may have included indices of movement behaviours, there was little interest in physical movement *per se*. Instead movement was simply looked upon as a register of cognitive and perceptual maturation.

Leaving aside the lack of interest from within developmental psychology, there has always been a separate literature available from outside psychology which has focused exclusively on movement development. Interestingly, early research in this area followed a similar approach to the naturalistic records and observations common within general developmental psychology in the first half of this century. There then followed a dormant period in movement development from the 1940s to 1960s but a renewed interest emerged in the 1970s largely as a result of practical issues such as a concern for children with learning problems, the rehabilitation of disabled children and the emergence of physical education as an academic discipline. The last 20 years have witnessed a tremendous growth in the area of motor development both through a greatly enhanced research base, and through the development of theories which are specific to motor development. Both these trends have produced a situation where motor development research is now able to shift its attention away from simply charting the course of behavioural change and towards an understanding of the psychological and biological processes which drive that change. Although many of the research methods remain similar (including detailed observations of movement), the theoretical approaches have expanded by integrating and cross-fertilizing ideas from the neurosciences and a range of other disciplines. Through this slow process of evolution, motor development research has become genuinely interdisciplinary, and has learnt to draw selectively from psychology's theories and methods but only as one part of a larger package of contributions.

Research in this field has traditionally adopted one of two methodologies, best categorized as either naturalistic or experimental (Thomas, 1989). The naturalistic approach relies upon the gathering of a large amount of descriptive data in natural settings in an effort to determine what changes our behaviour. For example, many of the early studies in motor development provided detailed and precise observations of young children's movements. Current studies adopting this approach use what are known as 'kinematic' and 'kinetic' analyses of movements to yield precise descriptions of specific actions. The experimental approach, on the other hand, normally uses controlled laboratory settings to examine the effects of particular manipulations on changes in motor behaviour. Whichever approach is adopted, it is normally the case that one of two research designs are used, either a longitudinal or a cross sectional design. The former monitors subjects over an extended period of time, periodically taking repeated measures of behaviour. For example, a study examining the development of throwing skills in children would measure a child's throwing ability at two years and once a year for each following year until the age of say 14 years. Using this method researchers claim to be able to observe directly development 'in the flesh' rather than having to infer change over time from different subject groups. A cross sectional design uses different subjects within each of the age groups of interest and tests all subjects at the one time. Development is therefore not directly observed but inferred from observed differences in performance of different age groups.

Both of these research designs have their inherent strengths and weaknesses, and arguments have been advanced in support of each, often depending on the researcher's vested interest. To overcome these problems, Schaie (1965) developed the sequential approach which essentially tries to bring together the best of both worlds. The three components normally included in a sequential design are age, cohort and time of measurement. Different cohorts are tested at the same time initially but then are followed up longitudinally, thus providing a time-lag component. However, although the sequential approach was originally proposed to circumvent existing design shortcomings it too has come under attack (Adam, 1978). The problem is basically a statistical one and stems from the fact that all results of a sequential study must be analysed three times using two of the three factors at a time. This type of repeated analysis can produce validity problems, and naturally increases the risk of 'type two' statistical errors (that is the more often you test, the more likely you are to find significant results on the basis of chance).

Beyond these methodological concerns, probably the most important problem still facing motor developmentalists is how to develop a comprehensive theoretical framework which is capable of explaining growth and change and which can encompass both physiological, biological and psychological considerations. From the biological or physiological perspective the primary concern is with understanding how the various body parts and systems contribute to developmental changes. From the psychological perspective the emphasis shifts to the role of the individual as a thinking and feeling human being whose behaviour is a reflection of cognitive and emotional development. In order to understand thoroughly motor development, both perspectives are equally important. The role of biological or physiological factors is especially salient to understanding physical growth changes and the physiological demands of various activities, as well as age-related differences in performance. At the same time it is equally important to acknowledge the role played by psychological factors such as an individual's decisions or emotions in affecting motivation and participation.

The early developmentalists studied changes in movement behaviours as they related to the maturation of the human organism. Prominent amongst these early writers was Gesell who argued that maturation was the regulatory mechanism that stabilized the process of development. Development itself was considered to be synonymous with growth and therefore he postulated a continuous process which 'beginning with conception, proceeds stage by stage in orderly sequence, each stage representing a degree or level of maturity' (Gesell and Amatruda, 1947). It was assumed that maturation was an unfolding process whereby observed behavioural changes were presumably directly linked to concomitant neurological changes, and indeed the link between the maturation of the central nervous system and the emergence of behaviour became the principal focus of much of the early motor development research work (see Haywood, 1986).

Gesell is also credited with developing the experimental method of co-twin control (a method later to be used so controversially by Sir Cyril Burt (Hearnshaw, 1992)). In the case of Gesell's work, one of the twins received specialized training (for example, climbing stairs) while the other was allowed to develop without specific intervention. The twins were then compared at a later date to determine the influence of genetic or biological factors on specific skills. The theory predicted, and generally proved, that additional training would not affect the appearance of skills until the organism's genetic blueprint had reached the point of readiness to learn the skill. Despite methodological problems, Gesell's work became crucial in the drawing up of sequences of skill development, and these subsequently have become very important in defining the order of appearance of the basic motor patterns. Not only has the maturational perspective continued to retain pole position in the motor development literature but it has also served as a pitprop supporting the argument that motor development is strongly determined by the genetic code (Newell, 1986).

More recently, and some would say radically, a new concept of coordinative structures and constraints has been proposed which represents a direct challenge to Gesell's and a host of other traditional perspectives. According to this dynamical perspective, the development of coordination is viewed as a property which emerges from the coming together of various constraints (both organismic, task and environmental) which are imposed upon the child's action (Kugler *et al.*, 1982). The theory suggests that as biological organisms, we naturally exhibit patterns of coordination that are both stable and optimal. That is, these patterns represent a 'best fit' given the constraints imposed on our action. Understanding the nature of the constraints on actions then becomes a major concern. The dynamical perspective tends to focus on understanding how complex movements are learned and controlled by examining the acquisition of phylogenetic skills, for example posture, locomotion and grasping. This approach is currently gaining in popularity not only amongst motor developmentalists but the ideas are now being taken up by mainstream psychology and are being used to further our understanding of developmental processes across psychology as a whole. This has to be an optimistic sign for the future for at long last there are signs that integrative approaches have secured a firm foothold across the area as a whole (see Eisenberg, 1987).

Contemporary Concerns

As a bare minimum, any list of the main areas of interest within the field of motor development during the past decade would have to include the following: first, the influence of growth on motor performance; second, the development of movement patterns and motor performance; third, physiological development and the effects of exercise across childhood and adolescence; fourth, the role of information processing on learning and controlling movements; and finally, the involvement in sport and its effect on psychosocial development.

Growth and Motor Development

Most research on physical growth and development has been descriptive in nature and more than anything else, has focused on establishing norms (for example Shephard, 1982). These norms have assisted practitioners in designing programmes for teaching motor skills, as well as being used extensively by clinical practitioners such as pediatricians and physiotherapists. Growth and maturation are essential concomitants to the development of many skills but obviously not all individuals grow and mature at the same rate. This means that a teacher or coach may face a group of 6-year-old children where some may be taller than some 7-year-olds and some may be shorter than some 5-year-olds. This makes it difficult for the teacher to know what to expect of the group as a whole. Before we can assess a child's sporting potential it is helpful to know the course of 'normal' development and to understand what are considered to be normal and abnormal variations to that course. This kind of information may then be useful in determining if a particular child is ready for involvement in a formal sports programme and at the same time will also be of great value to pediatricians and other clinical personnel who may be called upon to deal with atypical development.

Traditionally, the term growth was used to refer to structural changes alone and was often limited to concepts such as size. However, most developmentalists now consider functional changes including the growth of the bones and tissues, as well as the maturation of the major systems, as each having an important influence on motor development. As Keogh and Sugden (1985) point out, each plays a vital role in determining the influence of biological changes on motor development. For example, the basic body structure is provided by the increase in length of the bones and the increase in dimensions and proportions of muscle, fat and other tissues. In addition, from a psychological perspective the neuromotor system which links nerves and muscles to control movement and the cardiovascular and pulmonary systems which service energy needs and metabolic functions, all mature at varying rates but with an underlying organization and order.

An important aspect of growth and development for motor skill acquisition and involvement in sport concerns not absolute but relative growth. Relative growth refers to the fact that the many body parts all exhibit differential growth rates which cause notable changes in the overall form. In fact, body form changes dramatically over the first 25 years. For example, the head constitutes one quarter of the height at birth but only represents one eighth of the adult height. Similarly, the legs are approximately three eighths of height at birth but this proportion increases to almost half of the adult height. It is quite likely that these changes in form can cause major problems for the growing child who is involved in sport yet very little empirical research has been undertaken to examine their impact. One exception is the work of Jensen (1981) who examined the effects of a 12 month growth period on the principal whole body moments of inertia (defined as the amount of resistance to angular movement) of 12 boys aged between four and 12 years.

On the basis of this and related applied research conducted over the past 10 years, the need to consider scaling sports equipment to meet children's needs and requirements has been clearly demonstrated. For example, in basketball the average male adult height is estimated as 58 per cent of the height of a basketball hoop, whereas the average male 9-year-old is only about 43 per cent of that height. This means that the child would have to produce much greater force to hit the same target yet at the same time the child is disadvantaged because s/he has proportionately less muscle than an adult and the child's limb-trunk proportions are different which in turn will affect the biomechanics of throwing. In the USA, research which considered the effects of manipulating the size of the basketball for women has subsequently resulted in the introduction of a smaller and lighter ball for adult women. Perhaps this line of investigation should be followed through into the future design of children's sporting equipment as undoubtedly the kinds of form changes experienced over the growing years have significant effects on children's sporting performance.

Movement Patterns and Motor Performance

Sport scientists have long charted the appearance of various movement patterns, from the basic motor behaviours of posture, locomotion and grasping, to the more identifiable sports-related activities of running, hopping, jumping, throwing and catching. As already mentioned, early investigations adopted a very descriptive approach to research and hence were able to amass a number of naturalistic records of how the fundamental motor patterns progress through childhood. Many of these investigations were actually no more than individual case histories of selected individuals, and often involved the researcher's own children as subjects. Following on from this line of study came the contributions of Gesell and his followers who provided detailed records of the early developmental progressions. Indeed, many of the normative scales and charts developed at this time are still in use today by educationalists, health visitors and pediatricians. These scales provide us with the average age at which landmark achievements should be reached and also show an acceptable range of deviation which can be regarded as 'normal'.

A similar descriptive approach was used to examine the development of those basic motor skills which were assumed to be fundamental to sports skills (Roberton, 1982). These included throwing, catching, running, jumping and striking. As a result of this work a number of motor development textbooks now provide guidelines on what should be considered 'normal' or 'mature' motor patterns (for example, Roberton and Halverson, 1984). One of two lines of investigation is usually followed in this type of work. The first is close to the traditional descriptive approach in which total body actions are described. The second examines changes in body movements by breaking down the total action into separate components. For example, the throwing pattern would be described in relation to individual body segments, such as the forearm, arm, trunk, and leg.

The usefulness of these descriptions of movement patterns is open to debate. On the one hand some motor developmentalists argue that by describing the actual movement patterns exhibited by young children they are providing teachers and other practitioners with guidelines for development. On the other hand, there is the argument that we need to move beyond mere description and should now use the descriptive data as a starting point for testing theoretical constructs in the real world. However, although movement patterns have been well documented, the question needs to be asked as to whether teachers, working in the real world, are able to observe accurately the documented developmental sequences. Perhaps this is the next issue for research in this area to address but certainly at least an awareness of the need to marry good theory with good practice sits easily alongside recent trends in developmental psychology which we have already discussed.

Physiological Development and Exercise Effects

Without doubt, the advent of the health and fitness boom in the 1980s and 1990s has had a profound influence on the research agenda in this area. Traditionally, it was assumed that children naturally and automatically will take necessary exercise through voluntary and active play. Therefore the promotion of physical fitness amongst children, as opposed to adults, was not seen to be important. Recent studies from Europe and the USA have revealed that this is no longer true and that children nowadays are showing a number of risk factors for coronary heart disease and at an alarmingly young age (Dishman and Dunn, 1988). These findings have been related to the more sedentary lifestyles associated with leisure interests centring around videos and computer games, as well as diets based on convenience or junk foods. Gone are the days when physical fitness was seen as synonymous with youth. The young may be equally likely to be physically unfit and the more elderly may equally derive great benefit from physical activity (Willis and Campbell, 1992). This change in attitude represents a major social revolution over recent years, and one where sport psychology, or more correctly exercise psychology, has played and will continue to play a dominant role.

Information Processing and Skill Development

Another area of considerable interest concerns the perceptual and cognitive mechanisms which underlie skills development. In the main, two approaches have been adopted. The first is grounded in information processing theory and the second in the Piagetian and neo-Piagetian traditions. The information processing approach proposes a model of the various functions of the organism in response to stimulus from the environment. For example, when a soccer player is faced with a situation in which he has control of the ball but a defender is about to tackle him, he must respond immediately and decide whether to keep the ball, shoot or pass it to a teammate. In making any such decision a number of processes are involved. These include perceiving and interpreting the environmental situation, noting the options which are available, making a decision based on the situation as well as knowledge of capability and past performance, coordinating the correct muscles to produce the required action, and finally perceiving and interpreting feedback during and after the action. The information processing approach to motor development sets itself the task of examining children's, adults' and older adults' information processing abilities, memories and mental capacities in an effort to explain the limits of processing abilities and how this impacts on motor performance (see Thomas *et al.*, 1988).

Research based on the information processing approach suggests that children under the age of 12 years have limited information processing ability in comparison to adults in terms of factors such as selective attention, feedback, neuromuscular control and speed of processing (Thomas *et al.*, 1993). However, each of these factors can be significantly improved through experience, thus immediately suggesting that the limitations are not entirely due to cognitive or structural differences at particular stages of development. At the other end of the age spectrum, older adults also exhibit limitations in their information processing although these are qualitatively different to those in childhood. Most limitations at this stage of life affect only rapid movements requiring a high speed of processing.

Memory functions are also thought to be limited in both young children and older adults. In young children memory deficits are believed to result from reduced efficiency of the control processes that shift information through the memory system leading to lowered ability in rehearsing, labelling, chunking and recoding information to be recalled

(McPherson and Thomas, 1989). The speed of processing information is also slower in children under the age of 11 than in adults. All of these memory functions may also be impaired in the older adult although it is thought that at this stage of life some of these deficits may reflect structural changes in the brain, such as loss of neurons with old age.

With regard to cognitive development, Piaget's stage model of cognitive development still enjoys widespread popularity amongst motor developmentalists. According to Piaget, the behaviours that children exhibited with increasing maturity tended to appear in distinct stages, namely the sensorimotor (birth–2 years), preoperational (2–7 years), concrete operational (7–11 years) and formal operational (over 11 years). A major criticism of Piaget's theory has been the lack of attention to the functional process by which learning is proposed to occur. In direct reply to such criticisms the neo-Piagetian Pascual-Leone (1976) proposed the notion of M-space which is hypothesized as the mental space which grows with age. It is thought that a child develops certain rules and strategies to accommodate the tasks s/he is performing and as s/he grows older and has more experience s/he is capable of more difficult tasks by either calling up more 'rules' or by integrating more movements. This idea enjoys popular support in motor development circles as researchers have demonstrated that both the capacity and use of the M-space increases for motor performance with increasing age (Todor, 1978).

Children's Sport Participation

The study of young people's involvement in sport was spearheaded in the USA by a number of sport psychologists who became concerned with the effects of competitive sport involvement on young children (see Smoll *et al.*, 1988). Over the years this area has mushroomed and has been successful in bringing together contributions from a variety of disciplines including psychology, sociology, anthropology and medicine. There are two primary issues which confront researchers in the area. The first is to discover the factors which influence socialization into sport and exercise, and the second is to examine thoroughly the consequences of participation in competitive sport.

According to a recent review by Greendorfer (1992: 201), 'sport psychology has had only a passing interest in sport socialization either as a general or a specific area of research.' This may well have been true in the past but over very recent years the growth of interest in this field has been exponential, and outstanding theoretical advances have been made, most notably in relation to work on social cognition and intrinsic motivation (see Brustad, 1993). This includes the contribution of Bandura's self-efficacy theory, together with Harter's theory of perceived competence, Deci's cognitive evaluation theory and the work of Dweck, Maehr and Nicholls on achievement orientation (see Roberts, 1992). This work has been instrumental in demonstrating the significance of personal expectancies and values in terms of the reasons why people take up and often leave sport, and are beginning to be included alongside other factors in models which describe the determinants of sport participation. According to Greendorfer (1992), three principal clusters of factors can be identified. These are personal attributes (including expectancies, values and attitudes), significant others (for example family, peers, siblings, teachers, coaches and sporting role models) and socialization situations (or opportunity sets). Of the three clusters, personal attributes and significant others have received the most attention. With regard to the latter, the influence of social learning perspectives becomes immediately obvious. Above all else, social learning theories have been instrumental in alerting us to children's great capacity for learning by observing others and imitating their behaviour. This process is very evident when examining the influence of significant others on children's sport involvement. In general, it is has been shown that the family, and often the father, has a considerable effect on whether or not a child becomes involved in sport (Lewko and Greendorfer, 1988). If a child is used to seeing his or her parents involved in sport then it is more likely that the child will see sport involvement as natural in comparison to the child whose parents show no interest in sport. At the same time, a number of studies point to other influential factors contributing to this socialization process, such as the role of teachers/coaches, influence from siblings or peers, and the influence of socio-economic status on the opportunities for involvement in more costly sports (Greendorfer, 1992).

Whichever factors are more or less important it appears clear that an individual's motivation to take up sport will be influenced by the reinforcement which is offered, the rewards (both intrinsic and extrinsic) which accrue, and the feedback which is received. Those who are familiar with process models of work motivation (see Chapter 7) will immediately recognize the pieces of a jigsaw falling into place here, as these are all terms which are routinely used in expectancy-value models of work motivation. Only very recently have attempts been made to use these models to describe sport socialization as a whole, but the work in this area looks extremely promising (Brustad, 1993).

As part of any integrative model, gender must play an important part in the sport socialization process (Colley *et al.*, 1992). Numerous studies point to the different ways parents treat children of different sexes. When a small boy hurts himself playing football he is told 'big boys don't cry' but when a young girl goes out to play with her friends she is told not to get dirty. It is statements like these which quite unintentionally influence children's perception of what are appropriate gender roles. The same socialization process may influence a child's perception of sport, with boys often given greater encouragement and opportunity to become involved in competitive sport. The small number of studies which have looked at this issue certainly suggest that gender differences in sport involvement can often be attributed to social learning influences and many researchers agree that some of the physical differences found in motor development and skill acquisition research are attributable to social rather than biological differences between the sexes.

On the other side of the participation–motivation coin lie attrition and drop-out, concerns which have interested sport psychologists for some time but which have been quietly forgotten for too long by others in the world of sport. Indeed it could be argued that one of the very reasons why so many young people continue to drop out from organized sport is that because policy makers, coaches and educators alike have for too long neglected to identify the reasons why people choose to participate in the first place and whether these needs continue to be met by their chosen sport. For example, two of the primary reasons which young children consistently give for becoming involved in sport are 'fun' and 'improving skill', and not competition, health and fitness which are often higher on a list of a mature athlete's priorities (Brodkin and Weiss, 1990). The drop-out rate from children's organized sports programmes remains worryingly high. In the USA, Roberts (1984) declared that drop-out was the most serious problem facing contemporary children's sport, with an estimated 80 per cent drop-out rate between the ages of 12 and 17 years. Statistics from elsewhere confirm this depressing picture worldwide. In order to understand primarily attrition from sport Gould (1987) has proposed a motivational model applicable to youth sport. An initial descriptive study by Gould and Horn (1984) revealed that children give several different motives for becoming involved in sport, but reasons primarily centre on improving skills, having fun, being with friends, enjoying excitement, experiencing success and developing physical fitness. More significantly, children who had ceased involvement in sport cited several motives for their withdrawal including conflicts of interest, lack of playing time, lack of success or skill improvement, competitive stress, lack of fun, dislike of the coach, boredom, and injury. Subsequently, Gould (1987) developed a motivational model of youth sport withdrawal, a model which has three main components.

The first component, sport withdrawal, deals with the way in which children withdraw from a sport. Often they do not necessarily cease to participate in all sport but instead withdrawal is sport-specific. For example, Gould (1982) discovered that 80 per cent of swimming drop outs re-entered or planned to re-enter sport (an example of sport-specific withdrawal). In contrast Petlichkoff (1982) found that 59 per cent of school sport drop-outs did not subsequently re-enter any organized sport (an example of domain general withdrawal). It is therefore immediately important to regard drop-out not as all or nothing but as a continuum ranging from sport-specific drop-out to complete cessation of organized physical activity.

The second component involves the young athlete engaging in a costs-benefits analysis, an approach firmly based in social exchange theory. This theory proposes that individuals weigh up the perceived benefits or costs of particular situations by comparing outcome (in terms of reward or cost) against two standards. The first standard is known as the comparison level (CL) and can best be described as one's expectations about a given activity. Satisfaction or attraction to an activity is determined by comparing outcomes with CL (Schmidt and Stein, 1991). The second comparison is known as comparison level for alternatives (CL_{alt}) and is the lowest level of an outcome that a person uses to judge something as being attractive or otherwise. Dependence on an activity is determined by CL_{alt} as it represents the individual's best alternative to the current activity. Gould (1987) suggests that an individual will withdraw from sport if the perceived costs of involvement outweigh the perceived benefits and if the alternative activities (for example other sport, schoolwork or discos) are seen as more attractive.

The third component, motivation for withdrawal, is made up of two components, explanations given (as derived from the descriptive research to date), and theoretical constructs (as used to explain suggested motives for withdrawal). Gould draws freely on a number of approaches here, including Maehr and Nicholls's cognitive interpretation of achievement goals, Harter's competence motivation theory; and Smith's cognitive-affective model of stress. Maehr and Nicholls (1980) argue that withdrawal from activity is based on the individual's achievement goals and their perceived chances of success. Harter (1981) suggests that an individual's perception of competence will affect their decision to withdraw or participate, and that individuals with low self-concept will have a greater tendency to withdraw. Such perceptions of competence will depend on the individual's perceived control of his/her environment and motivational orientations. Finally Smith (1986) emphasizes how burn out may occur when competitive stress becomes too much.

Gould attempts to do more than just describe the process of withdrawal from youth sports, he also attempts to understand attrition by applying a similar approach to understanding sport participation. Whether this is feasible remains to be seen but certainly it is a worthwhile endeavour. Thus, for example, it is necessary to establish the individual's achievement orientation in order to predict both sport involvement and/or subsequent withdrawal. In applying the model of youth sport participation and withdrawal Gould and Petlichkoff (1988) emphasize the need for leaders of youth sport to recognize individual differences in motivational patterns, their level of perceived competence, their level of trait anxiety and their ability to cope with stress. Once this is achieved it is proposed that leaders should be responsible for structuring the environment so that motives are fulfilled and confidence remains high, the costs and benefits should be openly discussed and the reasons for departing also discussed.

Once more the movement here towards process models of motivation is extremely encouraging, and mirrors work mentioned earlier and in other chapters which deals not so much with why people may leave sport or how they may be encouraged to stay, but rather with why people take part in sport in the first place. As time passes, it is almost inevitable that all these research strands will fuse together and already the signs of this fusion are clear and the future looks optimistic (for example see Roberts, 1992).

It is a commonly held belief that involvement in sport is good for character development. Somewhat surprisingly, research does not always support this notion. This is not to say that no good comes of involvement in sport, it merely points out that not all sport is always good. Four main points emerge from a review of this area. First, parent–child relationships can be affected either positively or negatively through involvement in sport. What may have started as initial enthusiasm and encouragement from a parent may later be interpreted as pressure by a child if s/he perceives that the parent is spending a lot of money and time on the child's involvement in sport. Second, there is some evidence to suggest that involvement in organized formal sports programmes may interfere with and undermine a child's ability to create, develop and organize their own play and games. Third, there is some concern that children involved in organized formal sport may become obsessed with winning and playing well rather than with being fair and having fun. However, recently it has been suggested that although this may happen within the organized sport itself, it rarely carries over into other areas of a child's life. Finally, the influence of the coach on children's sport experiences has received some attention although almost certainly more attention is warranted. Generally, it is agreed that coaches can occasionally become a significant role model for young athletes, particularly if the child is lacking a family role model for sport. Despite the bad press which coaches often receive, research suggests that most coaches have a positive rather than a negative influence on children's involvement (Smith and Smoll, 1990).

Teaching Sport

Already we see some evidence of the significant role which teachers and coaches play in the development of sporting competence, and it is specifically towards the teacher and/or the coach that we now turn our attention. Psychology has long been recognized as a hunting ground for generating advice for the world of education, and sport and physical education is no exception. Unfortunately, the translation of psychological principles into classroom and coaching practice has not always been easy and over the years has been the subject of great controversy (Newell, 1990). There is not the time to delve into these complex issues too deeply here. Suffice it to say that those working with young athletes, whether in schools or sport clubs, have not always found it easy to put into practice the principles which psychology would espouse (see Singer, 1990). For example, Hoffman (1990) states quite categorically that he believes modern day motor learning research is of virtually no benefit to teachers of motor skills. Primarily this is because researchers have become removed from the real world, focusing their efforts on unravelling the complexities of human motor action but ignoring practical concerns such as how this knowledge may assist teaching practices.

The rationale behind this experimental research was the search for a global theory of motor learning which presumably would provide a set of general principles applicable to all types of skill learning, including the classroom. To achieve this goal, simple tasks took the place of real-world actions, relatively short practice times were built into learning experiments, and assumptions were made that the principles of movement learning would be similar for both simple and complex tasks (Schmidt, 1989). Of course, the consequence of this approach was that much research conducted under the guise of motor learning came to be regarded as esoteric and irrelevant to the teaching of physical education.

This is not to deny that motor learning and motor control research could be used to help the teaching profession, just that the process of transfer is not easy (see Magill, 1990). In the words of Hoffman (1990: 145–6),

> Most motor skill instructors, including those who teach under the very best of conditions, will not be the better for having read the past 20 years of literature on motor learning or for having taken a course that covers the territory traditionally covered by modern textbooks. Some of the most learned of motor learning scholars confess that they have had little to offer in the way of concrete suggestions to gym teachers, tennis professionals, or coaches at any level (Christina, 1989; Schmidt, 1989).

Fortunately there are signs that matters may be improving. Two recent motor learning textbooks both make serious attempts to take on board the criticisms levelled against the research over the last 20 years (Magill, 1989; Schmidt, 1991). Both books cover the basic research and yet also discuss practical implications and/or applications for the teacher or coach. As to how valid these extrapolations and generalizations from simple artificial laboratory tasks are to practise in the complex world of sport and exercise remains a further question to be answered.

One further issue worthy of brief mention here is the ethos or philosophy which underpins the teaching of physical education, and how this may impact upon young people's perception of sport. The new national curriculum in the UK has precipitated a radical rethinking of the physical education curriculum and has forced the profession to scrutinize what it has to offer in the education of children. Over the years physical education has had a variety of aims and objectives. It could well be argued that current debates surrounding health related fitness (HRF) have brought us around full circle to the ancient Greeks supposed motto *'mens sana in corpore sano'* (a saying which strangely sport scientists present not in Greek but in Latin and which is thought to derive from Juvenal's *Satires*!). The health related fitness movement is concerned with encouraging an understanding and awareness of the health benefits of an active lifestyle while also educating children in various types of exercise and physical activity. In more recent years, aspects of HRF are considered through cross-curricular themes such as health education, rather than solely through the subject matter of physical education. HRF gathered impetus during the 1980s when it became the latest buzz word with many arguing for its rightful place at the core of the physical education curriculum (Thomason and Almond,

1988). However, the approach has also had its critics who argue that its underlying values and assumptions are out of line with the aims of physical education (Coloquhoun, 1988), and that it fails to offer children an educational experience. These arguments are mainly based on the perceived notion that the HRF movement 'assumes that an homogenous culture exists in which we are all free to choose our lifestyles' and that if people are unfit or lead an unhealthy lifestyle it is because they choose to do so (see Sparkes, 1989). Furthermore, it has not yet been demonstrated that typical physical education programmes focusing on health related fitness necessarily lead to a more active adult lifestyle.

The Way Forward

The 1990s represent a genuinely interesting and challenging time for motor development research and for work relating to sport socialization. However, as Haywood (1986) points out, prospective researchers should temper their enthusiasm with an awareness that there are a number of unresolved issues standing in the way of progress. One concerns the famous, or perhaps infamous, nature vs nurture controversy. The well rehearsed arguments, familiar to all introductory psychology students, go right back to the 1930s when researchers attempted to establish whether hereditary (nature) factors or environmental (nurture) factors were primarily responsible for determining subsequent behaviour. Many branches of psychology openly acknowledge that the debate has never been satisfactorily resolved, nor can be resolved, but then press on regardless. Unfortunately it is impossible for those working in the field of motor development quietly to put aside this issue given that it manifests itself at the core of so many fundamental research issues. In terms of sport behaviour, arguments abound concerning whether athletic skills are born or made and not surprisingly, common wisdom now acknowledges here as elsewhere that an either/or approach to the issue is not helpful. Rather, it is appreciated that genetic and environmental influences are intricately related but the precise nature of this interaction has yet to be determined.

An equally difficult problem area concerns sensitive periods during development. The existence of critical periods remains an issue for debate in developmental psychology where it has been established that such periods may well be significant with regard to certain human cognitive skills. However, this proves little with regard to human motor development where, for both ethical and practical reasons, it has been difficult to accumulate substantial evidence either for or against critical periods. Cross cultural studies and work with institutionalized and deprived children suggest that normal motor development of locomotor and reaching and grasping skills may be delayed by a child experiencing a deprived environment, or lacking sufficient stimulation, or being subjected to restrictive cultural practices. Nevertheless, all of these data also show that unless the deprivation is severe and extends over a long period of time, that individuals eventually 'catch up' and achieve a normal standard in terms of a particular motor skill. Whether there is an adverse effect on later and perhaps more sophisticated motor behaviour has yet to be resolved.

On a more positive note, reviews of the major areas of concern within motor development highlight the interdisciplinary nature of enquiry and indeed point the way for other areas of developmental psychology. In terms of the future of research, as already noted, there are problems with both observing and describing changes in behaviour as they occur, and with the use of experimental methods in an attempt to determine the underlying causes of a person's behaviour. In general, it is now recognized that there is a need to loosen the experimental reins a little, and to be prepared to look at the individual in his or her natural setting. This may involve extended periods of collecting purely descriptive data which will serve as the foundation on which to build further work. This type of descriptive research has long been seen as valuable in other sciences (for example anthropology, paleontology and geology) but in psychology has typically been looked down upon as less robust and reliable when compared to more rigorous experimental approaches. In the field of motor development, Roberton (1989) makes the case for description to take on a new role in the experimental process. She argues that after theories have been developed researchers then need to examine the applied setting to see if the theories can be verified in the real world.

Theoretical or 'pure' research has often been afforded higher status than applied research but this status differential begins to look increasingly redundant. In terms of motor development research, a coming together of the pure and the applied is revealed in the number of studies aiming to outline developmental sequences so that teachers, coaches and parents have some reference points for their children's developing movement patterns. Thomas (1989) claims that this line of applied work can only be fruitfully developed through interdisciplinary research using sport-specific theories and paradigms. He maintains that motor developmentalists have so far only taken mainstream psychology theories and applied them to sport rather than developing theories of their own and he believes that when they start to create sport-specific theories then they will also start answering the applied issues which are of concern to practitioners. One recent development of this type is coordinative structures theory (Kugler and Turvey, 1987), as previously outlined.

Another area where theory and application is moving ahead rapidly is participation motivation. Great strides have been made over recent years in understanding and explaining how and why children take up and leave sport. Sport specific models have been developed which have borrowed ideas freely yet critically from a number of disciplines, and which show a willingness to accept complexity in recognition of the complexities which exist out there in the real world. Whether this work will come to represent a good example for the future of sport psychology as a whole, or whether it represents a false dawn, only time will tell but at the moment there appears to be light on the horizon.

References

ADAM, J. (1978) 'Sequential strategies and the separation of age, cohort, and time-of-measurement contributions to developmental data', *Psychological Bulletin*, 85, pp. 1309–16.

BRODKIN, P. and WEISS, M. R. (1990) 'Developmental differences in motivation for participating in competitive swimming', *Journal of Sport and Exercise Psychology*, 12, pp. 248–63.

BRUSTAD, R. J. (1993) 'Youth in sport: Psychological considerations', in SINGER, R. N., MURPHEY, M. and TENNANT, L. K. (Eds) *Handbook of Research on Sport Psychology*, New York: Macmillan, pp. 695–717.

CHRISTINA, R. (1989) 'Whatever happened to applied research in motor learning?', in SKINNER, J. S., CORBIN, C. B., LANDERS, D. M., MARTIN, P. E. and WELLS, C. L. (Eds) *Future Directions in Exercise and Sport Science Research*, Champaign, IL: Human Kinetics, pp. 411–22.

CLARKE, J. E. and HUMPHREY, J. H. (Eds) (1990) *Advances in Motor Development*, Volume 3, New York: AMS Press.

COLLEY, A., EGLINTON, E. and ELLIOTT, E. (1992) 'Sport participation in middle childhood: Association with styles of play and parental participation', *International Journal of Sport Psychology*, 23, pp. 193–206.

COLQUHOUN, D. (1988) 'Health as an issue in the physical education curriculum: A questioning of assumptions', invited lecture, School of Education, Exeter University, November.

DISHMAN, R. K. and DUNN, A. L. (1988) 'Exercise adherence in children and youth: Implications for adulthood', in DISHMAN, R. K. (Ed.) *Exercise Adherence: Its Impact on Public Health*, Champaign, IL: Human Kinetics.

EISENBERG, N. (Ed.) (1987) *Contemporary Topics in Developmental Psychology*, New York: John Wiley and Sons.

GABBARD, C. (1992) *Lifelong Motor Development*, Dubuque, IA: Wm C. Brown.

GESELL, A. and AMATRUDA, C. (1947) *Developmental Diagnosis*, 2nd edn, New York: Harper and Row.

GOULD, D. (1982) 'Sport psychology in the 1980s: Status direction, and challenges in youth sports research', *Journal of Sport Psychology*, 4, pp. 203–18.

GOULD, D. (1987) 'Understanding attrition in children's sport', in GOULD, D. and WEISS, M. R. (Eds) *Advances in Pediatric Sciences: Volume 2 Behavioral Issues*, Champaign, IL: Human Kinetics, pp. 61–85.

GOULD, D. and HORN, T. (1984) 'Participation motivation in young athletes', in SILVA, J. and WEINBERG, R. (Eds) *Psychological Foundations of Sports*, Champaign, IL: Human Kinetics, pp. 359–70.

GOULD, D. and PETLICHKOFF, L. M. (1988) 'Participation motivation and attrition in young athletes', in SMOLL, F. A., MAGILL, R.A. and ASH, M.J. (Eds) *Children in Sport*, 3rd edn, Champaign, IL: Human Kinetics, pp. 113–35.

GREENDORFER, S. (1992) 'Sport socialization', in HORN, T. (Ed.) *Advances in Sport Psychology*, Champaign, IL: Human Kinetics, pp. 201–18.

HARTER, S. (1981) 'The development of competence motivation in the mastery of cognitive and physical skills: Is there a place for joy?' in ROBERTS, G. C. and LANDERS, D. M. (Eds) *Psychology of Motor Behavior and Sport — 1980*, Champaign, IL: Human Kinetics, pp. 3–29.

HAYWOOD, K. M. (1986) *Life Span Motor Development*, Champaign, IL: Human Kinetics.

HEARNSHAW, L. S. (1992) 'Burt Redividus', *The Psychologist*, 5, 4, pp. 168–70.

HOFFMAN, S. J. (1990) 'Relevance, application, and the development of an unlikely theory', *Quest*, 42, pp. 143–60.

JENSEN, R. K. (1981) 'The effect of a 12-month growth period on the body moments of inertia of children', *Medicine and Science in Sports and Exercise*, 13, pp. 238–42.

KEOGH, J. and SUGDEN, D. (1985) *Movement Skill Development*, New York: Macmillan.

KUGLER, P., KELSO, J. A. S. and TURVEY, M. (1982) 'On the control and coordination of naturally developing systems', in KELSO, J. A. S. and CLARK, J. E. (Eds) *The Development of Movement Control and Coordination*, New York: John Wiley & Sons, pp. 5–78.

KUGLER, P. N. and TURVEY, M. T. (1987) *Information, Natural Law and the Self-assembly of Rhythmic Movement*, Hillsdale, NJ: Erlbaum.

LEWKO, J. H. and GREENDORFER, S. L. (1988) 'Family influences in sport socialization of children and adolescents', in SMOLL, F. L., MAGILL, R. A. and ASH, M. J. (Eds) *Children in Sport*, 3rd edn, Champaign, IL: Human Kinetics.

MAEHR, M. L. and NICHOLLS, J. G. (1980) 'Culture and achievement motivation: A second look', in WARREN, N. (Ed.) *Studies in Cross-Cultural Psychology*, New York: Academic Press, pp. 221–67.

MAGILL, R. A. (1989) *Motor Learning: Concepts and Applications*, 3rd edn, Dubuque, IA: Wm C. Brown.

MAGILL, R. A. (1990) 'Motor learning is meaningful for physical educators', *Quest*, 42, pp. 126–33.

McPHERSON, S. L. and THOMAS, J. R. (1989) 'Relation of knowledge and performance in boys' tennis: Age and expertise', *Journal of Experimental Child Psychology*, 48, pp. 190–211.

NEWELL, K. M. (1986) 'Constraints on the development of coordination', in WADE, M. G. and WHITING, H. T. A. (Eds) *Motor Skill Acquisition in Children: Aspects of Coordination and Control*, Amsterdam: Martinies NIJHOS, pp. 341–60.

NEWELL, K. M. (1990) 'Physical activity, knowledge types and degree programs', *Quest*, 40, pp. 234–68.

OSTROW, A.C. and DZEWALTOWSKI, D. A. (1986) 'Older adults' perceptions of physical activity participation based on age-role and sex-role appropriateness', *Research Quarterly for Exercise and Sport*, 52, pp. 216–27.

PASCUAL-LEONE, J. (1976) 'Metasubjective problems of constructive cognition: Forms of knowing and their psychological mechanism', *Canadian Psychological Review*, 17, pp. 110–25.

PETLICHKOFF, L. M. (1982) 'Motives Interscholastic Athletes have for Participation and Reasons for Discontinued Involvement in School Sponsored Sport', unpublished Masters thesis, Michigan State University, East Lansing.

ROBERTON, M. A. (1982) 'Describing "stages" within and across motor tasks', in KELSO, J. A. S. and CLARK, J. E. (Eds) *The Development of Movement Control and Coordination*, New York: John Wiley and Sons, pp. 293–307.

ROBERTON, M. A. (1989) 'Developmental sequence and developmental task analysis', in SKINNER, J. S., CORBIN, C., LANDERS, D., MARTIN, S. and WELLS, D. (Eds) *Future Directions in Exercise and Sport Science Research*, Champaign, IL: Human Kinetics, pp. 369–81.

ROBERTON, M. A. and HALVERSON, L. (1984) *Developing Children — Their Changing Movement: A Guide for Teachers*, Philadelphia: Lea and Febiger.

ROBERTS, G. C. (1984) 'Achievement motivation in children's sport', *Advances in Motivation and Achievement*, 3, pp. 251–81.

ROBERTS, G. C. (Ed.) (1992) *Motivation in Sport and Exercise*, Champaign, IL: Human Kinetics.

SCHAIE, K. W. (1965) 'A general model for the study of developmental problems', *Psychological Bulletin*, 64, pp. 92–107.

SCHMIDT, R. A. (1989) 'Toward a better understanding of the acquisition of skill: Theoretical and practical contribution of the task approach', in SKINNER, J. S., CORBIN, C. B., LANDERS, D.M., MARTIN, P.E. and WELLS, C.L. (Eds) *Future Directions in Exercise and Sport Science Research*, Champaign, IL: Human Kinetics, pp. 395–411.

SCHMIDT, R. A. (1991) *Motor Learning and Performance: From Principles to Practice*, Champaign, IL: Human Kinetics.

SCHMIDT, G. W. and STEIN, G. L. (1991) 'Sport commitment: A model integrating enjoyment, dropout and burnout', *Journal of Sport and Exercise Psychology*, 8, pp. 254–65.

SHEPHARD, R. J. (1982) *Physical Activity and Growth*, Chicago, IL: Year Book Medical Publishers.

SINGER, R. N. (1990) 'Motor learning research: Meaningful for physical educators or a waste of time?' *Quest*, 42, pp. 114–25.

SMITH, R. and SMOLL, F. (1990) 'Self-esteem and children's reactions to youth sport coaching behaviors: A field study of self-enhancement processes', *Developmental Psychology*, 26, pp. 987–93.

SMITH, R. E. (1986) 'Toward a cognitive-affective model of athletic burnout', *Journal of Sport Psychology*, 8, pp. 36–50.

SPARKES, A. (1989) 'Health related fitness: An example of innovation without change', *The British Journal of Physical Education*, 20, pp. 60–2.

SMOLL, F., MAGILL, R. and ASH, M. (Eds) (1988) *Children and Sport*, 3rd edn, Champaign, IL: Human Kinetics.

THOMAS, J. (1989) 'Naturalistic research can drive motor development theory', in SKINNER, J. S., CORBIN, C., LANDERS, D., MARTIN, S. and WELLS, D. (Eds) *Future Directions in Exercise and Sport Science Research*, Champaign, IL: Human Kinetics, pp. 349–67.

THOMAS, J. R., FRENCH, K. E., THOMAS, K. T. and GALLAGHER, J. D. (1988) 'Children's knowledge development and sport performance', in SMOLL, F., MAGILL, R. and ASH, M. (Eds) *Children and Sport*, 3rd edn, Champaign, IL: Human Kinetics, pp. 179–202.

THOMAS, J. R., THOMAS, K. T. and GALLAGHER, J. D. (1993) 'Developmental considerations in skill acquisition', in SINGER, R. N., MURPHEY, M. and TENNANT, L. K. (Eds) *Handbook of Research on Sport Psychology*, New York: Macmillan, pp. 73–105.

THOMASON, H. and ALMOND, L. (1988) 'Health and physical education in the National Curriculum', *Physical Education Review*, 11, pp. 119–22.

TODOR, J. I. (1978) 'A neo-Piagetian theory of constructive operators: Applications to perceptual-motor development and learning', in LANDERS, D. M. and CHRISTINA, R. W. (Eds) *Psychology of Motor Behavior and Sport — 1977*, Champaign, IL: Human Kinetics, pp. 507–21.

WILLIS, J. D. and CAMPBELL, L. F. (1992) *Exercise Psychology*, Champaign, IL: Human Kinetics.

Further Reading

CLARKE, J. E. and HUMPHREY, J. H. (Eds) (1990) *Advances in Motor Development*, Volume 3, New York: AMS Press.

GALLAHUE, D. L. (1989) *Understanding Motor Development: Infants, Children, Adolescence*, 2nd edn, Indianapolis: Benchmark Press.

GOULD, D. and WEISS, M. (Eds) (1987) *Advances in Pediatric Sciences*, Volume 2, *Behavioral Issues*, Champaign, IL: Human Kinetics.

ROBERTON, M. A. and HALVERSON, L. (1984) *Developing Children — Their Changing Movement: A Guide for Teachers*, Philadelphia: Lea and Febiger.

ROBERTS, G. C. (Ed.) (1992) *Motivation in Sport and Exercise*, Champaign, IL: Human Kinetics.

SMOLL, F., MAGILL, R. and ASH, M. (Eds) (1988) *Children and Sport*, 3rd edn, Champaign, IL: Human Kinetics.

THOMAS, J. R., THOMAS, K. T. and GALLAGHER, J. D. (1993) 'Developmental considerations in skill acquisition', in SINGER, R. N., MURPHEY, M. and TENNANT, L. K. (Eds) *Handbook of Research on Sport Psychology*, New York: Macmillan, pp. 73–105.

Chapter 9

Sport and Drugs and Runner's High

(Psychophysiology)

Marie H. Murphy
(University of Ulster at Jordanstown)

Introduction

A man's body and his mind, with the utmost reverence to both I speak it, are exactly like a jerkin and a jerkin's lining: rumple the one — you rumple the other.

Sterne, *Tristram Shandy.*

Since the time of Descartes and indeed much earlier, the interplay between the functions of the body and of the mind has been a topic for speculation and debate amongst writers, poets, philosophers and athletes alike. Despite such long term interest, the emergence of the area of psychophysiology as a separate academic/scientific discipline dealing with the physiology of psychology (and occasionally vice versa) did not occur until the 1950s. Subsequently the approach found a natural and comfortable home and has been applied with gusto to research problems in the relatively modern field of sport and exercise science.

To begin at the beginning, just what is psychophysiology? According to Stern, in 1964 it was defined as 'any research in which the dependent variable is a physiological measure and the independent variable is a behavioural one' (Stern *et al.*, 1980). He goes on to maintain that while such a description of the field was valid, over time it has become far too limiting. From a sport and exercise psychology perspective, this original definition would exclude, for example, experiments which have considered the effect of exercise on analgesia (that is the ability to tolerate pain). Here the independent variable is physiological (changes in the body due to exercise) and the dependent variable is behavioural or psychological (pain tolerance).

Certain authors have differentiated the work caried out in this area into two distinct disciplines (Porges and Coles, 1976). *Psychophysiological* studies manipulate psychological variables and then observe a physiological response (for example the effects of stress on heart rate) whereas *physiological psychology* studies manipulate the physiological status of the subject while observing the effects on behaviour (for example the effects of exercise on aggression). In a similar vein, Bennett (1982) actually defined physiological psychology as the study of the physiological foundations of behaviour.

However they are defined, both of these fields, psychophysiology and physiological psychology, may provide insight into the workings of the mind and/or body for the student of sport and exercise. Sport and exercise have both psychological and physiological dimensions and it seems logical that a psychophysiological approach which attempts to integrate psychological and physiological variables in a common conceptual framework would provide a fruitful avenue towards the fuller understanding of exercise and sport behaviour (Hatfield and Landers, 1987). Therefore for the purposes of the present chapter, psychophysiology will be defined more broadly as 'a scientific discipline that examines the interrelationships between psychological and physiological variables' (Hatfield and Landers, 1983).

In a thorough review of the psychophysiology of exercise and sport in the late 1980s, Hatfield and Landers (1987) have suggested that the development of the area has been hampered by the research being traditionally carried out by investigators who are based outside the sport and exercise sciences. Even in those areas where exercise scientists have attempted to answer psychophysiological questions, this has largely been left to physiologists or psychologists working in isolation.

Looking more specifically at the exercise and sports science literature, the research which could be classified as psychophysiological according to our working definition appears to be less than systematic. A chapter of this sort could not hope to give a comprehensive review of the many applications of psychophysiology to exercise and sport. Instead it will focus on a selection of topics which have received empirical attention in an attempt to illustrate how attention to psychological and physiological variables, and more critically the application of the theoretical constructs of psychophysiology, can enhance the study and application of sport and exercise psychology. The reader will note something of a departure in content from the rest of the book. While sport has been the major focus so far, this chapter will deal predominantly with exercise but not necessarily competitive sport, as it is in the exercise domain that the majority of research efforts which use psychophysiological methods and constructs have been concentrated.

Psychophysiological Effects of Exercise

Sport almost invariably involves some form of physical exercise, and exercise brings about wholesale alterations in the physiological functioning of the individual. These changes can be both acute and chronic in nature and are well documented in exercise physiology literature (for example, Brooks and Fahey, 1985). The direction and magnitude of these changes are affected by many factors including the intensity, type and duration of the activity as well as a host of individual factors. The aphorism *'mens sana in corpore sano'* dates back to ancient Greece and indicates an association between a healthy mind and a healthy body, a relationship which is much cited in the sport and exercise literature. Indeed one major impetus for research in this area has been an attempt to confirm and elucidate mechanisms behind the intuitive belief that exercise has a positive effect on an individual's psychological state. It is towards this topic that we now turn.

Exercise and Mood State, Depression, Anxiety and Analgesia

An interesting if somewhat inconclusive literature has accumulated rapidly over recent years charting the relationship between exercise and psychological well-being (Biddle and Mutrie, 1991; Willis and Campbell, 1992). The bulk of this literature is made up of experimental work dealing with the impact of exercise regimes, complemented by large scale descriptive studies. An example of the latter is the work of Stephens (1988). Basing his conclusions on four surveys carried out during the 1970s and early 1980s, and involving over 56,000 individuals from across the USA and Canada, Stephens concluded that physical activity appeared to be associated with positive mood and reduced anxiety and depression. Unfortunately, even according to Stephens, this positive and well-documented association between exercise and the psychological well-being of an individual does not substantiate the claim that exercise is the cause of such states. Rather, it could be that individuals who have more positive mood states, and experience less anxiety and fewer bouts of depression, are more inclined to participate in physical activity. Additionally the observation fails to uncover whether the purported effects of physical activity on mood are the result of a single bout of exercise (acute effects) or the result of regular participation (chronic effects).

For causality to be established, there was clearly a need to turn to experimental work where variables could be manipulated in a more systematic way. Often such research has been designed to consider the impact of exercise on mental state. An example of an empirical study in this area was that carried out by Boutcher and Landers (1986). They considered both brainwave (EEG) measures and subjective anxiety (as assessed by the Profile of Mood States questionnaire; see Chapter 2) of regular exercisers in response to 20 minutes' running at a relative exercise intensity of 80–85 per cent. Results were compared with scores obtained from a control group who sat quietly reading for a similar period of time. The researchers noted decreased anxiety and increased alpha-wave activity in the regular runners following exercise, but no changes were noted for the control condition.

Folkins and Sime (1981), Biddle and Mutrie (1991) and LaFontaine *et al.* (1992), amongst others, have reviewed the literature on exercise and psychological well being. The common conclusion is that exercise, and particularly that of an aerobic nature (exercise which relies predominantly on oxidative metabolism for the production of energy), is inversely related to depression and anxiety. The most striking elevation of mood state attributable to physical exercise appears in individuals who are initially depressed or anxious. Indeed much of the research in this area has been carried out with clinical populations as an adjunct or alternative to traditional psychotherapeutic and psychopharmacologic treatments. In such clinical settings, several researchers (for example Simons *et al.*, 1985) have suggested that exercise was equal or superior to results achieved by more orthodox psychotherapies in treating depression. Indeed a related but separate body of literature exists which relates exercise solely to the mood attribute of depression. For reviews of this literature the reader is recommended Dunn and Dishman (1991) and North *et al.* (1990). For psychophysiology, this relationship clearly opens up many research opportunities and there has been no shortage of attempts to explain the mechanisms which are responsible for the enhancement of psychological state which is attributed to exercise. The three most significant psychophysiological explanations are presented below but alongside these could be presented other psychological or psychosocial models. One example here is the distraction or 'time out' hypothesis which does not emphasize any psychobiological connection but instead argues that exercise may be therapeutic insofar as it simply provides breathing space to take one's mind off other concerns and worries (Bahrke and Morgan, 1978). Appealing as this hypothesis may be, and particularly to those who are drawn towards the more social models of mental health, the general consensus would be that social effects interact with more basic psychophysiological changes. It is towards the latter that we now turn.

The Thermogenic Hypothesis

One of the proposed mechanisms is known as the thermogenic effect (Morgan and O'Connor, 1988). This suggests that the increase in body temperature brought about by exercise reduces tonic muscle activity (measured by EMG), thus in turn reducing somatic anxiety (de Vries, 1981). In support of this argument, Raglin and Morgan (1985) noted decreased state anxiety (see Chapter 4) after a hot shower (at a temperature of 38.5°C) lasting five minutes. It has been suggested that the increase in temperature may alter the levels of brain monoamines (these include neurotransmitters such as noradrenaline, adrenaline, serotonin and dopamine; see 'Catecholamine Hypothesis' below). The increase in temperature during exercise and the subsequent subjective psychological effects, when paired with similar effects of increasing body temperature in the absence of exercise, makes the thermogenic hypothesis a plausible if an underresearched explanation.

The Catecholamine Hypothesis

Catecholamines is a collective name for a group of chemicals which include adrenaline, noradrenaline and dopamine. These function as transmitters in the central nervous system and are strongly implicated in the control of movement, mood, attention and endocrine, cardiovascular and stress responses (for a more thorough introduction to this area, see McMurray, 1991). Adrenaline is produced largely by the adrenal gland while the majority of noradrenaline is produced by the sympathetic nervous system or by the brain. Catecholamines act quickly (measured in milliseconds) and operate by sending messages directly through the nervous system to specific sites. The catecholamine hypothesis, as proposed by Kety (1966), suggests that exercise activates the release of catecholamines and the high levels of catecholamines are associated with euphoria and positive mood state while low levels may cause depression.

Exercise is known to bring about a significant alteration in levels of plasma catecholamines (those carried in the bloodstream). The actual level is thought to depend on the intensity type and duration of the exercise as well as individual factors. Although there is no conclusive proof that the level of catecholamines in the brain itself are increased by exercise in humans, research with rats has shown this to be so (Brown and van Huss, 1973). Since monitoring of chemicals in the brain of intact humans involves a difficult and dangerous methodology, the levels of the metabolites (that is chemicals remaining when a compound is broken down) excreted by the body have been used to infer what and how much is being produced in the brain. MHPG (3-methoxy-4-hydroxyphenylglycol) is a metabolite of noradrenaline and some researchers have noted an increase in MHPG in urine as a result of exercise (Chodakowska *et al.*, 1980), thus supporting the proposal that brain catecholamines (and in particular noradrenaline) increase with exercise. However, whether this increase causes an alteration in mood is still unknown.

Despite a growing understanding of the nature and operation of catecholamines, research has failed to support the original hypothesis and the thesis remains largely unproven. Although interest in the role of these neurotransmitters in psychological functioning has remained, a full knowledge of their behavioural functions is still a matter for investigation and debate rather than being regarded as a scientific certainty (Morgan and O'Connor, 1988, provide a thorough review of the catecholamine hypotheses which is recommended for the interested reader). McMurray (1991) suggests that what are needed are studies which measure psychological status before and after the injection of catecholamines in order to clarify their psychological effects. Such a seemingly obvious methodology (which borders on psychopharmacology) is not, however, without its problems, as we shall see when we discuss the next hypothesis.

Endorphin Hypothesis

The discovery of a group of chemicals collectively called endorphins in the 1970s and the subsequent identification of their opiate-like effects (causing euphoria and analgesia) heralded an unprecedented interest in the function of endorphins by exercise scientists. It has become widely accepted in the media, especially in the popular exercise literature, where the phrase 'endorphin high' or 'runner's high' was first coined, that endorphins are elevated by exercise and this in turn leads to enhanced mood state. This explanation for the mood enhancing effects of exercise has received the most empirical attention. In addition to elevation with exercise, endorphins have been hypothesized to increase with sex and the ingestion of food and/or alcohol. This has led to their being considered the basis of pleasure or the 'pleasure peptides'. The empirical evidence to date however remains far from compelling.

Endorphins, previously known as endogenous morphines, are produced endogenously (i.e. in the body, hence the root of the word, 'endo') and act in a similar manner to the drug morphine (hence 'orphin') extracted from the opium poppy. The term endorphin refers to both a specific type of opiate-like transmitter as well as a general class of transmitter which includes other opioids such as enkephalins and dynorphins. No physiological function of any of these endorphins has been conclusively demonstrated to date, but they appear to bind with specific receptor sites in discrete parts of the central nervous system which contain pathways that convey pain information and in areas which are involved in mood and emotion. Exercise has been shown by several investigators to cause a significant phasic increase in endorphins released into the bloodstream from the pituitary (Farrell *et al.*, 1987).

To test further the proposed effects of endorphins on the central nervous system, several investigators have considered the effects of administering naloxone. This is an exogenous drug (produced artificially) which, it is claimed, binds to the endorphin receptors in the brain thereby blocking the effects which might be attributed to endorphins. Janal *et al.* (1984) among others found naloxone to reverse some of the positive mood effects attributed to endorphins. Although others such as Markoff *et al.* (1982) reported no alteration in the mood elevation effect, this may be due to the low dosage of naloxone administered. Other investigators have tried to determine the effects of plasma endorphins (i.e. endorphins carried in the blood) on mood by artificially elevating their levels in the body by injecting them directly into the bloodstream. Foley *et al.* (1979) injected betaendorphins (generally regarded as the most powerful member of the endorphine family) into normal individuals and failed to notice any alteration of mood. In contrast, Kline *et al.* (1977) did record a mood change amongst schizophrenic and depressed patients following an injection of betaendorphins.

Overviewing this literature, the evidence would suggest that since exercise is associated with positive mood state, and that since endorphins have been shown to cause an elevation in mood and exercise elevates plasma endorphins, then *ergo*, there is an endorphin mediated exercise effect on mood. Unfortunately the major flaw in this line of investigation, and explanation, is that in most human studies the elevation in endorphins has been noted in the blood plasma (i.e. as part of the periphery) rather than in the cerebrospinal fluid or in the brain itself (i.e. the central nervous system), where it is supposed that the endorphins actually have their effect. These endorphins are unable to cross the blood–brain barrier in order to exert their effects on the central nervous system. Therefore it is very unlikely that the levels of endorphins in blood plasma will have a direct effect on an individual's psychological state. To account for this unresolved problem, some investigators have suggested that increased synthesis of endorphins at peripheral sites (and hence their appearance in the blood plasma) actually directly mirrors an increase in their synthesis in the CNS (Harber and Sutton, 1984). On a different tack, McArthur (1985) suggests that it could be that exercise, in some as yet undefined way, increases the permeability of the blood–brain barrier thus allowing endorphins safe passage into the brain and central nervous system. These theories may eventually explain how peripheral endorphin elevation is related to positive mood state but as yet they both remain purely speculative.

It is therefore reasonably well-established that exercise elevates endorphin levels in the blood; however the evidence for the actual effects of this elevation are far from conclusive. Sforzo (1988) has provided a comprehensive review of the effects of exercise not only on endorphins but also of the other known opioids. He suggests that further research should attempt not to replicate the established exercise effect on endorphins but to address the mechanisms for the numerous physiological roles that opoids may have. This would include their impact on metabolism, immunity, cardiovascular function, growth and development, as well as the effect that peripheral elevation of opoids may have on central nervous system levels and any subsequent psychological effects. One factor which may be holding research back is quite simply cost. The methodology involved in isolating and measuring these opoids, radioimmunoassay, is at present prohibitively expensive and is likely to remain so for the foreseeable future.

Conclusions

Despite the establishment of the mood enhancing effect of exercise, two important questions still remain for exercise psychophysiologists. First there remains little conclusive evidence indicating a precise mechanism of effect. Second the type of exercise necessary to secure the mood elevating response has not yet been clarified. The protocols used in many studies in this area differ widely in the type, intensity and duration of exercise used. In any worthwhile exercise study the relative exercise intensity (as a percentage of each subject's maximal capacity) should be clearly defined, the type of exercise (progressive and incremental or steady state) and the mode (for example cycle ergometry or running) must be carefully considered. When as rigorous attention is paid to these variables as to the others in the study (for example blood sampling, experimental design and questionnaire administration) researchers will be that much closer to determining the criteria necessary for producing an effect. In turn they will then be able to discover whether this effect is subject to a graded, dose-response relationship or whether thresholds exist beneath which no effect occurs, or above which no further elevation can occur.

Exercise and Stress Responsivity

As well as the alterations in psychological states which are associated with a single bout of exercise, there has been considerable interest in how regular exercise or training affects the psychophysiology of an individual. One popular layperson's notion which has been widely investigated in the psychophysiology literature is the contention that a physically fit person is less susceptible to the ill-effects of stress.

When subjected to the stress of exercise the body responds by transporting more oxygen to working musculature through increased heart rate, cardiac output and stroke volume. This occurs by reducing blood flow to non-exercising areas through vaso-constriction (a decrease in the diameter of the blood vessels), and by increasing the circulation of certain substances (specifically catecholamines and hormones) which assist in the release of the fuels needed for muscular work. (Brooks and Fahey, 1985)

In response to psychological stress, many similar sympathetically mediated responses (i.e. those associated with the sympathetic nervous system, the system which prepares us for action) appear to occur. When faced with a stressor the individual first of all assesses the situation. If the person perceives it as threatening there is an increase in neurohormonal activity (release of chemicals from neurons into the bloodstream) and a stimulation of the secretion of hormones which are used to mobilize fat and other energy-rich molecules in the body. For example, the perception of stress stimulates the secretion of adrenaline and noradrenaline. To date the list of hormones whose secretion rates are altered by stress is by no means complete; in fact it is more than likely that the secretion of every known hormone may be affected in some way by stress (Vander *et al.*, 1990). The physiological changes which then take place are well documented. For example, heart rate increases, total peripheral resistance changes and cardiac output (i.e. the volume of blood pumped by the heart in one minute) increases.

The effects on the brain itself are also noteworthy. The energy demands made upon the brain in its decision-making capacity can only be met by glucose, as the brain is physically incapable of metabolizing fat. (Brooks and Fahey, 1985). Thus during periods of stress or arousal, extracerebral cells (those away from the brain) are more inclined to rely on free fatty acids and glycogen to provide the energy, in this way sparing glucose for the brain (Atkinson and Milsum, 1983).

What do these changes mean in terms of the effects of fitness on stress responsivity? In the first instance, fitter individuals are able to adapt more efficiently to a given physical workload than those who are less fit (Astrand and Rodahl, 1986). They experience less sympathetic nervous activation in the form of less catecholamine secretion, less heart rate acceleration and a smaller amount of vasoconstriction in areas not involved in exercise, for a given absolute workload. Several authors therefore have suggested that since increased fitness alters responsivity to exercise it may also have a beneficial effect on the psychophysiological response to stress (van Doornen *et al.*, 1988; van Doornen and de Geus, 1989). There is now a substantial literature which has considered whether regular exercise alters the way in which an individual responds to a psychological or psychosocial stressor. Initially many of the studies in this area were cross-sectional in design, placing subjects into fit and unfit groups according to one of a variety of tests of 'fitness', and subsequently observing differences between groups using a range of biochemical, ventilatory, electrodermal, cardiovascular and subjective measures.

The majority of these cross-sectional studies have noted some difference in responsivity between fit and unfit groups. In general, studies found either greater magnitude of response to the stressor in unfit subjects and primarily in the cardiovascular system (van Doornen and de Geus, 1989) and in catecholamine response, particularly plasma noradrenaline (Sothmann *et al.*, 1987) or a quicker recovery to baseline of the cardiovascular system (Moses *et al.*, 1987) and/or catecholamines (Brooke and Long, 1987) after the removal of the stressor in fit individuals. At the same time, several studies using a similar cross-sectional design have failed to note any significant differences between fit and unfit groups (Claytor, 1988).

Somewhat predictably, several criticisms have been raised against this cross-sectional research. First, the accuracy of the fitness assessment used to categorize subjects as fit and unfit varies widely. This ranges from self-report of activity, through actual tests of muscular strength and endurance, to submaximal exercise tests, to the 'gold standard' for operationalizing aerobic capacity, the maximal exercise test. Additionally in many experiments the fit and unfit subjects were not sufficiently differentiated so as to provide discrete fitness groups. Fitness, like most human attributes, lies along a continuum. It seems apparent that only by comparing extreme ends of this continuum will the researcher be able to infer fitness correlates to the stress response. The second criticism is the quasi-experimental research design used. A cross-sectional design may mean that internal validity is threatened, i.e. individuals who are active and fit may share some other factor which alters their responsivity to stress.

An experimental design which may circumvent many of these problems does exist. This is where subjects of equal fitness are tested for responsivity and are then divided into training or control groups. They are then retested after the experimental group have experienced a period of training which has brought about a significant and measurable fitness improvement. Unfortunately such well designed studies are relatively scarce, yet approximately half of the projects which have used this design have found significant differences between experimental and control groups' responsivity in the retest condition. Most recently Sothmann *et al.* (1992) used a 16-week programme of closely monitored aerobic exercise sessions (three times per week, 25 to 30 minutes of treadmill running at 70 to 75 per cent maximum), resulting in a 20 per cent increase in aerobic capacity (determined by a maximal treadmill test). This well-controlled study failed to find any changes in responsivity of the variables measured (heart rate, subjective response or catecholamine levels) to laboratory stressors.

Such mixed results throw into doubt the intuitive belief that because exercise training produces adaptations which decrease the magnitude of the body's response to the stress of such exercise it will also decrease the response to psychological stress. Indeed Cox (1991), drawing primarily on animal research, suggests that exercise training actually increases the transmitter content of neurons, the size of the adrenal gland and the amount of catecholamines produced. In turn these may have quite unexpected effects on the stress response, and in particular two salient points derived from Cox's research are worth mentioning. First, an individual may show both an attenuated reactivity and an exaggerated response to stress after physical training, depending on which variable is observed. Second, the short duration of many stressors used may disguise differences in reactivity, that is variables show no differences on initial exposure to the stressor but these may appear if the stressor is continued.

In addition to physiological variables, several studies have included subjective tests of the individuals' 'feelings' or affective state before, during or after exposure to the stressor. Sinyor *et al.* (1983) found no fitness correlates of trait anxiety or subjective levels of arousal in response to a stress. The authors did however find that the trained group in the study had lower scores on Spielberger's State Anxiety Inventory (see Chapter 4) after the stressor. In a later study where individuals were trained over a 10-week period, Brooke and Long (1987), using a 5-point, eight-adjective pair mood checklist (Hull *et al.*, 1984) noted a faster recovery from subjective anxiety among aerobically fit subjects than among the unfit. Descriptive studies of fit and unfit individuals suggest that unfit subjects may be more likely to perceive significantly more distress in their lives than fit subjects (Tucker *et al.*, 1986), and that taking part in an aerobic conditioning programme is associated with reduced anxiety (Long, 1983). However, the mechanisms for this improved psychological status have not been determined and there remain a number of key issues still waiting to be resolved (see Chapter 4 for further discussion).

Over recent years, the complexities of the underlying concepts have been brought under the spotlight, and certain assumptions which have guided previous research have at last been critically examined. For example, van Doornen *et al.* (1988) have challenged the assumption that the physiological response to stress should be regarded as being synonymous with the physiological response to exercise. During exercise, the heart rate increase is dictated by the oxygen needs of the muscles performing work, whereas psychological stress usually requires only minor movements and therefore the heart rate response occurs in the absence of immediate metabolic needs. In some respects while at times this may be an appropriate response in terms of providing a readiness to respond, on other occasions it may actually be 'metabolically inappropriate' (Obrist, 1981). Heart rate, cardiac output and stroke volume increase in proportion to oxygen consumption during exercise but in stressful situations all may increase with hardly any change in oxygen consumption. The increases in cardiac response to stress may originate in the sympathetic nervous system, whereas in exercise they are in part due to the chronotropic effects of vagal withdrawal (i.e. determined by the parasympathetic nervous system which regulates the body's function to conserve energy).

In addition, during exercise peripheral resistance in the blood vessels decreases to allow more oxygen to reach the working muscle and this leads to a decline in diastolic blood pressure. However, during stress, depending on the difference in sympathetic activity of the intestines (vasoconstriction) and the muscles (vasodilation), diastolic blood pressure may actually tend to rise (van Doornen *et al.*, 1988).

Furthermore, Dimsdale and Moss (1980), among others, have reported a threefold increase in noradrenaline and a 50 per cent increase in adrenaline during exercise, whereas during stress the hormonal response represents a doubling in the output of adrenaline coupled with a 50 per cent increase in noradrenaline. Again, the function of the increase in catecholamines in exercise is in response to metabolic needs (for fuels) whereas in stress it is largely inappropriate.

These findings indicate that the long-established psychophysiological analogy linking stress and exercise may be questionable. However, some of the empirical evidence available does indicate a differential physiological response to stress among fit and unfit individuals. The equivocal findings in the literature reviewed points perhaps not to the lack of effect of fitness upon response to psychological stress but rather to methodological differences, experimental design and inadequacies of measurement techniques. Additionally, the stress response appears to be complex and multi-dimensional with some individual variation in response pattern. With one exception (Brooke and Long, 1987), in all the empirical studies mentioned here the stressors have been laboratory tasks. Laboratory studies that rely on a purely contrived stress, such as doing mental arithmetic or attempting to solve unsolvable puzzles, may have limited applicability to the psychophysiology of emotional arousal outside the laboratory. Dimsdale and Moss (1980) suggest that if we wish to explore catecholamine and cardiac response to emotional arousal (and then the effects of fitness on these changes), it seems likely that the most striking data will come from those studies that capitalize on the subject's exposure to naturally occurring stimuli, the stressors that s/he may realistically encounter and find stressful in everyday life.

Exercise Addiction

Considering the mood enhancing and analgesic properties tentatively associated with exercise, and the contention that these may in part be influenced by chemicals which are akin to opiates, it is perhaps not surprising that attention has also been directed towards the notion of exercise addiction. Exercise elevates the levels of catecholamines in the body. In addition to mood elevation the level of catecholamines has been linked to those neural pathways which control food intake and obsessive–compulsive disorders. This may represent one psychophysiological explanation of exercise addiction. Addiction to exercise was first noted in the late 1960s by Baekeland (1970) when attempting to study the effect of exercise deprivation on sleep patterns. In the course of this work he encountered great difficulty in persuading heavy exercisers to stop taking exercise. By 1979, Sachs and Parmagan had coined the term running addiction, defining it as 'addiction, of a psychological and/or physiological nature upon a regular regimen of running, characterised by withdrawal symptoms after 24 to 36 hours without participation'. They went on to describe withdrawal symptoms which include feelings of anxiety, restlessness, guilt, irritability, tension, bloatedness, muscle twitching and discomfort.

Support for the existence of some sort of exercise addiction is provided by a small number of empirical studies. In one such study Morris *et al.* (1990) divided a group of 40 regular male runners into two groups and required one of these groups to stop exercising for two weeks. During the period of enforced rest, symptoms of depression, anxiety and insomnia were greater in the non-exercising group but these symptoms disappeared as soon as they recommenced training. As you may expect this type of research is difficult to set up, and Baekeland's original problem of persuading regular exercisers to stop exercising is one which unquestionably hampers empirical efforts in this area. If subjects are asked to volunteer for a study in which they may be required to stop exercising, almost inevitably it will be the more seriously addicted individuals who will not volunteer, thus decreasing the potential of the study to draw conclusions about more severe forms of exercise addiction. One possibility for examining withdrawal from exercise is to use injured athletes to form the experimental group. Chan and Grossman (1988) used 30 such individuals who, due to injury, had to cease exercise for two weeks. They discovered higher levels of depression, anxiety and confusion amongst the injured athletes than in the control group. This type of design however presents problems of validity, in that the injury itself may be exerting considerable effects on the subject and this may confound any exercise withdrawal effects. In addition Solomon and Bumpus (1978) suggest that many exercise addicts will continue training through injuries regardless of the adverse effects.

Whether the mechanism for this addiction is based on psychological factors (for example, personality type), physiological factors (for example, endorphin dependence) or an interplay between these two, has yet to be properly established. Although the area is fraught with methodological difficulties a growing recognition of the exercise addiction phenomenon in our increasingly 'exercise literate' society has to be healthy, and certainly warrants further research into the underlying causes, symptoms and mechanisms.

Anabolic-Androgenic Steroids, Exercise and Addiction

The disqualification of British athletes during the Barcelona Olympics, positive drug tests on well-known former East German athletes and the second positive drug tests on Canadian sprinter Ben Johnson are just a few of the incidents which have recently heightened public interest in the use of drugs in sport. In particular the use of anabolic-androgenic steroids has become a widespread phenomenon among élite and indeed non-élite, junior athletes (Buckley *et al.*, 1988). Androgenic-anabolic steroids are synthetic chemicals (that is they are anabolic) which resemble the male hormone testosterone (that is androgenic) and which cause an increase in protein synthesis. The physiological effects of such drugs are reasonably well documented. These include accelerated muscle growth, more rapid recovery from training and an ability to endure higher training loads. (Lamb, 1984). Surprisingly these changes have not been widely confirmed by empirical evidence but this is undoubtedly due in part to the dosages of the drugs used in the studies. In addition to the physiological benefits which have been proposed, several authors have suggested that there may be psychological benefits such as increased self-confidence, increased pain threshold (Holzbauer, 1976), mental alertness and mood elevation (Itil *et al.*, 1974). In addition to research dealing with the artificial elevation of testosterone levels, a small number of studies, including Hakkinen *et al.* (1988), have shown increases in resting testosterone after extended periods of exercise training, in the case of Hakkinen's study, weight training for a period of at least two years.

The perceived benefits which may accrue from using anabolic steroids are not gained without serious physiological side-effects. These include alterations in liver function, lipid chemistry, cardiovascular efficiency and the reproductive function (Brooks and Fahey, 1985). Not surprisingly given these side-effects, only a limited number of researchers have considered the experimental effects of these exogenous drugs on psychological and behavioural parameters. In terms of psychological effects, increases in testosterone have been linked to aggressive behaviour (Archer, 1991). One may therefore expect that an artificial elevation of testosterone in the body by the administration of anabolic-androgenic steroids will cause increases in aggressive behaviour. Several personal accounts in the literature from athletes who have taken anabolic steroids suggests that the possible psychological side-effects may include increased aggression, mania, paranoia, anxiety, irritability and depression. For obvious ethical reasons (not being able to administer drugs with possible harmful side-effects), empirical support of this notion is difficult to obtain. In humans therefore many of the observations come from case studies of athletes who have taken the drugs (Donohue and Johnson, 1988; Mottram, 1988). In addition, a more recent clinical literature is becoming available which looks at the effects of withdrawal from anabolic steroids, and most especially the short term effect on depression which has been shown to be considerable (Choi, 1993).

Given the justifiable shortage of human experimental research, not unexpectedly several animal studies have attempted to throw light on the psychological effects of anabolic steroids. Rejeski *et al.* (1988) used primates as part of a double-blind experimental design. They noted increases in dominant and submissive behaviours in those monkeys who received injections of anabolic steroids over a period of eight weeks (monkeys in one enclosure received steroids; monkeys in the other enclosure received a placebo solution). Whether it was dominant or submissive behaviour which increased was chiefly dependent on social factors and especially the existing dominance hierarchy. This study suggests that anabolic steroids cause an intensification and amplification of existing behavioural predispositions, perhaps extending to cognitive and affective predispositions as well. In a follow-up study (reported in Gregg and Rejeski, 1990) the monkeys were housed together where again some received anabolic steroids and some received a sham injection, only on this occasion the dose of steroids was increased. On this occasion quite similar changes in behaviour were noted among both drug and control groups. This suggests that the psychological and behavioural effects of steroids reflect upon an interaction between the psychophysiological effects of the drugs themselves, personality variables and social context. Although the aggressive and submissive behaviours returned to normal after the treatment was stopped, the authors also noted decreased affiliative behaviour in the anabolic steroid group which remained long after the cessation of anabolic steroid treatment.

Given that the physiological and psychological consequences of anabolic steroid use are not fully understood but that the limited evidence associating their use amongst humans suggests negative effects on physical and psychological health, it is not surprising that they are widely condemned. The International Society of Sport Psychology (1993) in a recent position statement concluded that:

> beyond the ethical issues, the use of AAS (anabolic-androgenic steroids) is potentially dangerous, both psychologically and physically and should not be part of sport and physical activity.

> (ISSP, 1993:6)

Anxiety, Arousal and Biofeedback in Sport

In sport psychology, considerable attention has been focused on anxiety in competitive sport settings and the attainment of optimal arousal levels for peak performance (see Chapter 4). Anxiety and arousal are discussed in terms of both cognitive and somatic elements, and there is an obvious niche here for the sports psychophysiologist in helping to understand the interrelationship between the psychological and the physiological.

The link between mind and body upon which psychophysiology is founded has so far only been discussed in unidirectional terms, that is from the body to the mind or the effect of physiology on behavioural and psychological processes. There is equally good reason to expect an effect of psychological processes on physiological functioning and some of the studies investigating such links provide interesting conclusions for the sports psychologist considering competitive anxiety and arousal in sport. For example, several studies have shown that physiological activity particularly heart rate can be controlled or in some way altered by psychological processes. Goldstein *et al.* (1977) demonstrated that with appropriate feedback on heart rate, subjects could learn to reduce their heart rate and blood pressure during submaximal exercise. Similar and consistent findings suggest that the cardiovascular response to mild exercise are controlled by central neural mechanisms which reduce symapthetic arousal and enhance vagal tone. (Hatfield and Landers 1987)

Feedback regarding physiological functioning is termed biofeedback and has been embraced enthusiastically by many sports psychologists. Biofeedback has been described as 'the use of instrumentation to monitor a covert physiological process so that it becomes overt' (Bilodeau, in Sandweiss and Wolf, 1985:160). In other words individuals are made aware of some aspect of their physiological response (for example heart rate) in an effort to learn to exert control over this response and so enhance performance. The application of biofeedback to sport and exercise science is still in its infancy but has already yielded some interesting results. Hatfield *et al.* (1992) studied twelve trained cross-country runners to determine what effect biofeedback (in the form of ventilatory and EMG information) had on response to exercise. Subjects performed 36 minutes of treadmill running during which time they were either first distracted by having to do a timing task, second given feedback every 15 seconds on how much air they were inhaling and how much tension existed in their biceps (upper arm) and trapezius (neck/upper back) muscles, or third left to run without distraction or feedback. In this way subjects were able to act as their own control group. The authors noted that during the feedback condition subjects altered their ventilation so as to become more efficient. Although obviously requiring the same amount of oxygen to perform the same exercises, subjects became more efficient in their extraction of the available oxygen from the air which they breathed. Through physical training alone, runners hope to improve their oxygen extracting capacity; this study would suggest obvious advantages to runners of biofeedback training where they can produce the same effects simply by attending to their physiological responses. This increase in efficiency could eventually mean that they are able to run faster or more probably that they will be able to maintain pace for longer.

The study described above is just one recent example of the potential of biofeedback and psychophysiology in sport science research. The interested reader is directed to Sandweiss and Wolf (1985) for a further discussion of possibilities in this area.

The Way Forward

Just as some sport and exercise psychologists have come to realise the potential of psychophysiology for developing understanding in their areas of interest, so too have a growing number of psychophysiologists begun to acknowledge the great possibilities that exist within sport and exercise. Magina (1990) in a presidential address to the 4th International Conference of Psychophysiology concluded that,

> Physical activity and sports are generally healthy endeavours for adequate development in good physiological condition. Psychophysiology is also useful in evaluating and improving athletic skills in sports and it can be applied in order to optimize the performance of élite athletes in highly competitive situations. The future of Sports Psychophysiology appears to be inviting further exploratory work.
>
> (Magina, 1990, p. 100)

Such enthusiasm for the application of psychophysiology is encouraging for the sport psychologist. However such ardour for application should not preclude the development of appropriate theoretical frameworks for research. Psychophysiology in sport to date has been used largely to describe physiological and psychological responses to, or antecedents of, sport and exercise, rather than to integrate these into a cohesive conceptual schema. Hatfield and Landers (1987) argue strongly for the development of this theoretical framework if the advances in measurement sophistication are ever to be used to their full advantage.

To answer many of the questions currently being posed in sport psychology (and indeed in exercise physiology) requires the integration of psychological and physiological parameters. Psychophysiology by its definition seeks to do this and although perhaps more onerous for the researcher the rewards from this type of research should be greater and will surely provide a greater understanding of exercise and sport. As Morgan (1981) has explained:

> it is certainly more convenient to study problems at a psychological or physiological level, but unfortunately most of the answers will probably be found at a psychophysiological level — not just a psychological or physiological level alone.
>
> (Morgan, 1981, p. 389)

References

ARCHER, J. (1991) 'The influence of testosterone on human aggression', *British Journal of Psychology*, 82, pp. 1–28.

ASTRAND, P. O. and RODAHL, K. (1986) *Textbook of Work Physiology*, New York: McGraw-Hill.

ATKINSON, C. and MILSUM, J. H. (1983) 'A system model of the metabolic response to stress', *Behavioural Science*, 28, pp. 268–73.

BAEKELAND, F. (1970) 'Exercise deprivation', *Archives of General Psychiatry*, 22, pp. 365–69.

BAHRKE, M. S. and MORGAN, W. P. (1978) 'Anxiety reduction following exercise and meditation', *Cognitive Therapy and Research*, 2, pp. 323–33.

BENNETT, T. C. (1982) *Introduction to Physiological Psychology*, Mayfield, CA: Brooks/Cole.

BIDDLE, S. and MUTRIE, N. (1991) *Psychology of Physical Activity and Exercise*, London: Springer-Verlag.

BOUTCHER, S. H. and LANDERS, D. M. (1986) 'Anxiety reduction in conditioned and unconditioned subjects following vigorous exercise', *Medicine and Science in Sport and Exercise*, 18, p. 518.

BROOKE, S. T. and LONG, B. C. (1987) 'Efficiency of coping with a real-life stressor: A multimodal comparison of aerobic fitness', *Psychophysiology*, 24, 2, pp. 173–80.

BROOKS, G. A. and FAHEY, T. D. (1985) *Exercise Physiology, Human Bioenergetics and its Applications*, New York: Macmillan.

BROWN, B. S. and VAN HUSS, W. (1973) 'Exercise and rat brain catecholamines', *Journal of Applied Physiology*, 34, pp. 664–9.

BUCKLEY, W. E., YESALIS, C. E., FRIEDL, K. E., ANDERSON, W. A., STREIT, A. L. and WRIGHT, J. E. (1988) 'Estimated prevalence of anabolic steroid use among male high school seniors', *Journal of the American Medical Association*, 260, pp. 3441–5.

CHAN, C. and GROSSMAN, H. Y. (1988) Cited in GRANT, E. 'The exercise fix', *Psychology Today*, 22, pp. 24–28.

CHODAKOWSKA, J., WOCIAL, B., SKORKA, B., NAZAR, K. and CHWALBINSKA-MONETA, J. (1980) 'Plasma and urinary catecholamines and metabolites during physical exercise in essential hypertension', *Acta Physiologica Polonica*, 31, pp. 623–30.

CHOI, P .Y .L. (1993) 'Alarming effects of anabolic steroids', *The Psychologist*, 6, 6, pp. 258–60.

CLAYTOR, R. (1988) 'Aerobic power and cardiovascular response to stress', *Journal of Applied Physiology*, 65, pp. 1416–23.

COX, R. H. (1991) 'Exercise training and response to stress: Insights from an animal model', *Medicine and Science in Sports and Exercise*, 23, 7, pp. 853–9.

DE VRIES, H. A. (1981) 'Tranquilliser effect of exercise. A critical review', *The Physician and Sports Medicine*, 9, 11, pp. 47–53.

DIMSDALE, J. and MOSS, J. (1980) 'Plasma catecholamines in stress and exercise', *Journal of the American Medical Association*, 243, 4, pp. 340–3.

DONOHUE, T. and JOHNSON, N. (1988) *Foul Play: Drug Abuse in Sport*, Oxford: Blackwell.

DUNN, A. L. and DISHMAN, R. K. (1991) 'Exercise and the neurobiology of depression', *Exercise and Sport Sciences Reviews*, 19, pp. 41–98.

FARRELL, P. A., GUSTAFSON, A. B., MORGAN, W. P. and PERT, C. B. (1987) 'Enkephalins, catecholamines, and psychological mood alterations: effects of prolonged exercise', *Medicine and Science in Sports and Exercise*, 19, pp. 347–53.

FOLEY, K. M., KOUNDES, I. A., INTURRISI, C., KAIKO, R. F., ZAROULIS, C. G., POSNER, J. B., HOUDE, R. W. and LI, C. H. (1979) 'B-endorphin: Analgesic and hormonal effects in humans', *Proceedings of the National Academy of Science of the USA*, 76, pp. 5377–81.

FOLKINS, C. H. and SIME, W. (1981) 'Physical fitness training and mental health', *American Psychologist*, 36, pp. 373–89.

GOLDSTEIN, D. S., ROSS, R. S. and BRADY, J. V. (1977) 'Biofeedback heart rate training during exercise', *Biofeedback and Self-Regulation*, 2, pp. 107–25.

GREGG, E. and REJESKI, W. J. (1990) 'Social psychobiologic dysfunction associated with anabolic steroid abuse: A review', *The Sport Psychologist*, 4, pp. 275–84.

HARBER, V. J. and SUTTON, J. R. (1984) 'Endorphins and exercise', *Sports Medicine*, 1, pp. 154–71.

HATFIELD, B. D. and LANDERS, D. M. (1983) 'Psychophysiology — A new direction for sports psychology', *Journal of Sport Psychology*, 5, pp. 243–59.

HATFIELD, B. D. and LANDERS, D. M. (1987) 'Psychophysiology in exercise and sport research: An overview', *Exercise and Sport Science Reviews*, 15, pp. 351–88.

HATFIELD, B. D., SPALDING, T. W., MAHON, A. D., SLATER, B. A., BRODY, E. B. and VACCARO, P. (1992) 'The effect of psychological strategies upon cardiorespiratory and muscular activity during treadmill running', *Medicine and Science in Sports and Exercise*, 24, 2, pp. 218–25.

HAKKINEN, K., PATARINEN, A., ALEN, M., KAUHANEN, H. and KOMI, P. V. (1988) 'Neuromuscular and hormonal adaptations in athletes to strength training in two years', *Journal of Applied Psychology*, 65, pp. 2406–12.

HOLZBAUER, M. (1976) Psychological aspects of steroids with anaesthetic properties', *Medical Biology*, 54, pp. 227–42.

HULL, E. M., YOUNG, S.H. and ZEIGLER, S. H. (1984) 'Aerobic fitness affects cardiovascular and catecholamine responses to stressors', *Psychophysiology*, 21, pp. 353–60.

INTERNATIONAL SOCIETY OF SPORT PSYCHOLOGY (1993) 'The use of anabolic – androgenic steroids (AAS) in sport and physical activity: A position statement', *The Sport Psychologist*, 7, pp. 4–7.

ITIL, T. M., CORA, R., AKPINAR, S., HERRMAN, W. M. and PATTERSON, C. J. (1974) 'Psychotropic action of sex hormones: Computerized EEG in establishing the immediate CNS effects of steroid hormones', *Current Therapeutic Research*, 16, pp. 1147–70.

JANAL, M. N., COLD, W. D., CLARK, C. W. and GLUSMAN, M. (1984) 'Pain sensitivity, mood and plasma endocrine levels in man following long distance running: Effects of Naloxone', *Pain*, 19, pp. 13–25.

KETY, S. S. (1966) 'Calecholomines in neuropsychiatric states', *Pharmacological Review*, 18, pp. 787–98.

KLINE, N. S., LI, C., LEHMAN, H. E., LAJHTA, A., LASKI, E. and COOPER, T. (1977) 'B-endorphin-induced changes in schizophrenic and depressed patients', *Archives of General Psychiatry*, 34, pp. 1111–3.

LAFONTAINE, T. P., DI LORENZO, T., FRENSCH, P. A., STUCKY-ROPP, R.C., BARGMAN, E.P. and MCDONALD, D. G. (1992) 'Aerobic exercise and mood — A brief review 1985–1990', *Sports Medicine*, 13, 3, pp. 160–70.

LAMB, D. R. (1984) 'Anabolic steroids in athletics: How well do they work and how dangerous are they?', *American Journal of Sports Medicine*, 12, pp. 31–38.

LONG, B. C. (1983) 'Aerobic conditioning and stress reduction: Participation or conditioning?' *Human Movement Science*, 2, pp. 171–86.

MCARTHUR, J. (1985) 'Endorphins and exercise in females: Possible connection with reproductive dysfunction', *Medicine and Science in Sports and Exercise*, 17, pp. 82–88.

MCMURRAY, R. G. (1991) 'Exercise, mood states and neuroendocrinology', in DIAMANT, L. (Ed.) *Mind-Body Maturity, Psychological Approaches to Sports, Exercise and Fitness*, New York: Hemisphere, pp. 237–54.

MAGINA, C. A. (1990) 'Some beneficial present and future applications of psychophysiology', *International Journal of Psychophysiology*, 7, pp. 99–104.

MARKOFF, R. A., RYAN, P. and YOUNG, T. (1982) 'Endorphins and mood changes in long distance running', *Medicine and Science in Sports and Exercise*, 17, pp. 82–88.

MORGAN, W. P. (1981) 'Psychophysiology of self-awareness during vigorous physical activity', *Research Quarterly in Exercise and Sport*, 52, pp. 385–427.

MORGAN, W. P. and O'CONNOR, P. J. (1988) 'Exercise and mental health', in DISHMAN, R. K. (Ed.) *Exercise Adherence: Its Impact on Public Health*, Champaign, IL: Human Kinetics, pp. 91–121.

MORRIS, M., STEINBERG, H., SYKES, E. A. and SALMON, P. (1990) 'Effects of temporary withdrawal from regular running', *Journal of Psychosomatic Research*, 34, 5, pp. 493–500.

MOSES, J., EDWARDS, S., MATHEWS, A. and STEPTOE, A. (1987) 'Age, aerobic fitness, type A behaviour pattern and reactivity to psychological stress in women', *SPR Abstracts*, 24, 5, 603.

MOTTRAM, D. R. (1988) *Drugs in Sport*, New York: Spon.

NORTH, T. C., McCULLAGH, P. and TRAN Z. V. (1990) 'Effect of exercise on depression', *Exercise Sport Sciences Reviews*, 18, pp. 379–415.

OBRIST, P. A. (1981) *Cardiovascular Psychophysiology, A Perspective*, New York: Plenum Press.

PORGES, S. W. and COLES, M. G. H. (Eds) (1976) *Psychophysiology*, Pennsylvania: Dowden, Hutchinson and Ross Inc.

RAGLIN, J. S. and MORGAN, W. P. (1985) 'Influence of vigorous exercise on pain sensitivity, and mood state', *Behaviour Therapist*, 8, pp. 179–83.

REJESKI, W. J., BRUBAKER, P. H., HERB, R.A., KAPLAN, J. R. and KORITNIK, D. (1988) 'Anabolic steroids and aggressive behaviour in cynomolgus monkeys', *Journal of Behavioral Medicine*, 11, pp. 95–105.

SACHS, M. and PARMAGAN, D. (1979) 'Running addiction: A depth interview examination', *Journal of Sport Behaviour*, 2, pp. 143–55.

SANDWEISS, J. H. and WOLF, S. L. (Eds) (1985) *Biofeedback and Sports Science*, New York: Plenum Press.

SFORZO, G. A. (1988) 'Opiods and exercise: An update', *Sports Medicine*, 7, pp. 109–24.

SHERWOOD, A., LIGHT, K. C. and BLUMENTHAL, J. A. (1989) 'Effects of aerobic exercise training on hemodynamic responses during psychosocial stress in normotensive and borderline hypertensive Type A men', *Psychosomatic Medicine*, 51, pp. 123–36.

SIMONS, A. D., McGOWAN, C. R., EPSTEIN, L. H., KUPFER, D. J. and ROBERTS, R. J. (1985) 'Exercise as a treatment for depression: an update', *Clinical Psychology Review*, 5, pp. 553–68.

SINYOR, D., SCHWARTZ, S., PERRUNIT, F., BRISSON, G. and SERAGANIAN, P. (1983) 'Aerobic fitness level and reactivity to psychosocial stress: Physiological, biochemical and subjective measures', *Psychosomatic Medicine*, 45, pp. 205–17.

SOLOMAN, E. G. and BUMPUS, A. K. (1978) 'The running meditation response, an adjunct to psychotherapy', *American Journal of Psychotherapy*, 32, pp. 583–92.

SOTHMANN, M. S., HART, B. A. and HORN, T. S. (1992) 'Sympathetic nervous system and behavioural responses to stress following exercise training', *Physiology and Behavior*, 51, 6, pp. 1097–103.

SOTHMANN, M., HORN, T., HART, B. and GUSTAFSON, A. B. (1987) 'Comparison of discrete fitness groups on plasma catecholamines and selected behavioural responses to psychological stress', *Psychophysiology*, 24, pp. 47–54.

STEPHENS, T. (1988) 'Physical activity and mental health in the United States and Canada: Evidence from four population surveys', *Preventative Medicine*, 17, pp. 35–47.

STERN, R. M., RAY, W. J. and DAVIS, C. M. (1980) *Psychophysiological Recording*, Oxford: Oxford University Press.

TUCKER, L. A., COLE, G. E. and FREIDMAN, G. M. (1986) 'Physical fitness: A buffer against stress', *Perceptual Motor Skills*, 61, pp. 1031–8.

VANDER, A. J., SHERMAN, J. H. and LUCIANO, D. S. (1990) *Human Physiology, the Mechanisms of Body Function*, 5th edn, New York: McGraw-Hill.

VAN DOORNEN, L. J. P. and DE GEUS, E. C. B. (1989) 'Aerobic fitness and the cardiovascular response to stress', *Psychophysiology*, 26, 1, pp. 17–28.

VAN DOORNEN, L. J. P., DE GEUS, E. C. B. and ORLEBEKE, J. F. (1988) 'Aerobic fitness and the physiological stress response: A critical evaluation', *Social Science and Medicine*, 26, pp. 303–7.

WILLIS, J. D. and CAMPBELL, L. F. (1992) *Exercise Psychology*, Champaign, IL: Human Kinetics.

Further Reading

ARCHER, J. (1991) 'The influence of testosterone on human aggression', *British Journal of Psychology*, 82, pp. 1–28.

BROOKS, G. A. and FAHEY, T. D. (1985) *Exercise Physiology, Human Bioenergetics and its Applications*, New York: Macmillan.

CHOI, P. Y. L. (1993) 'Alarming effects of anabolic steroids', *The Psychologist*, 6, 6, pp. 258–60.

DONOHUE, T. and JOHNSON, N. (1988) *Foul Play: Drug Abuse in Sport*, Oxford: Blackwell.

GALE, A. and EDWARDS, J. A. (Eds) (1983) *Physiological Correlates of Human Behaviour, Vol. 1: Basic Issues*, London: Academic Press.

GREGG, E. and REJESKI, W. J. (1990) 'Social psychobiologic dysfunction associated with anabolic steroid abuse: A review', *The Sport Psychologist*, 4, pp. 275–84.

HATFIELD, B. D. and LANDERS, D. M. (1987) 'Psychophysiology in exercise and sport research. An overview', *Exercise and Sport Science Reviews*, 15, pp. 351–88.

MORGAN, W. P. and O'CONNOR, P. J. (1988) 'Exercise and mental health', in DISHMAN, R. K. (Ed.) *Exercise Adherence: Its Impact on Public Health*, Champaign, IL: Human Kinetics, pp. 91–121.

MCMURRAY, R. G. (1991) 'Exercise, Mood States and Neuroendocrinology' in DIAMANT, L. (Ed.) *Mind-Body Maturity, Psychological Approaches to Sports, Exercise and Fitness*, New York: Hemisphere, pp. 237–54.

NORTH, T. C., MCCULLAGH, P. and TRAN, Z. V. (1990) 'Effect of Exercise on Depression', *Exercise Sport Sciences Reviews*, 18 , pp. 379–415.

SANDWEISS, J. H. and WOLF, S. L. (Eds) (1985) *Biofeedback and Sports Science*, New York: Plenum Press.

SFORZO, G. A. (1988) 'Opioids and exercise: An update', *Sports Medicine*, 7, pp. 109–24.

Index

6127

DATE DUE